APR 1 7 2015

W9-BYF-744

ALONE ATOP THE HILL

ALONE ATOP THE HILL

The Autobiography of Alice Dunnigan,
Pioneer of the National Black Press

_____

Edited by Carol McCabe Booker
With a foreword by Simeon Booker

The University of Georgia Press | Athens and London

A Sarah Mills Hodge Fund Publication
This publication is made possible in part through a grant from the
Hodge Foundation in memory of its founder, Sarah Mills Hodge, who
devoted her life to the relief and education of African Americans in
Savannah, Georgia.

Published by the University of Georgia Press
Athens, Georgia 30602
www.ugapress.org
© 2015 by Robert W. Dunnigan and Carol McCabe Booker
All rights reserved
Designed by Melissa Bugbee Buchanan
Set in 10.75/14 Minion Pro
Printed and bound by Thomson-Shore, Inc.
The paper in this book meets the guidelines for
permanence and durability of the Committee on
Production Guidelines for Book Longevity of the
Council on Library Resources.

Most University of Georgia Press titles are
available from popular e-book vendors.

Printed in the United States of America
19 18 17 16 15 C 5 4 3 2 1

Library of Congress Control Number: 2014957344
ISBN: 978-0-8203-4798-1 (hardcover: alk. paper)
ISBN: 978-0-8203-4860-5 (ebook)

British Library Cataloging-in-Publication Data available

If I can so live to inspire others to strive to achieve,

I will not have lived my life in vain.

Alice Dunnigan, letter to Claude A. Barnett, January 20, 1948

CONTENTS

FOREWORD

I knew Alice Dunnigan for all the years I worked in Washington, first as a reporter for the *Washington Post*, and then as bureau chief for *Jet* and *Ebony* magazines, until her death in 1983. Quiet, unassuming, and plain-spoken, she had a passion for both journalism and politics, and she was successful at both.

Alice arrived in Washington, D.C., in 1942, almost a decade before I joined the *Washington Post* toward the close of 1951 for a two-year stint that almost killed me, so difficult was it to function as a reporter in a city where even the pet cemeteries were segregated. In 1956, when I returned from Chicago as bureau chief of John H. Johnson's growing magazine empire, I found that Alice was still making her rounds as chief of the Associated Negro Press's one-person bureau. Never having given up despite incredible obstacles, she was actually thriving—not financially by any means, but in reputation and political access. Even without the backing of a daily newspaper, or the paycheck and connections that such employment guaranteed, Alice in 1947 had doggedly and successfully pursued the credentials to join both the White House press corps and the Capitol Press Galleries as the first black woman journalist accredited by either. When blocked from the latter because she did not represent a daily paper, she campaigned for a rule change so that a news agency and the weekly newspapers it served—a staple in the black community—would no longer be denied access. She went right on to pursue the same access to the White House. Although encountering, as she later reported, more discrimination as a woman than as an African American, she managed within months to secure a berth on the Presidential Special carrying Harry S. Truman cross-country on a whistle-stop trip to the West Coast—albeit on her own dime when the newspapers she represented refused to pay her expenses.

Alice's story did not begin in 1947, although from that point on her world was very different from the one she left. If, as she requests, we judge her not by what she achieved but by the depths from which she rose (paraphrasing Frederick Douglass), her journey from sharecropper's daughter—and, in fact, a sharecropper herself as well as a laundress, cook, and nanny at points in her early life—Alice's journey from a red clay hill in rural Kentucky to the marble columns of the White House is an incredible success story.

Originally titled *A Black Woman's Experience—from Schoolhouse to White House*, Alice's description of her struggle to become and to sustain herself as a schoolteacher in rural Kentucky is as jaw-dropping as her later account of making it as a reporter in pre-civil-rights-era Washington. The original title did not reflect the steep slope of her early climb out of the rural poverty of her birth, and it was also ridiculed by detractors who substituted "outhouse" for "schoolhouse."

Reading like a novel and told in her own words, painstakingly recorded in retirement after her successive careers as a rural schoolteacher, White House correspondent, and finally political activist, Alice's story should give hope to anyone who has ever doubted his or her ability to make it through tough times or, much more painfully, his or her own worth. Alice's experience offers a resounding, "Yes, you can!" as long as, in the words of the Negro spiritual, you "keep-a inching along."

Simeon Booker, *Jet/Ebony*
Washington Bureau Chief, 1956–2007

EDITOR'S NOTE

It wasn't the poverty of a washerwoman's life in rural Kentucky that drove young Alice Allison relentlessly to succeed as a professional. Poverty would be with her for most of her life, even as a national reporter for more than one hundred black weekly newspapers. What spurred her on was a keen intellect, immense determination, and a yearning for dignity and respect despite intractable racial and gender barriers. Alice so hungered for learning that nothing—not even her father's taunts—would keep her from walking miles to the Negro schoolhouse, staying at the top of her class, and earning a teaching certificate in record time. But even with these accomplishments, she still had to confront a system in which, like her mother, she might spend her life either washing the clothes or caring for the children (or both) of white families. With too few Negro schools, teaching positions for blacks were scarce, and there were no other viable options for a woman in a state where Jim Crow still held sway. None of those realities stopped Alice Dunnigan from pursuing and achieving much more, including a long and impressive litany of historic "firsts" as a black female reporter:

- accredited to the White House
- traveled with a U.S. president (Truman)
- credentialed by the House and Senate Press Galleries
- accredited to the Department of State
- accredited to the Supreme Court
- voted into the White House Newswomen's Association

- voted into the Women's National Press Club
- broke into the all-male bastion of Washington sports reporting

Despite all this, few people today know her story. Alice Dunnigan's historic achievements during the 1940s and 1950s are largely forgotten, in large part due to the tsunami of civil rights battles and victories that swept over the nation during the 1960s. The exceptions are largely among the small cadre of surviving veterans of the 1950s and 1960s black press, the civil rights movement, and the administrations of Presidents Kennedy and Johnson. They remember her with admiration and respect.

This historical breach was rectified to some degree at the Newseum in Washington, D.C., on January 17, 2013, when the National Association of Black Journalists (NABJ) inducted Alice Dunnigan posthumously into its hall of fame. Also among the honorees that evening was another legend of the black press, Simeon Booker (my husband), who at ninety-four was one of a handful of attendees (besides her family) who had actually known Dunnigan. I recalled seeing her only once, at one of the famous Christmas parties hosted by the Washington bureau of Johnson Publishing Company's popular *Ebony* and *Jet* magazines, but that was long after she'd moved on from journalism.

Dunnigan's hall of fame induction prompted my search for a copy of her autobiography, *A Black Woman's Experience—from Schoolhouse to White House* (self-published in 1974). I discovered it was scarcely available beyond the reference collections of a few major libraries. The few online used booksellers offering it were charging one hundred dollars or more. I chose to read it at the Library of Congress, under the splendid dome of the Jefferson Building's Main Reading Room. And that's where my fascination with Alice Dunnigan's inspiring story began.

She tells it well, describing in journalistic detail the terrain, the players, and the politics in Depression-era/prewar Kentucky as well as in the rough-and-tumble of a national capital struggling to make its way through a nascent, postwar racial revolution. I was convinced that this was a narrative that should be read today—not only by scholars or students of American history, civil rights, journalism, politics, or women's rights but by a general audience looking for a really good read, as well as an inspiring one. The problem, it seemed to me, was not only the book's unavailability but its length of more than 670 pages, approximately the last 200 of which lacked the compelling poignancy of the preceding chapters. My goal was to offer an edited text that presented the central thread of Dunnigan's story while preserving her voice and viewpoint.

As Dunnigan observes in her preface, part 1 of her three-part memoir reads like a novel. My only editorial challenge there was to peel away the parts of the text that detracted from the core of her recollections. For each incident or anecdote included in the original, I asked a set of questions: Had the author indulged in too much introspection? Had she focused too much on youthful insecurities or disagreements with parents or a sibling that didn't seem to affect her later life? Did an anecdote contribute in a meaningful way to the reader's understanding of the author and her place in history?

This section covers the first four decades of the twentieth century in Kentucky, a Border State that, along with Missouri, Delaware, and Maryland, had allowed slavery but did not secede from the Union during the Civil War. For Alice, life was a struggle to take advantage of any break that might come her way. She describes it matter-of-factly, without a trace of self-pity, even when she leads us through the Depression years, when she rummaged through garbage at the town dump for produce still fit to cook and eat. She married twice, but each time the union was doomed from the start by a system that restricted the options of black men in ways different from those of women but no less oppressive.

With that background, Dunnigan sounds almost flippant when she says of the fourteen years between 1947 and 1961 during which she crashed through more barriers than any other national reporter in history, "Being a pioneer was no bed of roses."[1] Repeatedly pawning her watch on Fridays to get by until her weekly paycheck arrived on Monday was a step up from scavenging from a trash dump, but not a very big one. This second world of Alice Dunnigan played out in the politically—and racially—charged world of Washington, D.C. She arrived in the nation's capital as a typist for the federal government and, when faced with unemployment at the war's end, convinced Claude Barnett, founder and head of the Associated Negro Press (ANP) news agency, to give her a job covering Washington for half a cent per word.

Strapped for cash himself, Barnett had been unable to recruit a male journalist to work full-time as bureau chief for his struggling news agency.[2] He was full of doubt about hiring a woman, and even more so one with limited journalism experience.[3] What he didn't count on was her determination to succeed.

In Dunnigan's first months with ANP, Chicago editor Frank Marshall Davis, an experienced journalist, editor, and poet, instructed her to follow the ANP style sheet more closely and to watch her grammar and punctuation but added in several letters that her copy was "good."[4] She soon let Barnett know that she didn't intend to be confined in her reporting to Washington, D.C., but intended to take to the road when she saw a promising story elsewhere. Furthermore, she decided that, despite her boss's advice to the contrary, she would not get her information from "backdoor" sources such as butlers, chauffeurs, or messengers but would fight for admission to journalism's front lines as an accredited correspondent in the Congressional Press Galleries, the Supreme Court, and even the White House.

At first, Barnett was reluctant to support her efforts, asking why she thought she could succeed at breaking down barriers when his male reporters had not.[5] Realizing she was on her own when it came to gender issues, she pursued White House credentials without Barnett's help and then secured an invitation to join President Truman's press entourage on a cross-country whistle-stop tour. As it turned out, however, she had to pay her own way, not just because the ANP couldn't get its subscribers to contribute toward her expenses but because Barnett admittedly did not see it as an assignment for a woman.

This would not be the last instance in which Alice Dunnigan proved that Barnett had seriously underestimated her. Although she had little formal journalism training, within a very short time Dunnigan proved herself not only to Barnett but to front-page editors of dozens of black newspapers. In 1951, she was the first woman awarded the Capital Press Club's "Newsman's Newsman" award, and eventually her boss's critiques of her copy would include observations such as "quite well done" and even "extremely well done."[6] Furthermore, in 1957 one of the foremost (and most competitive) of the black newspapers, the *Pittsburgh Courier*, asked her to send copies of her articles at the same time as she submitted them to ANP for the purpose of identifying "possible front page leads." *Courier* editor Percival L. Prattis also negotiated with her for regular exclusives, in addition to a byline column dubbed "Washington Inside-Out." *Courier* managing editor George F. Brown promised to give her "top priority" if she kept "feeding us those top stories and a hot column." Prattis even called one of her columns "superb."[7]

Throughout his White House years, President Truman welcomed Dunnigan's questions at his press conferences. But when Dwight D. Eisenhower took the presidency, his irritation at her civil rights focus led to headlines in the daily press about his blatant snubbing of her persistent efforts to get answers on race issues.

In Congress, where Harlem's Adam Clayton Powell Jr. in 1945 had joined Chicago's William Dawson as the second black member of the House, Dunnigan was stunned to hear blacks referred to as "niggers" in debates in which racial ridicule was used without hesitation to satisfy Dixie constituents. However, it wasn't politics that posed her biggest challenge as she raced from Capitol Hill to the White House, a legion of federal agencies, and the occasional round of parties on Embassy Row. Her biggest challenge was financial survival. When she finally got her per-word payments converted into a weekly salary, it was barely enough to support herself as well as her son from her second marriage. It wasn't until she retired and wrote her autobiography that readers of the more than one hundred newspapers for which she reported would learn what she had to do just to keep body and soul together as America's first black, female national correspondent.

Part 3 of Dunnigan's original memoir chronicled her life after journalism—when she worked for nearly a decade as a political appointee in the federal government. I found this section anticlimactic after she'd gone toe-to-toe with such formidable figures as Jim Crow during her longer journalism career.[8] Furthermore, many journalists at some point have traded in the deadlines and uncertainties of the daily or weekly press for regular hours and the guarantee of a substantially larger paycheck. Dunnigan's account of these government years not only seemed familiar but tended to detract from the powerful recollections of her hand-over-fist climb from sharecropper to schoolteacher, painfully backsliding at times, until finally, by sheer grit, she ascended to the press galleries of the U.S. Congress and the White House press office. Similarly, the chapters on her foreign travel seemed less compelling than the core narrative. For that reason, I opted to omit those chapters.

The following narrative includes many of Dunnigan's original annotations, to which I have added others. Where necessary to distinguish between the two, I have added her initials ("—AD") to the endnote.

Many of Alice Dunnigan's peers recognized the importance of her book. Washington correspondent John W. Lewis Jr. praised it in a review carried by members of the National Newspaper Publishers Association (NNPA). Under an eight-column streamer headline, Lewis wrote that it answered "a desperate need for information about the black press."[9] Press clips saved in scrapbooks now held by the Moorland-Spingarn Research Center at Howard University echo that assessment, chronicling the applause of audiences at numerous book talks and signings, including one that particularly pleased her because it was sponsored by an association of her peers. Shortly after her book was published, the National Association of Media Women hosted a party at its annual convention in New Orleans, where it bestowed on her honorary membership and a merit award.[10]

The autobiography of Alice Dunnigan is a slice of history recounted by a woman whose struggle paved the way for many others and, in so doing, led to a better America. It's a story that merits telling over and over again—a clear message that success can be achieved, even against all odds. Alice Dunnigan proved it!

Carol M. Booker, Editor

PREFACE

The story of my life is an account of the struggle and accomplishments of an ambitious country girl who began life with the determination to reach a definite goal and worked hard to achieve it.

The first part of my story tells bluntly and simply what life was like in most backwoods communities of the South in the first half of the twentieth century. Based on raw facts, it is uninhibited, unembellished, and unvarnished. It may read at times more like a novel than an autobiography, but this is the way it was. While it relies exclusively on my own recollections of my early years, in the end it is a portrayal of a lifestyle pattern of the old rural South.

The second part of the book, beginning with my departure from "my old Kentucky home," draws initially upon the diary of memory, but my account of later years, including the civil rights movement; increased participation of minorities in America's political, economic, and social activities; and other contemporary issues, is based almost entirely upon clippings of my own newspaper stories, as well as unpublished material from my personal confidential or correspondence files and other sources as necessary to verify important facts. My scrapbooks demonstrate the role the Negro press has played in a people's upward struggle. The clippings prove that the black press of my generation had just as important a role in recording facts relating to the battle for equality of opportunity for minority citizens as it had in 1827, when John B. Russwurm and Samuel

Eli Cornish put out the first black newspaper—*Freedom's Journal*—as an organ of protest against man's inhumanity to man.

While the role of the black press, like other newspapers, is that of objectively reporting the news as it happens, it has had another function equally as important—that of fighting oppression. Without black reporters constantly on the national scene to record contemporary history of the Negro's role in the fight for civil rights, equality, and justice, and without black authors and historians to compile these facts into permanent record, the deeds, efforts, and struggles of the black man in his progressive fight for security and recognition would forever be lost to history.

Without black writers, the world would perhaps never have known of the chicanery, shenanigans, and buffoonery employed by those in high places to keep the black man in his (proverbial) place by relegating him to second-class citizenship through the denial of social, economic, and political rights and forcing him into poverty, shame, and disgrace.

More historical than autobiographical, the latter chapters of this book might well serve as a guide to the social revolution of the forties. It should be especially useful in answering those who contend that no advancement toward civil and human rights was evident in this country until the sixties.

It is my fondest hope that the story of my life and work will, by interpretation, investigation, information, and inspiration, encourage more young writers to use their talents as a moving force in the forward march of progress and that their efforts will soon result in giving Americans the kind of nation that those of my generation so long hoped and worked for.

Alice A. Dunnigan, 1974

PART I
THOSE EARLY YEARS

1

NO GREATER THRILL

I arrived at the northwest gate of the White House at nine o'clock on a typically hot, muggy Washington morning in August 1947. Trying to appear composed and nonchalant, while anything but, I announced to the uniformed Secret Service officer that I was there for the president's news conference. I had gone over this in my head for two hours since waking to music from a clock radio at seven o'clock and riding a street car the three miles from my apartment to Fourteenth and G Streets Northwest, then walking among office workers and tourists the two blocks to the executive mansion at 1600 Pennsylvania Avenue.

"I must not be late," I'd repeated too many times as I waited impatiently through each stop of the trolley before arriving at mine. I had heard that no one enters these conferences late, and even if someone wanted to, the Secret Service would have locked the doors so that no latecomers could enter. So I had given myself an hour for transportation and an hour for orientation before the scheduled start time of ten o'clock. The guard at the gate, although stern faced, was friendly enough as I fumbled in my purse for the precious White House press pass that I was using for the very first time.

"You're too early for the press conference," he advised, taking the pass from my hand and scrutinizing it, comparing the likeness on the card with the woman in front of him. "It doesn't begin for another hour or so." Despite my outward coolness and calm, he had obviously identified me as a newcomer to the White House press corps since my face was not familiar. No matter how much I tried to impress him with my composure, I wasn't fooling anybody because everyone will admit that his or her first adventure at the White House is an exciting experience.

I laid it all on the line. "May I go in and wait? I'm afraid if I leave, I might not get back in time. I don't want to be late for the conference." Apparently amused at my anxiety, the guard tried to restrain a smile as he motioned for me to enter the grounds.

I proceeded around the circular driveway to the west portal of the White House, where I was stopped by another uniformed guard seated at a desk just inside the doorway. Once again I proffered my credentials and was allowed to enter the spacious lobby.

A large, round table with fancy carved legs occupied the center of this great room. Overstuffed chairs and couches lined the walls. The expensive-looking furniture, upholstered in red and black leather, showed signs of long, hard wear, with sagging cushions and frayed armrests. A few newsmen, who I later learned were regularly assigned White House reporters, sat around glancing at the morning papers. Some puffed on pipes or smoked cigarettes while others sipped coffee from paper cups as they exchanged views on the issues of the day. Attractive, well-dressed girls (secretaries and aides in the press office) darted in and out of the lobby, occasionally exchanging a few pleasantries with the loitering newsmen.

I sat there alone and apparently unnoticed, taking in all the activity while glancing now and then at my newspaper. If anyone wondered who I was, or why I was there, they made no effort to find out. As time passed, other reporters began to drift in, indicating the time for the conference was drawing near. Some of the reporters had met me on Capitol Hill and came over to exchange a word or two. Some wanted to know what I was doing there. When I proudly responded that I had been accredited to the White House press corps, they extended a casual congratulation, implying this was no big thing.

To them it was nothing unusual because white reporters with reputation and status had always been accredited to the White House. But for me it represented progress for my race, recognition of the black press, consideration of women reporters, and a personal honor because I was the very first woman of my race ever to receive such accreditation. I appreciated and cherished this honor even though I felt that I had actually earned it the hard way—through strenuous preparation, perseverance, hard work, acceptable qualifications, persistence, a heroic fight, and proven ability.

As the hour for the conference drew nearer, the reporters began to drift toward the door leading into the president's Oval Office. At a given time, the door swung open and newsmen pushed and scrounged like herded cattle through the open doorway and down the narrow hall, elbowing their way into the office, pushing and shoving to get as near as possible to the president's desk. Since newsmen had to stand throughout the conference in those days, it was apparent that each was trying to grab a choice spot so as to get a good view or to be seen and recognized by the president if the reporter raised his hand for a question.[1]

President Truman stood to greet reporters, gave a brief statement on some pressing issue of the day, then made himself available for questions. After half an hour the conference was abruptly dismissed with a brisk, "Thank you, Mr. President!" spoken by a dapper, black-haired reporter. At the same time, he dashed from the room, practically running into everybody in his way, and sprinted through the lobby like a professional track star, into the pressroom on the opposite side, where he immediately closed himself tightly into a tiny telephone booth.

Later I learned that this man was Merriman Smith of United Press International, who, because of his excellent work and years of seniority, had earned for himself the title of dean of White House correspondents and had acquired the responsibility of dismissing all presidential press conferences. The well-known Pulitzer Prize winner kept this title and performed this task until his suicide in April 1970.

As Smith scurried through the White House lobby on that particular day, a few other reporters were right on his heels racing to see who could be the first to get his story on the wire. These "scoop-seekers," I learned, were all wire-service reporters or representatives of daily papers that were nearing their deadlines. Those who were not pressed for time scattered in different directions, making their way to their respective bureaus or to other assignments.

I took a taxicab to the Capitol, where I had spent most of my time since becoming accredited to the Senate and House Press Galleries a few months earlier. As the doors of the special press elevator to the Senate gallery closed behind me, it occurred to me that on this day I had reached a goal that I'd set for myself many years before when I vowed that someday I would reach the top in my chosen profession of journalism. I had just about hit the mark. One can't get much higher in the newspaper field than a Capitol and White House correspondent. But even then I had no idea of the many opportunities that would eventually open up to me as the only reporter of my sex and race working from this vantage point. Neither could I ever have imagined the many experiences—both pleasant and unpleasant—that would come my way. One thing was certain: I was far from the ramshackle, unpainted, one-room schoolhouse tucked away at the edge of a scrubby, unsightly thicket on a red clay hill in rural Logan County, Kentucky. I couldn't help but marvel, "You've come a long way, sister."

2

THE FAMILY TREE AND ITS BITTERSWEET FRUIT

Frederick Douglass once said, "Do not judge me by the heights to which I have risen, but by the depths from which I have come."

My father, as the story goes, was the grandson of Jack Allison, a plantation owner. Grandpa Jack (as we called him) was never married but sired a son named Alex by one of his slaves. It is not known what happened to Alex's mother, who most likely either died or was sold down the river. Grandpa Jack took Alex to live with him in the big house, rearing him as if he were a legitimate child of his own race. In due time, Jack bought another attractive, half-Indian, half-Negro slave named Martha to serve as his housekeeper and concubine. Along with this purchase came Martha's own little girl named Alice, who was fathered by her former master. Little Alice (for whom I was named) also lived in the big house, along with her mother, Martha, Massa Jack, and his mulatto son, Alex.

Jack was often charged with the offense of adultery and fornication by county law enforcement officers. He would always pay his five-dollar fine and continue to cohabit with his black paramour. These charges were made so frequently that Grandpa Jack adopted a policy of voluntarily riding into town on horseback the first of each month to post the five-dollar fine before the arrest was made, then go right on living with Grandma Martha.

As time went on, the union between Jack, the white plantation owner, and Martha, the colored slave, produced six children. In the meantime, the two older, mulatto children, Alex and Alice, who as stepbrother and sister shared the same house but were not actually blood relations, became infatuated with each other and were married. To this union were born seven children including my father, Willie. All of these children were permitted to attend elementary school until at least completing sixth grade. The Allison family stayed together and cultivated the farm—not as master and slaves but as one big family—until Grandma Martha passed away.

MAMA: LENA PITTMAN

My mother came from quite a different background. Her story, as she related it to me many times, went something like this. She, with an older sister, Lou, and a younger sister, Annie, lived on a farm with their mother, Minerva, and their grandfather, Jake Pittman. The girls knew nothing about their fathers since their mother was never married. Because my grandmother had three children out of wedlock, she was considered a "softy" by men of her acquaintance and described by neighbors as being incapable of taking care of herself. In addition, she had a speech impediment that caused people to brand her as mentally retarded or, as they called it, feeble-minded. Even her father treated her in this manner, never discussing any business matters with her, never giving her any responsibility or ever allowing her a chance to develop her mental capabilities.

Grandpap Jake (as we called Grandma Minerva's father), was a strong-willed, hardworking, shrewd businessman. Only a few years out of slavery, he had managed to acquire a sizable farm, with mules, cows, a wagon, and other farm tools such as plows, harrows, and the like. The entire family worked with him on the farm, helping to cultivate the two principal crops, tobacco and corn. The children were never allowed to go to school or any other place. Once a year, on circus day, my mother recalled, Grandpap would load the three grandchildren and their mother into the wagon and carry them to town to see the circus.

In the fall when the tobacco was sold, he would buy each of the grandchildren a pair of shoes, which they wore for the entire winter. If the shoes wore out or became too small before warm weather, the girls would have to wrap their feet in rags because there would be no more shoes until the next year. They all went barefoot during the entire summer.

One thing Mama remembered most vividly about her grandfather was that he was "saving." You might call him sort of a pack rat, she said. He would pick up everything he saw on the road or in a field, be it an old crooked nail, a rusty screw, a tap, a bolt or nut, or even a twisted horseshoe. He piled all of this junk beneath a huge poplar tree in their yard with the warning that "these things might come in handy someday." From this lesson my mother learned to be economical and never wasted anything. This was also a trait she passed on to my brother and me.

When Grandpap Jake died, he left his family completely helpless. None of them knew what to do or which way to turn. My mother was ten years old at the time, but she remembered white people coming in and taking everything they had. One white man would come in and take a mule, saying, "Uncle Jake owes me and I'm going to take this mule for the debt." Another would come in with the same explanation and take a cow. Still another took the wagon, and so on until everything was gone, even the farm. None of them showed any papers or other evidence that "Uncle Jake" owed them anything. It was then that Mama realized that her mother didn't know what to do and that each child had to look out for herself.

So, without any family consultation or knowledge of what her mother and sisters planned to do, she struck out on her own. Donning her one good dress, she started walking down the road toward town, stopping at every house she passed, asking if they wanted to hire a little girl to help with the housework. She had reached the edge of town before anyone showed an interest. This was the Wilson family who showed a willingness to hire her to take care of their baby, Cyrus. "How much do you want for your work?" Mrs. Wilson asked.

"Vittles and clothes" was the reply, and with this, she was hired.

First, she was taught to care for the baby. As time went on, she was given additional chores such as cleaning house, washing dishes, doing the laundry, and finally cooking. Mama recalled how pleased she was when Mrs. Wilson bought calico and made her some new dresses. As she grew older, she was also taught to sew and had to make her own clothes. She remembered how she used to cry if she sewed the seam wrong and was made to rip it out and do it over again until it was done right. She thought Mrs. Wilson was awfully mean but was later proud that she had been taught to do her work right.

Mama was an excellent worker but was never allowed to spend much time in school. Mrs. Wilson would let her go to school only now and then, she said, until she finally reached the third grade. Mama often said, "About all I learned was how to write my name. I'm an awful poor reader. I wish I could read good."

My mother had reached her teens and was doing all kinds of house-work before she received any wages. She was quite shy, but one day she asked Mrs. Wilson for a little spending money. "Don't you think my work is worth something?" The "madam" agreed to allow her fifty cents a week. That amount was gradually increased until it reached two dollars per week, the amount she was receiving when she left the Wilson household as a grown young lady.

Lou and Annie, my mother's sisters, each found jobs with white families, but she never knew how it was managed. They both died soon after at very early ages.

The (white) Albert Wilhelm family, who owned the farm adjoining my great-grandfather's and who took over his land after his death, later deeded one acre back to my grandmother and built her a one-room cabin with a lean-to kitchen. They allowed her to do odd jobs around their house for food and a little spending money, an arrangement that lasted until her death. As she grew older, my mother realized that the Wilhelms must have taken her grandfather's land unfairly or they never would have been so generous as to later give a plot of land to her mother and build her a house.

Growing into young womanhood, my mother became dissatisfied working for, and living with, the Wilsons. She wanted a social life, and the opportunity to be with young people of her own age and race. She was anxious to attend church and participate in other social activities. So she left the Wilsons and obtained a cooking job with another white family in

Lena Pittman
(Dunnigan Papers,
MARBL, Emory
University)

Willie Allison (right) with his father, Alex Allison
(Dunnigan Papers, MARBL, Emory University)

town. She got a room with a colored family and helped the landlady with laundry work at night to pay for her lodging. She began to go out with fellows like other girls her age were. Unfortunately, she also became pregnant. When Richard was born, she arranged for her mother to keep him while she continued working.

LENA AND WILLIE

Richard was four years old when my mother, Lena Pittman, met and married my father, Willie Allison. A tall, rather attractive, light brown woman with high, Indian-like cheekbones and short, reddish-brown hair, my mother had accepted my father in matrimony against the wishes of her mother. My father was a tall, medium-built, handsome man with fair skin, straight black hair, and a heavy mustache, who, despite his meek, kind, congenial personality, was rejected by his mother-in-law for no reason other than his color. My grandmother had the notion that "them yellow Allison niggers think they're better than my Lena and I don't want any part of them." Nevertheless, the young couple added another room onto Grandma Minerva's cabin and went to live with her. They were married three years before I came into the world. And it is from this point that my story really begins.

3

ALONE ATOP A HILL

My journey began in the three-room, whitewashed cottage where I was born on April 27, 1906. The house stood all alone atop a low, red clay hill about two hundred yards from the highway (or "pike" as we called it). A railroad track stretched along at about the same distance, crossing the pike directly in front of our house. So in giving directions, we would describe our place as the big white house on the hill at the railroad crossing. A two-mile trip south on this highway would lead to the nearest town, Russellville, Kentucky, a village of some five thousand people, where we attended school and church, as well as shopped for food and other necessities.

My first family recollection is that of my father earning a living as a tenant farmer and my mother pitching in as a hand laundress. I sometimes referred to my father as a dirt farmer and my mother as a washerwoman. These titles were not meant to be disrespectful but rather to point out antiquated methods of operation necessitated by the lack of modern conveniences.

Unlike the majority of tenant farmers who lived in rent-free shacks on the boss's farm, my family was a

Baby Alice Allison
(Dunnigan Papers,
MARBL, Emory
University)

bit more independent because we lived in our own home. Since that one acre of land surrounding our house did not provide sufficient space to eke out a living, my father found it necessary to raise an additional crop on shares on the adjoining Wilhelm farm. The little tract of land the Wilhelms had deeded to Grandma was just large enough to grow a sizable vegetable garden and a small plot of corn for feeding the hogs.

Several acres of tobacco, the chief money crop, and more corn for the market were grown on the Wilhelm farm. In raising the crops, my father supplied the labor and the landlord furnished the land and stock (mules) for use in cultivation. The tobacco was carefully nurtured through the many cycles of growth until it reached the curing stage. It was then stripped and sold at the auctioneers' market to the highest bidder. The profit was divided between the landowner and the sharecropper.

The corn was usually gathered in the field and divided between the two partners, who were at liberty to dispose of it as they wished. I don't recall the exact portion of the intake shared by each partner, but I am pretty sure it was not divided equally. It was more like two-thirds of the profit going to the landlord and one-third to the sharecropper.

When the work on his own crop was "all caught up," my father would hire himself out for a day or two each week to other farmers who needed extra help. For this labor he was paid $1.25 per day. This would provide some ready cash to supplement my mother's earnings in purchasing necessary food for the family.

We always had an abundance of food because we raised a variety in our garden, including asparagus and peanuts. My mother would can the surplus green beans, corn, and tomatoes for the winter months. Such vegetables as black-eyed peas, gray peas, navy beans, pinto beans, and butterbeans were allowed to dry on the vine, then picked and stowed away for winter.

At the end of the summer season, root vegetables such as turnips, beets, white potatoes, and sweet potatoes were put in something called a keel. This was nothing more than a hole in the ground, lined with straw and covered with soil, leaves, burlap bags, and pieces of plank. This served the same purpose in preserving food as the old-fashioned root cellars.

We also had a variety of fruit trees such as apple, peach, cherry, plum, greengage, and damson, as well as a strawberry patch and a grape arbor. The fruit was dried, canned, preserved, jammed, or jellied for future use. Wild strawberries, raspberries, and dewberries were gathered from the fields and put to the same use. Many of the berries and fruits were made into delicious wines. Cucumbers and watermelon rinds were made into pickles, cabbage into sauerkraut, tomatoes into ketchup, and green tomatoes into relish.

The hogs my family slaughtered in the winter supplied enough meat for year-round use. Pork provides a variety of cuts including hams, shoulders, bacon, roast, spareribs, backbone, liver, lights (lungs), heart, chitterlings, hogshead, brains, pig ears, pig feet, pig knuckles, pig tails, sausage, souse, and hogshead cheese.

Our cow supplied sufficient milk and butter to serve our family needs and often enough to share with the neighbors. We raised hundreds of chickens; many supplied food and others were kept as "layers." Thus we always had an abundance of fresh country eggs. Sometimes we raised our own Thanksgiving and Christmas turkeys. And sometimes my mother even tried her hand at raising ducks, geese, and guineas for food and for the market.

We carried our homegrown corn to the mill and had it ground into meal. Mother used much of the corn for making big pots of hominy, which we always kept on hand.

A WOMAN'S WORK

My mother contributed her share to the family budget by washing and ironing clothes for several white families, for which she was paid an average of one dollar per week per family. Her maximum earnings for this work never exceeded five dollars per week. She had no washing machine (nor did anyone else in that area in those days), so the clothes had to be scrubbed on an old-fashioned washboard, hand-rinsed, hand-wrung, and hung outside to dry. Imagine, if you can, what it was like hanging wet clothes outside in the winter with each piece freezing before it could be pinned on the line and your hands almost freezing in the process.

Since there was no running water in the house, the wash water had to be carried from a nearby pond and heated out-of-doors in a big kettle during the summer months or on the iron woodstove in the kitchen during the winter.

The ironing had to be done with old-fashioned "smoothing irons" heated around an outdoor brush fire in the summer or in front of an open wood fireplace in the winter. There was no rural electrification, and even if there had been, it would have made no difference since electric irons were unheard of, especially where I lived.

As I grew up, my household duties included setting the table, gathering vegetables from the garden, washing dishes, sweeping the floor, dusting the furniture, carrying water from the spring, washing and rinsing clothes, hanging them on the line to dry, bringing them in, and pressing the "rough" laundry such as towels, undies, and the like. By the time I reached my teens, I had learned to cook family meals, sew for myself, and iron all types of clothing, including the tedious white dress shirts. I also helped in the tobacco and cornfields and tackled almost any other task at hand.

We never had a lot of clothes, but we always had enough to keep clean and warm. My mother was a stickler for cleanliness and comfort. When we didn't have a car, we had a horse and buggy, the common method of transportation of the day. It wasn't many years, however, before my brother bought a brand-new Model T Ford. After that, the family was never without an automobile.

Our home was most unusual for a Negro family living in the country at this time because of its size. The three-room cottage where I was born was enlarged over the years, with rooms added as needed, until the roof was raised and a second story added, bringing the total number of rooms to seven, including the kitchen.

As I grew older and was able to analyze the circumstances of my youth, I realized that I was as well-off as any of the other schoolchildren—and maybe better off than most—who lived in the town and called me a country bumpkin because I didn't. My mother tried to dispel the stigma by telling me we lived in "the suburbs"—not the country, but the word meant absolutely nothing to me or to any of my classmates.

A LONELY GIRL

No neighbors lived in sight of our house, and no girls of my age resided anywhere in the community. However, there were several older children scattered around the neighborhood. The only one anywhere near my age was a little boy named Charles Dunnigan who visited our house often to play with my brother. Although Charles was five years older than I, he was two years younger than Brother Richard, and I felt that because his age fell between ours I also had a right to play with him. I was always pleased to see this little, dirty-faced, barefoot boy coming down the path through the thicket that blocked the view of the two houses.

Regardless of my happiness at his frequent visits, Charles consistently refused to play with me. He and Richard would trek off into the nearby "crusher-pond" to fish or skinny-dip, and of course I was not permitted to follow them. Even if I tried to join them in such games as marbles, catch (baseball), or top spinning, they would yell for my mother to "make this little girl let us alone. We don't want to play with her."

My mother would sternly warn me, "The boys don't want to be bothered with you. Why don't you let them alone and go back to your mud pies and dolls?" With tears in my eyes and a lump in my throat, I would slowly return to my favorite spot in the back of the house and again begin pouring water in the dirt to make mud cakes, talking to myself, and pretending to be talking with a playmate. This went on day after day during the summer months. On rainy days or during cold winter weather, I would entertain myself indoors with my dolls, busying myself cleaning my dollhouse, which my mother had arranged for me in the attic. I would play mother to the dolls, talking to them and pretending to prepare meals for an imaginary husband.

As I look back over those days, I realize that this was my introduction to sex discrimination. I wasn't sure how to deal with it and sometimes would just lie flat on the floor, giving vent to my emotions and crying for no discernible reason. My mother would rush to my side and ask, "What's wrong with you?"

"Nothing."

"Are you sick?"

"Noum" (for "No ma'am").

"Well, why are you crying?"

"I have a funny feeling."

"What sort of a 'funny feeling'?"

"I feel like Mama ain't wid me."

"You're talking foolish, child. I'm right here, ain't I?"

"Yessum."

Soon the crying would cease and I would go back to my playing. Little did I realize then that the "funny feeling" was nothing more than loneliness—a desire for attention, a longing to feel wanted, a yearning for love and affection.

When I was about four years old, I often cried to follow my brother around despite his hostility toward me. To placate me, my mother allowed me to go to Sunday school with him, but it didn't last long. Richard soon informed my mother that he was definitely not going to carry me to Sunday school anymore because I persisted in embarrassing him. "Every Sunday," he said, "as soon as Sunday school gets underway, Alice leaves her card class and comes over to my class whispering in my ear that she has to go to the 'closet'" (meaning the outdoor privy, which was used exclusively before indoor lavatories became prevalent). He went on to tell Mama that he always had to carry me out, unbutton my drawers, and wait for me to finish in the toilet so that he could button me up again before returning to class. His friends would laugh at him, tease him, and call him a nursemaid. This was just too humiliating, he complained.

Little girls in those days wore homemade, tight-legged, brown-domestic drawers with a trap door (three-button flap) in the back, buttoned up all around to what was known as a drawersbody. Little children couldn't manipulate these buttons and always had to have some help in an emergency. And what would one expect from a four-year-old who had hiked two miles, except that she would be forced to relieve herself at the end of the journey?

But my mother sided with my brother on the premise that "Alice seems to have a knack for embarrassing people," citing an incident during a typically long Southern Baptist church service when I had made a scene by crying and demanding a piece of cornbread after she offered me a cookie to satiate my hunger. I was too small to even remember the incident!

"YALLOW GAL"

My grandma Minerva also sided always with my brother, but she took it a step further. My little heart would practically break when Richard refused to play with me, but it was pierced almost beyond repair one day when I heard her tell my brother, who was brown-skinned like our mother, not to play with "that little ole yellow gal."

"I just can't stand yellow niggers," she said. "I never wanted none in my family. I can't understand why Lena [my mother] married that old yellow nigger."

Perhaps my brother would not remember our grandma's snide slurs regarding my color, but there was one incident he remembered all his life, even into his retirement. No doubt based on Grandma's disapproval of me, Richard developed a habit of mauling my head with his fist. He called it "putting the Nelson" on me. While it didn't hurt physically, it did hurt my feelings dreadfully. So I would cry and yell for Mama to make him behave. After speaking to him several times about this, she finally ordered him never to "put the Nelson" on me again. But he didn't heed her order.

The next time he did it, I cried and told Mama on him again. She became very angry, not so much for what he was doing as for disobeying her orders. She was sitting on the porch swing sewing, and without second thought she threw the sewing at him. Somehow the scissors got caught in the material and stuck in the top of his head. The blood gushed and she became terrified. Adding to her fear, Grandma shouted, "See what you've done! You're trying to kill that boy for that little old yellow gal!"

In due time the wound healed, but it left a jagged scar. It seemed also to have left a scar of guilt on my mother's conscience that never healed, because she appeared to spend the rest of her lifetime atoning for that one mistake. She humored Richard and catered to his every desire as long as she lived. Despite her humility, Richard often pointed to the scar on his head while telling people, "I'll carry it to my grave. Mama put this scar here about Alice when I was just a little boy." The scar that I carried was an unfavorable dimension to my character—a sense of intimidation, shyness, or fear of doing or saying the wrong thing at the wrong time. I cultivated the habit of quietness, refusing to speak up even when outspokenness was expedient or necessary. I found myself refraining from voluntarily reciting in the classroom, even if I knew the answers, for fear of making myself look silly. This introversion tended to create an image of stupidity, dullness, or lack of intelligence. Even today, I find myself holding back, for fear of becoming a bore.

Although Grandma Minerva failed to break up my parents' marriage (which lasted happily until my mother's death some fifty years later), she had started early in their married life to plant a wedge between my brother and me—based strictly on skin color. The color rivalry among Negroes was a holdover from slavery days, when lighter-complexioned slaves, who were obviously the offspring of the plantation owners, were frequently allowed to work, and sometimes even to live, in the "big house" with their fathers' families. They were usually assigned to the easier and more dignified jobs such as houseworker or handyman. This "class" often scorned the black slaves, to whom they felt superior. In return, this group—commonly known as "house niggers"—was resented and often despised by the darker slaves of pure African descent who were relegated to hard, dirty field work.

Using this caste system as a barometer for social standing, my father would have fallen into the category of house nigger, while my mother would have been looked upon as a product of the field nigger clan. This old status system was passing away with the ages until the 1960s, when it was revived by the Black Power movement. Only this time it was not applied to color alone but also to social attitudes. The more militant blacks branded the conservative Negroes as Uncle Toms or house niggers.

GRANDMA

We lived with my grandmother into my teens, even after she got married. Although she was in her late sixties, this was her first marriage. Her new husband, Jim Hardgrove, was a disabled widower who was no doubt seeking a home for himself. I didn't realize it then but later learned that he was suffering from an advanced stage of what was then called old-fashioned consumption. Although he was unable to work, he was up and around spending a great deal of time rabbit hunting. He often entertained the family in the evenings, picking the banjo and singing or telling horrible ghost tales. His nighttime stories were so scary that my brother and I would often be afraid to go to bed.

These family gatherings were short-lived. After a few months of marriage, Mr. Hardgrove stirred up dissension in the family by persuading my grandmother to have a will drawn up leaving all of her possessions to him after her death, with a special provision that the real property would convert to his heirs after his death. This would have deprived our family of the home on which my parents had spent a great deal of money, having enlarged the house from a one-room cabin to a comfortable six-room (later, seven-room) cottage. After this incident, the two families became somewhat estranged, each confining itself to its own quarters with little communication between them.

One evening just before retiring, I went into the dining room for a drink of water and heard a strange gurgling noise coming from my grandmother's room. As any uninhibited ten-year-old would do, I burst into the room without knocking. There I discovered my step-grandfather on his knees with his head resting in my grandmother's lap, hemorrhaging from the mouth and nose. She was just sitting there speechless with her arms around his neck, apparently not knowing what to do. I yelled for help. My mother, father, and brother came running, but within a matter of minutes he became limp and died in my grandmother's arms. I can recall how the puddle of blood on the old sandstone hearth left a stain that could never be removed no matter how much it was scoured. The entire hearth finally had to be replaced with new brick. With Mr. Hardgrove's death, the property feud was settled and once again we became a united family.

It must have been about four years later, in November 1920, when my grandmother passed away. I remember the date so well because it was the first election day after the adoption and ratification of the Nineteenth Amendment—women's suffrage—to the Constitution. My mother and grandmother, like all other women, were delighted to have the opportunity to cast a vote for their favorite candidates. They had planned to walk the two miles to town early that day to be there when the polls opened, thus avoiding the crowd. But on that election morning, Grandma woke up with a terrible headache and didn't feel like getting out of bed. This was not especially alarming because my whole family suffered from chronic migraine headaches ("sick headaches," as we called them). Mama went into town alone, leaving me to take care of Grandma and reminding me to "keep the fire up" in her room.

In the midst of my dishwashing, I got a sudden, strong urge to go put a log on Grandma's fire. As I entered the room, she was making a peculiar noise. I went to the bedside to ask what was the matter, or what I could do for her. She only glared at me with a strange, glassy look in her eyes, unable to speak a word. I hastily applied a cold compress to her forehead, and another and another as she continued staring at me, apparently trying to say something. Soon, the noise ceased. She closed her eyes and was gone.

I didn't know what to do. Fourteen-year-olds in those days were not as alert as teenagers are today. There were no telephones or close neighbors. I ran to the house of the nearest neighbor, asking her to come with me to see about Grandma. "She's very sick!" I emphasized. The neighbor calmly urged me to go on back home—she would be there in a little while. "Please come now," I pleaded. "I think she's dying." (I dared not admit that I thought she was dead.)

"Ah, go on back home, child," she ordered. "You know your grandma ain't dying."

Eventually the neighbor came, after she had finished whatever work she was doing. I was standing on the front porch when she arrived.

"How's she?" the neighbor asked.

"I think she's dead," I replied.

The neighbor rushed in and tried to find a pulse or a faint heartbeat. When none was discernible, she shouted, "Oh my God, she is dead!"

It was not the practice in that day to summon a doctor after someone had expired, since no death certificate was required. So we assumed that she had died of a cerebral hemorrhage. Although a decade had passed between the time that I'd overheard my grandmother castigating me because of my color, the incident crossed my mind as I stood beside her deathbed, and in my heart I secretly forgave her.

4

SCHOOL DAYS

Looking back now to that Sunday school incident of my very early childhood, I realize that out of it came some good. After my mother took me out of Sunday school at my brother's insistence, she was asked by my teacher, Miss Arletta Vaughn, why I no longer attended her class. When Mama explained the embarrassment I had caused my brother, Miss Arletta suggested that Richard drop me at her house on the way to Sunday school, and she would take it from there. She would bring me to the church and see that all my needs were taken care of. This arrangement worked out well.

My admiration for Miss Arletta, who taught regular school as well as Sunday school, helped build my confidence as I grew older. She was a stout, light-complexioned woman with a beautiful face and long, black hair that she wore in a bun at the back of her head. She was always pleasant and smiling, and she always showed a personal interest in everyone. She became my idol.

"Someday I'm going to be just like Miss Arletta," I said to myself. I realized that we already had some common traits, although I knew I would never have a pretty face like hers. However, our bodies were similar. "When I grow up," I vowed, "I'll be a big, fat, yellow woman like her. I'll never again feel guilty about my color. I'll never again feel ashamed of myself because I'm fat. I will no longer feel like a freak just because my hair is long, even if other children tease me. I'll be a schoolteacher when I grow up, just like Miss Arletta. I'll smile and be pleasant to people. I'll help them whenever I can. And I'll even do more. I'll write for a newspaper and let people know what other people are doing. I'll go around speaking to people about the proper way to live, and advise them on how they can have a better life."

I would then close my eyes and visualize myself in the future sitting on a speaker's platform wearing a wine-colored velvet dress. My black hair would be parted in the middle and loosely carried back in a soft chignon at the back of the neck. I would be welcomed and admired by my audience, and I would humbly, but gracefully, accept their praise and applause. Perhaps this daydream accounts for my spending the first money I ever earned on the purchase of a wine-colored silk-poplin dress (I couldn't yet afford velvet)—the first step toward my desired goal. And ever since, I've always managed to have a velvet dress in my wardrobe.

DROPOUTS

Unlike today, when there are local laws requiring children to stay in school until they reach a certain age, and truant officers to enforce these laws, the colored children of yesteryear were encouraged by their parents and white school authorities to leave school early and go to work. Boys dropped out at a much greater rate than girls. They had no incentive to do otherwise. There were no nationwide or government-sponsored "stay-in-school" campaigns as there are today. The adult community made no attempt to impress upon youngsters the necessity of getting an education. Therefore, children had no future to look forward to. This was especially true of boys since they saw no opportunity around them for anything more than hard manual labor like that in which their fathers and neighbors were engaged. Their parents encouraged them to leave school and go to work because it was the southern white man's theory that masculinity was measured by the amount and type of hard work that a man could endure. I saw that theory in action myself when I applied for a job in a rural school and was informed that a male teacher had applied for the same job. The white farmer, who was trustee in that community, favored me and willingly signed my application with the comment, "That big-old man should get out there behind a plow and go to work. I see no need for him sitting up in the shade on his 'hiny' all day. That's a woman's work."

It was the custom for white farmers to increase their productivity by having black farmhands compete with each other to see who could cut the most corn or set the most tobacco in the course of a day. The black men got a great kick out of these races, which they called "bucking" each other. There was no reward for the winner except a pat on the back and the spreading of word around the neighborhood that he was the "best" (most masculine) man in the community.

This old theory was handed down to boys, who concluded it would enhance their manhood to boast that they were hardworking men rather than sissy schoolboys. As a result of this culture, girls who managed to remain in school found upon graduation that they had no one to marry of their own caliber, at least not among their usual circle of friends.

As a preteen, my knowledge of the dropout problem was based on my limited experience with the two boys I knew best—Brother Richard, who dropped out of school in the sixth grade, and his buddy Charles, who dropped out about the same time. My brother sought work on the farm, while Charles ran away from home at the age of fifteen to escape family discipline. We learned later that he obtained a job in a coal mine in a nearby town.

America's entrance into World War I in 1917 brought on a nationwide scarcity of manpower. Industrial plants holding government contracts had to send recruiters into small southern towns seeking laborers. The companies paid their transportation to the factory sites, the majority of which were located in Pennsylvania. This was the first opportunity for black people to escape the southland en masse for a job that paid a decent wage. Some who took advantage of the opportunity never returned south, becoming permanent residents of northern cities.

Since my brother and Charles were both below the compulsory draft age (Charles around sixteen and Richard nearing eighteen), they both traveled "up north" seeking work. America's participation in the war lasted only one year. The armistice was signed on November 11, 1918. Factory recruits were discharged as veterans returned home to reclaim their jobs. Richard came home and made a deal with the Wilhelms to raise his own crop of tobacco on their farm "on shares," but Charles continued to drift from city to city, and from job to job, until family and friends completely lost track of his whereabouts.

From the days when I watched jealously as my older brother went off to school, neither rain nor snow nor even bullying by classmates about being a "hick" would keep me from wanting to go to class every single day. Even when my father would call me a fool for going to school on a day that "looked like rain" and call my mother a fool for letting me do so, I persisted. When the deep snow came, letting me go would sometimes be against Mama's better judgment, but she would wrap me up in long-john underwear, stuffed down in my black cotton ribbed stockings. Over this I would wear pink outing flannel or black sateen bloomers, a wool underskirt (made from one of Mama's old winter dresses), a cotton dress, a sweater, a coat, high-top button shoes, buckled overshoes, a long, wool-knit stocking cap that fit tightly on my head with the end wrapped around my neck like a scarf, woolen mittens, and a veil tied over my face. She would then reluctantly turn me loose in the cold for the long walk to school.

On one of those days, Dr. Ulysses Porter, the town's only Negro physician, passed me in his buggy en route to visit one of his patients in the country, and he smiled and waved at me. Some weeks later, when he was invited to address our student body about the importance of staying in school, he said he knew one student who would one day make good—Alice Allison, whom he had seen trudging for miles in knee-deep snow just to get to school. At first, the public pat on the back boosted my sagging ego and motivated me to strive even harder. But it also inspired my classmates to tease me all the more, saying that I looked like a stuffed rag doll, with a nose that resembled a rubber ball, and on and on.

LOOKING AHEAD

In spite of all of my social frustrations, I still managed to stay on top, or near the top, of my class, completing eight grades and passing into the high school department. The school was known as Knob City High, but it was actually a combination of an eight-grade elementary school and a two-year high school. I had a special interest in writing and drama, and if I had any talent at all, it was in these fields. My eighth-grade teacher had recognized my writing ability and encouraged me to develop it. This was especially gratifying because, since I was very little, I had wanted to be a newspaper reporter. I don't know where I got the inspiration for this because there was no Negro newspaper published in our town, nor did any circulate there. Negro newspapers were practically unheard of by most people in our community. There was only one white weekly in the entire county, and it certainly had no thought of employing black writers.

I shared my aspirations with a cousin, Virginia Herald, who taught school in Owensboro, Kentucky, a town about seventy-five miles from our home. She put me in touch with a friend who was editor of the *Owensboro Enterprise*, and he arranged for me to do a weekly column, composed of what I call "one-sentence stories," on happenings in our little community. This column, along with similar ones from other small towns around the state, made up an entire page under the heading "Home Town News." While I received no cash payment for the column, a number of papers were sent to me to sell for five cents each, out of which I got to keep three cents from each sale. The more papers I sold, the more space the editor would allot to my columns. The more space I had, the more names I could include, and more names would sell more newspapers. One item I wrote about, someone's automobile being struck by a freight train, caught the editor's eye during a week when hard news apparently was scarce. He lifted the one sentence from my column and elaborated on it (from his imagination), giving it a front-page spread with a bold black streamer. I was thrilled beyond description and vowed then and there that someday I would be a recognized journalist with many headlines and bylines. After two years as a columnist, my name was becoming known around the state as a prospective newspaperwoman.

As for my dramatic talents, except for a leading role in a high school play, I had no opportunity to pursue this. There was no demand for black actors in that era. Television had not yet been invented, radio employed only a few black people, and motion pictures still fewer. Whenever they were used on the screen, it was usually in servant type roles. So drama was not a profitable profession for Negroes to pursue. Public speaking, however, was something I became very good at, and it later became an important part of my professional political career.

The two-year Knob City High School was the only school for Negroes in the town of Russellville, while the whites had a fully equipped four-

Alice as a teenager
(Dunnigan Papers,
MARBL, Emory
University)

year high school and two colleges—one for girls, known as Logan College, and another for boys called Bethel College. The closest college for colored youth was in Frankfort, Kentucky, approximately two hundred miles away.[1]

Our school had no extracurricular activities. It taught no science because it had no laboratory. Since there was no demand for Negro typists or secretaries, nor for business administrators or executives, there were no provisions made to teach courses in office procedure such as typing, shorthand, bookkeeping, accounting, or any other business or commercial tasks.

HOME ECONOMICS

No vocational education was taught since there were no opportunities for the employment of black boys in skilled trades. No courses in woodwork were scheduled since there were no shops. Up until this time, there had been no courses in home economics, even though cooking for private families was about the only type of work available in that area for girls who did not qualify to teach school.

During my first year in high school, an interesting young woman named Octavia Bigbee came to town to live with her uncle, the Reverend C. P. M. Bigbee, pastor of the city's largest Negro church. Octavia could find no employment except in domestic service. Since it would have been rather degrading to have the niece of the town's foremost black leader working as a domestic, Reverend Bigbee worked out an arrangement with the board of education to have Octavia teach a course in cooking—called home economics—at our school.

There was no provision for any such course in the school curriculum, and no money available in the budget for another teacher. After some negotiation, an agreement was reached whereby if the school would provide the space, and the teachers would allow the high school girls some extra time, the home economics teacher would purchase the food for practice work, train the girls to cook, then sell the food they prepared as hot lunches to the students at a minimal cost. Through this arrangement, the girls would receive training in the art of cookery and at the same time the children would benefit from hot lunches for the very first time.[2] In lieu of an established salary, Miss Bigbee would be entitled to any profit, however meager, realized from the sale of the lunches.

After the plans were drawn, a large classroom was partitioned and converted into a kitchen and dining room. A secondhand coal stove was installed. Since there was no running water in the building, a sink was not needed. The water had to be drawn from an outdoor cistern and heated in teakettles on the stove. Dishes had to be washed from a dishpan kept on the stove at all times for that purpose. Dirty dishwater was disposed of by dashing it out the back door on the playground.

There was no thought of refrigeration in those days, so lunches had to be prepared from nonperishables such as dried or canned foods.

No theory of cooking was taught. No menu making was discussed. No consideration was given to balanced meals. No mention was ever made of calories. The word "nutrition" was unheard of among the students. "Vitamins" were not in our realm of knowledge.

We got right down to work on the very first day, preparing food for hot lunches. The first day was exciting as we prepared navy bean soup, salmon croquettes, and cottage pudding. The next day, the same menu was prepared, and the day after, and on and on for the entire two-year course, although the types of soup varied from day to day. Eventually we learned to make kidney-bean salad to add to the menu. These same items were prepared daily because they were inexpensive and good sellers. At that time, the price of a large can of plain white salmon was fifteen cents. When mixed with other ingredients such as eggs, diced potatoes, onions, and bread crumbs, at least a dozen croquettes could be made from a single can. I don't remember whether each menu item sold for five or ten cents, but whatever the price, it netted a fair profit.

As I recall, Miss Bigbee brought no extra cooking utensils for our convenience, not even a can opener. We were taught to open a tin can with a butcher knife. I thought that ridiculous at the time, but if there was a lesson in it, it was improvisation.

Although the girls did the cooking, selling, serving, and dishwashing, we were not permitted to eat any of the food—not even a cup of soup or one croquette. Everything was counted, including the squares of cottage pudding, and each item had to be accounted for. Octavia claimed that the margin of profit was so narrow that she couldn't afford to share any of the food with the girls who prepared it.

For me, that was almost too much to bear. I was still carrying my cold lunch to school in a little tin bucket. After preparing the hot lunch and smelling the appetizing aroma of onions, salmon, and other goodies, my cold biscuits and fat meat, or homemade jam between cold biscuits, just didn't seem palatable, and my mouth would water as I watched the other children enjoy the hot, seasoned food.

One day I asked my mother if she could give me ten or twenty cents a day to buy a hot lunch like the other children. She answered with an abrupt "No! If you think you're too good to eat my little stuff, you just get yourself a job and buy your own lunch." This was the first time I was made aware of my parents' financial status. While we had plenty of food, my mother was too proud to admit that their cash income was not adequate to cover additional expense, regardless of how small.

SOLVING THE PROBLEM

I racked my brain to come up with a way to earn some money out in the country. My situation was different from the girls who lived in town and could babysit in the evenings or find a little cleaning job in the mornings or dishwashing jobs in the afternoons after school. There was no one living near me who could use my services.

Then, one day on my way home from school, a white woman who lived on the edge of town asked if my mother could do another washing. I replied that I could do it for her. She seemed a little surprised and asked if I thought my mother would mind.

"No'm. Mama told me to get myself a job. And this is it," I gleefully replied.

"Since you'll be washing for only two people, my husband and myself, we will pay you seventy-five cents a week," the white woman stated.

"Get the clothes ready. I'll carry them now," I insisted.

She brought out the dirty clothes in a soiled pillowcase, and I "wagged" them all the way home along with my usual armful of books.

I was pleased to tell my mother that I had found a job and would now be making my own money so I could buy hot school lunches. She agreed to help me all she could. So together we worked out a plan for how the job could be done.

Mama instructed me that I must "pack" my own wash water from the nearby pond on Sunday afternoon, filling the kettle. She was referring to the big black kettle that was permanently perched on three tall legs in the backyard. Its specific purpose was for heating water to do her laundry work. Then, she said, I must drag up some brush from the woods, break it into short lengths, and place it under the kettle, ready for lighting a fire. She would light the fire on Monday afternoon in time to have the wash water hot when I arrived from school.

I would stop by the lady's house on my way home from school, pick up the dirty clothes, bring them home with me, and be ready to begin rubbing them on the old-fashioned scrub board as soon as I arrived. The scrubbed clothes would be packed in a tub of clean water, where they would remain overnight. I would have to get up early enough the next morning to rinse them out of the clean water then run them through another bluing water, starch them through a solution of homemade flour-starch, and hang them on the line for drying before leaving for school.

Mama would have the ironing fire made and the irons hot when I arrived home from school Tuesday afternoon so I could begin my pressing. The same would be true on Wednesday afternoon, when I could iron the better clothes. I should be able to finish my ironing on Thursday afternoon, pack the clothes in a little basket, and carry them back to the woman Friday morning on my way to school, at which time I would also collect my seventy-five cents for next week's rations.

Sometime later that same year, I took on another job, cleaning house for a second white family on Saturdays. This was the county sheriff's family, who lived in a big white house near town. It would take me the entire day, for which I was paid one dollar. Now I had enough for school lunches plus some other things I wanted, such as silk stockings like the town girls were wearing. I continued this work schedule throughout my two years in high school.

Prior to taking this job, Saturdays were the only days that offered any diversion in my weekly activities. When the weather was beautiful and warm, my mother and I would often spend the afternoons in town, visiting my father's sister, doing a little shopping, or just seeing and mingling with friends like other country folks came to town to do on Saturdays. They would congregate on the street corners and swap jokes or talk crops while eating cheese and crackers or chocolate drops from brown paper sacks, fingerpicking sardines from tin boxes opened with a pocketknife, licking ice cream from dripping cones, and drinking hot soda pop from tall bottles.

DISCOVERING JIM CROW

It was during those long Saturday afternoon street sessions that I first actually began to feel the sting of racial discrimination. I discovered that no public restrooms were available for colored women anywhere in the downtown area. A man could easily step into an alley, partially conceal himself behind a wagon or parked car, and relieve himself. But a woman found it necessary to go to the home of a friend somewhere in the residential section to take care of her needs. The stores provided no public accommodation for black customers, and the only public restroom, located in the county courthouse, was clearly marked "White Ladies."

Although just a child, I would walk right into the courthouse restroom whenever the urge arose, in spite of my mother's protest. "You stay out of that place," Mama warned. "You know that's against the law and it's dangerous. Them white folks are going to beat you half to death in there some of these times. And there ain't a thing we can do about it." But I kept going and nothing happened. The white women in there were just ordinary citizens who came in for the same purpose I did, and they had no authority to order me out. They would often give me dirty looks, but nobody ever openly challenged me.

I'd never heard the phrase "civil disobedience," but that is exactly what I was practicing in effect on my very own initiative. From that time throughout the rest of my life, I have worked to break down discrimination wherever I found it.

When high school closed for summer vacation, I took a third job, cleaning house every weekday morning for a family who lived in a small farmhouse about a mile from our home. I would arrive at about nine o'clock and clean the entire house by noon. After eating the midday meal, I would wash the dishes and be ready to depart by two o'clock. For this service I received $1.25 per week. My afternoons were devoted to doing my little washing, and Saturdays to cleaning house for the sheriff's family. This went along very well for a while, but it had gotten to be too much for me before the end of the summer.

The heavy work, plus the daily hike to the farm family's house and the mile-and-a-half walk to the sheriff's on Saturdays in the hot summer sun, took its toll, and I came down with malaria. When I recovered, it was time to go back to school, and I never worked for the farm family again.

GRADUATION

In 1923, at the age of seventeen, I was a happy person to receive a beautiful diploma from my two-year high school. I wanted in the worst way to continue my education as other classmates were planning to do, but my parents said this was not possible since they lacked the money to send me away to school. As a sharecropper, my father had no steady income. His wages came in a lump sum at the end of the year when the crops were sold. My mother contended that she could not keep up with their current living expenses and send me to school on her small weekly earnings as a washerwoman. While she seemed willing enough to send me if she could, my father was less interested. He kept asking why I wanted to continue in school, and "Why do you want to be a teacher? None of my folks ever made a teacher; why should you?" I reminded them that other classmates who seemed to have far less than us were enrolling in distant institutions of higher learning. I was the only one in my class with no hopes for the future, although I had probably struggled the most over the last ten years, and had graduated at the head of the class. But my parents stuck to their guns.

I wrote to top officials at Kentucky Normal and Industrial Institute

(KNII, later known as Kentucky State College), the only state school for colored students in Kentucky, and to Simmons University, a Baptist school in Louisville, asking for employment of any kind that might help pay expenses through school. Both schools replied that there were no in-school job openings, and out-of-town girls were not permitted to go outside of school for employment in those days. As far as I knew, there were no scholarships available during these years for needy or deserving youngsters.

The summer was passing swiftly, and as September neared I still had not figured out what I was going to do. I was still attending church regularly and serving as the Sunday school secretary, when one week before the opening date of Kentucky Normal, Sunday school superintendent Dr. William Russell, the town's only colored dentist, asked me where I was going to school that fall. He was shocked when I modestly replied that I wasn't going at all.

"What?" he asked in great surprise. "You were the best student in the whole class—the valedictorian—and you're not going any further in school?"

With tears in my eyes and a lump in my throat, I sadly replied. "My parents say they aren't able to send me."

"Tell your parents that I want to see them!" he exclaimed.

I did as he said, but as the week passed and he hadn't seen them, I became more despondent, finally going into a terrible mood where I couldn't eat or sleep and wouldn't talk. About midweek, my mother reminded me of a big picnic that was being planned for the following Saturday at Red River, a little rural settlement about ten miles away, and suggested that I go and then spend the following week with Ruth Spaulding, a good friend who lived there. The picnic was to be followed on Sunday by baptizing, one of two big affairs held annually at the rural churches throughout the area.

It was common practice for every rural church to hold an annual summer basket-dinner. This would be an all-day rally where members would bring great baskets of food and spread it out on tablecloths on the ground to be served free at noontime to all persons attending the meeting. People would come from far and near in buggies, wagons, and automobiles to meet and socialize with old friends, many of whom they had not seen in a long time. In that respect, these meetings served as homecoming events as well as religious fetes. During the autumn season, these same churches would hold big baptisms out-of-doors in a pond, creek, river, or whatever body of water happened to be located in the vicinity of the church. Like the basket-dinners, these occasions were as much social as religious gatherings and drew large crowds from around the country. I knew it would be an enjoyable event, and expected it might help take my mind off my unhappiness and disappointment, so I agreed to go.

As it turned out, I wasn't let down. Ruth and I had a wonderful time at the picnic on Saturday. Without parents or older brother around, I felt free to talk and flirt with the young farm boys without the usual parental restriction. The baptizing on Sunday was also like old home week. Hundreds of people who had moved away from the village to other sections of the country returned home to mingle with friends and relatives.

We were in the midst of it when I was shocked to see my mother and father driving up in their buggy. As soon as the ceremony ended, they summoned me to go to Ruth's house and get my things because they were taking me home.

Anger flared up in me and my face flushed. I all but choked out, "What have I done now? You said I could spend the whole week with Ruth."

"Yes," Mama replied calmly, "but you'll have to go home today. You've got to get ready to go to school tomorrow."

I couldn't fathom what she meant. "What school?"

"We're sending you to Kentucky Normal. Your other classmates, who were planning to leave tomorrow morning, have agreed to wait for you if you are ready by tomorrow night."

On the way home in the buggy, they filled me in. They had gone to church that morning and seen Dr. Russell. He had "jumped all over" them for not making a sacrifice to send me to school. He had reminded them of the many sacrifices I had made on my own initiative to stay in school, trudging the long distance through rain and snow to obtain what little education the school had to offer. This was an indication, he said, that out of the entire class I seemed the one most likely to succeed if I had the opportunity. Then he asked if they wanted to be guilty of denying me that opportunity. It would be a crime, he told them, to keep me out of school.

They quoted Dr. Russell as saying, "Send her! Do what you can to keep her there. If you get to the place that you don't have the necessary money, let me know and I'll lend it to you. And I won't hold either of you responsible for paying it back. I will wait until she gets out of school and finds a job, then she can pay me back. I have enough confidence in her to believe that she will make good and she will repay the loan. If she disappoints me, I will just be the loser, but I don't believe she will. At any rate, that's a gamble I'm willing to take."

With this assurance, my parents had no alternative but to get me ready and let me go. I will never forget Dr. Russell for that.

5

WHERE THERE'S A WILL

Monday was a busy day in the Allison household as we tried to get a few things ready for school. We had learned from the catalogue that girls wore uniforms. This was to my advantage, as it was to any poor girl, and the reason why the policy was adopted.

The girls' class uniforms for winter were navy blue serge middy suits, similar to the middies worn by sailors. In the fall and spring when the weather was warm, girls wore white cotton middies and the same blue skirts. The Sunday garb was a navy-blue suit (called a coat-suit) with a white blouse.

Fortunately, I had a blue middy suit since they were fashionable in those days and almost every girl owned one. I took some of my savings and bought two white cotton middies. Aunt Katie gave me her beautiful blue suit with a white lace dickey for dress-up wear. My blue taffeta dress with the gold-beaded sunburst, made for my high school class night exercise, was my only party dress. That completed my wardrobe, along with one change of undies and a change of stockings.

I didn't even have a trunk in which to pack my things. Again Aunt Katie came to my rescue. She searched her attic and came up with an old trunk with a broken lock. My father tied it on the back of the buggy, hauled it to the blacksmith shop to have the lock repaired, and had it back home in time to pack.

With all in order, I was ready to leave on the evening train with class-mates Mildred, John, and Willie, each of whom lived with a widowed mother. We left home happy and gay, but because it was the first time any of us had been away from home, we were already beginning to feel a little sad, homesick, and edgy with each other by the time we changed trains in Louisville around two o'clock in the morning. When we reached the Frankfort campus early Tuesday morning, we were still a little homesick and lonely, feelings that worsened when we found the students unfriendly to newcomers while welcoming their friends from previous years with open arms, kisses, and handshakes. Mildred and I were happy at least to be assigned to the same room since we'd been friends all through our earlier school years.

After unpacking and paying my registration fee and a month's board of fifteen dollars, I was sitting alone in the reception room of the girls' dormitory when a lady walked up and asked if I would help serve supper since I didn't seem very busy. I gladly agreed. After supper, I was asked to help wash dishes, which I also did without objection.

When the dishes were finished, I asked this lady (who I later learned was the stewardess, Mrs. Harrison) if I might have a regular job waiting tables and washing dishes.

"We have already assigned girls to these jobs," she stated coldly. "We're using the same girls we used last year. Some of them are just a little late arriving. That is why we are shorthanded tonight. We always use the same girls year to year until they graduate. Then others are selected from a long waiting list. You're new. You'll have to register for the job. Then your name will go on the bottom of the list, and you'll have to wait your turn."

Heavy hearted, I left the dining room thinking there was no reward for favors rendered. Early the next morning, around seven o'clock, I heard my name being paged in the hallway. I stuck my head out the door and was told that Mrs. Harrison wanted to see me in the dining room immediately. I dressed as quickly as possible and hurried down the stairs, where she told me that she wanted me to help serve breakfast. She then assured me that this job was mine if I still wanted it, explaining, "If those other girls were sincerely interested in their jobs, they should have reported for duty on time." I couldn't have been happier.

There was no cash with this job but a credit of "half-board." That meant my monthly board was reduced by $7.50, which made me very happy. But, even with the ten dollars my mother sent me each month, there was no money after paying board and buying secondhand books and supplies to pay for cleaning my clothes. I wore my blue serge skirt until it was stiff and smelly with grease and funk. As long as the weather permitted the wearing of white middies, I could get by washing them. But when I was forced into the blue serge middy, the situation changed, since it was not washable and soon smelled of body odor and dishwater, making me offensive to be near.

Finally it was so embarrassing that I wrote my mother explaining the situation, as much as I hated to burden her with my needs. She immediately sent me two homemade, navy-blue cotton middies. None of the other girls wore cotton middies in the winter, but I welcomed them because at least I could keep them clean and odorless. I actually cried when the box arrived—grateful for my mother's concern and undoubted sacrifice.

Next the waitresses were requested to wear white aprons on the job. Once again I reluctantly had to write home for them. My mother cut up an old white dress that I'd left behind and made aprons, which she bleached and laundered and sent to me. Although they were plain homemade aprons with no fancy, frilly ruffles like some of my coworkers were wearing, I kept them spick-and-span, neatly starched, and ironed, and I wore them with great pride.

However ragged my one change of underwear and stockings had become, I continued to wash them every night, and in winter I placed them on the radiator overnight to make sure they were dry enough to wear the next morning.

The duties of my job were very taxing. Breakfast was served from seven to seven-thirty, dinner from twelve to twelve-thirty, and supper from five to five-thirty. Waitresses had to be on the job a half hour before each meal, seven days a week, to see that the tables were set up properly and the food ready for service as soon as the students were seated. Each waitress was responsible for two tables seating twelve and fourteen, respectively. She also had to wash the dishes for her own tables after each meal. This required some real rushing, especially if she happened to have an eight o'clock or a one o'clock class.

Compulsory chapel exercises (for all except waitresses) were held daily from eleven-thirty to twelve. Many times visitors were invited to speak during these exercises. Although they were always instructed to keep their remarks brief, many would completely disregard time, prolonging the chapel period and thus delaying the midday meal. This would require the dishwashers to work overtime, causing them to be late or absent from their one o'clock classes. Making matters worse, most of the instructors showed no sympathy for the working student, who was expected to toe the mark in every respect, just like the students who had plenty of leisure time. These instructors neither accepted nor even listened to excuses.

Pantry work was not only a rush job but a heavy one. The kitchen was in the basement of the girls' dormitory, one floor below the dining room. Food was sent up on a dumbwaiter to a serving room, called the pantry, adjoining the dining room. Sometimes the food servers were so slow sending up the food that the waitresses would find it quicker to run down the steps, get the food, and rush back up in order to get their tables served within the allotted time.

In their rush to get the dishes cleared away after meals, waitresses often found themselves carrying big trays loaded with twenty-six glasses, many half-filled with water, making them entirely too heavy for a girl to carry. Then each dish had to be washed, rinsed, dried by hand, and stacked on the table, ready for the next meal.

As the year went on, dishes were broken until the supply got so scarce that there were not enough left to go around, and the school had no budget to buy another supply. If a waitress came into the dining room early and found she was short a plate or two, or a few glasses, she would swipe some from another table and then stand guard over them until mealtime. When the last waitress to arrive found her table short of dishes, someone at that table would be short of a meal. The waitress was always blamed. The deprived student would lambaste her, calling her all kinds of names while beating on the table with the silverware, usually leaving the poor girl in tears.

Instead of taking out their hostility on the administration as they should have (and would today), the deprived students targeted the helpless, harried waitresses. There were no pickets, no boycotts, no mass protests on the campus, and no confrontations with school authorities, who were responsible for not demanding necessary supplies from the state department of education.

Student protest for better food and better service would have been justified since our meals consisted almost daily of only beans (of different varieties) and bread for dinner, and canned peaches or stewed prunes and white bread and butter for supper.

One by one, the waitresses succumbed to the harassment from fellow students and gave up their jobs. When new girls were brought in, the remaining waitresses had the double hardship of having to train them. It became so bad that Mrs. Harrison resigned as well, leaving no supervision over the girls and making the situation even worse. The girl with the most experience was then elevated to acting supervisor, which the other girls resented. They gave her no cooperation or respect, making her so miserable that eventually she resigned, too.

By May, the month before school closed, every girl who had started work at the beginning of the term except me had quit the job. I tried desperately to hold on because I had hoped and prayed so hard for a job, and I needed it so badly. But finally I became ill, and the doctor ordered me to give it up. With that, my board doubled to the original fifteen dollars a month, which upset my parents terribly since it came at the end of the term, when they also had to send my train fare home.

Despite all the hard work and my impoverished status, campus life, in contrast to my existence back home, was great fun and an exciting experience. There were continuous activities and never a dull moment. The year chugged along with all kinds of adventures both pleasant and unpleasant, the latter due chiefly to my poverty and frequent hunger.

Some of the girls sneaked kerosene stoves into the dormitory to heat their straightening combs and curling irons. My roommate had one, and we would use it to cook tidbits we managed to slip out of the pantry. Sometimes I could persuade the school butcher to slice me a small hunk of beef. Our beef was raised and butchered on the school farm. At other times, I might sneak out a loaf of bread. Still, it was all worth it. It was with great sadness, therefore, that I realized I would not be able to return the following year since I would no longer have a job. Somehow I had to find a way to profit from the year's work completed. Finally I came up with an idea that I discussed with the dean.

Normal schools were composed of a regular four-year high school with two years of normal (or teacher training) equivalent to freshman and sophomore college classes. Graduates of eight-grade elementary schools, with sufficient financial backing, could enroll at KNII for the entire six-year course, which would give them a full high-school education and two years of college. Upon graduation, they would receive a certificate entitling them to teach for three consecutive years, after which their certificate would automatically be renewed for life. Eighth graders who were unable to stay through the full course could enroll in a special elementary teacher training course, which would award them a two-year teacher's certificate for work in elementary schools following two years of study.

Two-year high-school graduates such as me, who were unable to take the entire normal course, could enroll in an intermediate teacher training course. After two years of study, they would be qualified for a four-year teacher's certificate.

Regular spring sessions were conducted in these institutions for teachers who wished to continue their studies after the close of school. Since rural school terms were only seven months in Kentucky, teachers could return to KNII in early April for a three-month spring term plus an additional six-week summer session. This would amount to one semester's work. Thus teachers could continue their studies spring and summer until they completed the entire normal course.

I had enrolled in the intermediate teacher training course. Had I remained in this course for two years, I would have been qualified to teach in junior high schools for a period of four years. When I discovered that I would be unable to return for my second year's study, I asked the dean if it would be possible to be awarded a two-year elementary teacher's certificate since I had already done a year's work beyond the requirement for this type of certificate. I realized that this would downgrade my qualifications, but I was willing to make this sacrifice rather than lose what I had already accomplished. The dean took my request under consideration and discussed it with a faculty committee. Later he called me in for further information. They had checked my work record and found that I was dependable, conscientious, and sincere. I also had a good class attendance record. But since they had no exact knowledge of my academic attainment as the final grades for the year had not yet been released, the dean wrote a request for my record and had me hand-carry it to each of my instructors and return their replies to him.

I was a bit apprehensive because I did not know how well I had done scholastically. But I made the rounds and returned the sealed envelopes to the dean. He opened them in my presence, and, to my surprise, my lowest grade was about eighty-six and my highest around ninety-three.

Impressed with my grades, the dean smiled and assured me that anyone who could earn grades like this in spite of all the obstacles I had to face certainly deserved some reward. Before school closed for the year, I had in my hand a certificate authorizing me to teach in any elementary school in the state for a period of two years. I returned home the first student ever to leave Russellville and return after only one year's study as a licensed schoolteacher. Dr. Russell practically jumped with joy as he proudly told my parents, "I told you so!"

6

THE JOB HUNT

Back in Russellville, I spent almost the entire summer of 1924 searching for a job, and it was the most difficult and disappointing period of my life. I was proud of my two-year elementary teacher's certificate and clutched it tightly in a large manila envelope when I visited the Logan County school superintendent to apply for a position as a county schoolteacher. That certificate represented one hectic year marked with struggle, toil, and hardship at the only state institution of higher learning for Negroes in Kentucky.

My spirits were high when I entered the county office of education but were soon crushed by the superintendent when, after examining my transcript and newly earned certificate, he stated apologetically, "Your academic record is satisfactory. I have no doubt that your newly acquired teaching methods are adequate, if not superior, to those now used by my present teaching staff, but you have no experience. We could not justify the replacement of an experienced teacher with one as young and inexperienced as you. We'll keep you in mind, however, if anything opens up."

I left the office with tears in my eyes, a pain in my heart, a crimp in my spirit, and a puzzling question in my mind as to how a young teacher could ever get experience if she is not given a chance to work. I mailed applications to school authorities in almost every county in the state, and I visited the superintendents in adjacent counties—Todd, Warren, Simpson, Christian, and Muhlenberg. The results were practically the same everywhere—too young (eighteen), no experience, no vacancies. Some superintendents acknowledged the application with simple statements that it would be kept on file in case a vacancy occurred. Others didn't bother at all.

I had worked extra hard and made painful sacrifices to obtain my teacher's certificate in half the usual time because I knew I would be unable, both physically and financially, to return to school the following year. If I failed to find a teaching job, I would be forced to accept employment as a domestic servant. Then my whole year's work, sacrifice, and money at the teacher training school would have been lost. I was sure the experience would crush my spirits so badly I would never again be able to summon the courage to continue my education.

It was common knowledge during this period that the supply of teachers greatly exceeded the demand, especially among black people of the South. The fact was that no other type of dignified employment was available for Negroes. If a young Negro man had courage to seek higher education, he had no other alternative than to teach or preach, or perhaps become an undertaker or an insurance agent. There were no black lawyers practicing in any of the small southern towns and only a few, if any, doctors. Likewise, if a Negro girl received higher training, the only job available to her was that of school teaching. If she could find no employment in the public school system, her future would be relegated to that of domestic servitude as a cook, cleaning woman, nursemaid in a private family, or "washerwoman."

There were no office jobs since there were no Negroes in business who needed secretaries, typists, or even file clerks. There were no Negro salesgirls since no Negroes owned stores. There were no librarians since there were no libraries in these small towns. There were no jobs for trained nurses since there were no hospitals nearby. There were no social workers since there were no social welfare programs in existence. And even if there had been any jobs in these categories, no whites would employ blacks for them.

There was a small shirt factory in my hometown and a little hosiery mill nearby, but they employed only whites. Negro women were not even employed in commercial laundries, nor were they hired as charwomen in public institutions such as schools or municipal offices in government buildings. These types of jobs were filled by poor, illiterate whites who were qualified to do nothing else and were not willing to work as servants in private homes.

It became a common expression among Negroes in those days that "either you make a schoolteacher or you end up in the white folks' kitchen." I did not want to do that, and it grieved me the entire summer. I had been publicly praised by the minister of our church and other local educators for being the first from my school ever to earn a teacher's certificate in one year of study. My parents were proud of me, and it gave me joy to know that I had lived up to, or even surpassed, their expectations. Now I was to be humiliated by not being able to obtain a professional job and would be forced to end up "in the white folks' kitchen." I cried. I prayed. Nothing happened. I cut myself off from friends to avoid embarrassing questions. I shut out all social activities. I didn't wish to see or talk with anyone. I was hurt, and I was bitter.

And so I passed the summer in self-imposed isolation until, eventually emerging from this gloomy cocoon on the first Sunday of September, I finally determined to start life anew, accepting it as it came. The local sandlotters were playing their final game of the season, and I was trying my best to whoop up a victory in a sun-drenched cow pasture with most of the town's sports fans, shouting as though the loudest cheering section would clinch the game. Suddenly I felt a firm, steady tap on my shoulder and, turning, heard my brother, Richard, say, "We're going home."

I had already come to regard Richard as a regular killjoy. Seven years my senior, it seemed he was always on hand to jeopardize my pleasure whenever he thought I was having a good time. As usual, I raised no argument and quietly followed him to his Model T Ford, in which we rode away without another word, although I was furious that at eighteen, and with a hard-earned schoolteacher's license, I was still subjected to his paternalism.

But a short distance down the road I could bear it no longer, and a whole summer's worth of frustration poured out: "Why did you do it? Why did you drag me from the baseball game just as I was beginning to have fun? Have I not suffered enough anguish this summer? Or does your sadistic nature thrive on seeing other people squirm in an atmosphere of unhappiness and discontentment?"

"Mama sent me to bring you home," he replied, calmly but firmly.

"For what?"

"She said you must get ready for your new job tomorrow."

"What job?" I asked, more infuriated than ever because I thought Mama had hired me out as a cook or a maid to some "good white folks," as she would say.

"Your school-teaching job," Richard replied, showing no sign of emotion.

"What school?" I asked, getting madder all the time because I thought he was just pulling my leg.

"Mount Pisgah," he answered, adding after I exclaimed that I'd never heard of it, "It's in Todd County, somewhere near Trenton."

As the story unfurled, I learned that Mount Pisgah was a one-room country school four miles south of Trenton, a town with a population of about eight hundred, which, at some thirty miles from Russellville, seemed almost halfway across the country. (Model Ts in those days seemed to be flying if they made thirty miles an hour.) Just as school was about to open on Labor Day, the top school administrator discovered that Mount Pisgah had no teacher. A man who had taught there for years had died suddenly on the eve of the school's opening day. Looking over the applications filed in his office, he decided mine showed the best qualifications and tried to contact me for the job. Since, like most rural families, we had no telephone, he called the pastor of our church, whom I had used as a reference, and Rev. C. P. M. Bigbee drove out to our home to deliver the message. My parents, overwhelmed with joy, immediately sent Richard to the improvised baseball park to fetch me home.

The feeling that possessed me at the moment I heard the big news is indescribable. I would never feel the same sense of accomplishment, joy, and gratitude again until some thirty years later, when I entered the White House as an accredited news correspondent. It was a moment that confirmed my sorely challenged belief that sincere efforts are rewarded and that, as my mother was fond of saying, "Where there's a will, there's a way." It was a motto I would live by for the rest of my life.

7

THE UPS AND DOWNS
OF MY FIRST JOB

Reverend Bigbee picked me up at five o'clock on Labor Day morning, having offered to drive me to my
new post and see that I got started on the right foot.
Two hours later, we approached the school, stopping
nearby at a three-room double log house occupied by
two elderly ladies, the widow Frances Tutt and her
crippled, spinster sister, whom everyone called Miss
Molly. The sisters were reluctant to even consider
Reverend Bigbee's humble plea that they provide living accommodations for me because of convenience
to the school and because we could be of some help
to each other.

"We don't want to board no more schoolteachers,"
said Mrs. Tutt. "The last one we had was always complaining about something. We ain't got much, you
know. We can't afford the kind of fancy food that the
city folks been used to." (Because of the remoteness of
Mount Pisgah, its citizens considered the small village
from which I came a city and looked upon me as a city
gal.) "This woman would be dissatisfied here, and we
just don't want to be bothered."

Reverend Bigbee did not give up, assuring them that
I was not hard to please. "She's just a plain, country-

reared girl," he said. "She'll be satisfied with whatever you have to offer. She'll adjust to your way of life and will be little or no trouble at all."

Finally, after much persuasion, the ladies agreed to board me for sixteen dollars a month, which they considered "big money" and was indeed a sizable chunk in those days and in that locality. It was fortunate for me that they agreed because there was no other suitable place to stay for miles around. The nucleus of this little community consisted of a neat, well-kept, white frame church sitting on the hill at the bend of a dirt road. Down in the valley a few hundred feet, behind the church, stood the little schoolhouse where I was to work. It was a drab, ramshackle frame building with rough, weather-beaten sides, a rusty tin roof, and two small windows on either side. The several broken windowpanes were covered with squares of yellowing cardboard. The building had no steps since it sat flat on the ground.

Miss Frances and Miss Molly's house was just across a little cow path from the school premises. Adjoining their property was another tumble-in, one-room log cabin occupied by an aged couple who cared for their two grandchildren, Roberta Tyler, a teenager, and her younger brother. At the top of another rise a few hundred yards away stood a somewhat larger log-and-frame combination home occupied by the Dixon family. Mr. Dixon was a bigwig in the church—something like the chairman of the deacon board—and an influential community leader. His wife was a sister of my two landladies. The Dixons had five children: Veatrice, a teenage daughter; two grown sons, Turner and Scoot; and two school-age boys called Brother and Booty. This was the total makeup of the Mount Pisgah center; however, students enrolled in the school from many miles around.

Once I was settled in my new home, Reverend Bigbee and I went over to take a look at the interior of the school building before opening time at eight. The inside was as crude as the outside. The floor was rough and dusty. The unpainted walls and ceiling were graying with age. A rusty pot-belly stove sat near the center of the room with several joints of stovepipe shooting upward, then elbowing into a hole cut in the roughly constructed flue. The pipe was secured by a strand of rusty wire wrapped around it and stapled to the ceiling. The wall around the flue hole was blackened with smoke, and brown, jagged streaks ran down the wall, marking traces of rain that had from time to time poured through the leaky roof.

The seats were old, rough-hewn, discarded church pews in which odd initials and other funny markings had been carved by mischievous boys with their trusty jackknives.

I was completely disgusted at the appearance of a place supposedly representing a center of learning. But I was too proud of my new job to complain. Instead I made a mental note of what I could do to improve the school's appearance.

Soon the children began to arrive, wide-eyed and curious to see what the new teacher looked like. Many were accompanied by their parents, who were just as anxious to see the new schoolmam. While I stood shyly in the background, Reverend Bigbee went forward and greeted them, introducing himself and reminding them of the years he pastored in nearby Trenton. After more small talk, he introduced me.

Most of the parents looked at me disapprovingly. Some even expressed fear that I would not be successful because, they said, "She's too young. She can't manage these kids. Some of our students are older than she is!" After being assured by Reverend Bigbee that I would be a success, not only in properly instructing their children but also in helping build up the community, the parents ultimately pledged cooperation with the new teacher. Finally, with the formalities out of the way, Reverend Bigbee departed for home and the parents left shortly thereafter, leaving me on my own to enroll the students and announce plans for the next day.

ESTABLISHING PRIORITIES

As some of the parents had observed, all three of my senior (eighth-grade) students were around my own age. Veatrice Dixon, my landladies' niece, was eighteen; Roberta Tyler, the girl next door, was seventeen; and Miss Frances's granddaughter, Louise Dickerson, was about sixteen. Because her family lived several miles away, Louise also lived with my landladies during the school year. I spent much of my time giving special instruction to these girls to prepare them to pass the county examination at the end of the term. It was the policy of the board of education to have identical final examinations for all seniors in the county—black and white. I had been told that very few black students passed this examination, not because of racial prejudice nor any inability to learn but perhaps because of improper coaching by uninterested teachers, lack of self-confidence, or nervousness generated by fear of competing with white students on questions prepared and graded by white people. I was told that there had never been a graduate from Mount Pisgah during my predecessor's years there, nor could anyone remember ever having a graduate from that school. Pupils dropped out, refused to take the county exam, or flunked the finals. I was determined to see that my senior class compared favorably with students from any school in the county and made this goal my number-one priority for the year's program.

My total enrollment was around sixty-five, with an average daily attendance of about forty-five, a good record for a rural school. Traditionally, rural children attended school very irregularly, partly due to the distance they had to travel but mainly because parents kept them out about half the time to help with farmwork.

The heavy curriculum imposed upon rural schools required a carefully planned daily program. The upper classes carried a schedule of ten subjects including spelling, reading, arithmetic, English, history, geography, agriculture, general science, art, and public school music. Once I'd worked out the schedules for all eight grades and ensured it was running smoothly, I began to concentrate on improving the physical plant, seeking and welcoming student and community participation. This proved so popular that I suggested we organize a parent-teacher association, something unheard of in this community. They were delighted with the idea, and the school's first PTA was formed.

I was delighted when the month ended and I was able to go to Elkton, the county seat, and pick up my first check of sixty-three dollars. This was more money than I'd ever seen in my lifetime. After paying my landlady her sixteen dollars for board, I sent my mother twenty dollars, the exact amount that she earned in a month as a five-dollar-a-week laundress. The balance was my own to use as I pleased.

While visiting the office of education, I discussed with the superintendent the many things needed at our school. While he didn't take too kindly to the lengthy list, he at least agreed that a new roof was necessary to keep out the rain and that windowpanes were essential to keep out the cold and let in more light. He also offered me some secondhand desks that were stored in an old warehouse if I could get them hauled to the school, as the county would not furnish delivery. Also agreeing that dust is detrimental to the health of children, he gave me some cheap oil to liven up the floor and abate the dust.

Soon we had a shiny new tin roof, and the yellowing cardboard over the broken window panes had been replaced with glass. Mr. Dixon and his two adult sons, Turner and Scoot, picked up the desks and delivered them to the school, where they replaced the carved-up church benches. These improvements served as an incentive to all of us to do more to beautify the old building. Toward that end, the newly formed PTA began planning for our first program, a Halloween night entertainment with poems, songs, and little dialogues appropriate for the occasion. Since we had no music to accompany the songs, we asked Mr. Dixon to have the church organ brought down for the evening, but we still needed someone to play it. Walter Dickinson, the church organist, volunteered to do it. Walter, in his twenties, was the oldest of the six Dickinson offspring and lived a short distance from the church with his parents and four younger siblings. Although he had no formal musical training, he had a great deal of talent and could strike up, by ear, any tune he heard. He enjoyed coming to rehearsals early, arriving during the noon recess and taking part in playground activities, which was the only help I had during the day.

The PTA's Halloween affair attracted an overflow crowd, each of whom paid ten cents for admission, providing sufficient profit for the organization to paint the walls and ceiling (a restful baby-blue), the blackboard, and even the rusty stove. The older girls made sash curtains, on the border of which the younger children traced and painted animals, giving the appearance of a circus parade. The old school was shaping up and looking good!

As Thanksgiving approached, we planned another celebration, and again Walter volunteered to play the borrowed organ. Admission this time was free, and instead money was made on a box supper following a short pageant in dialogue and song on the story of Thanksgiving. The women and older girls of the community each packed a box of food, which was auctioned off to the highest bidder. The rule was that the packer and the purchaser would share the box together. The older men tried to outbid each other for the box packed by their own wives or the favorite neighborhood cook, while the younger men outdid themselves to buy the box belonging to their favorite girlfriend. The outcome was a lot of fun and a handsome sum of money that went into the PTA treasury.

During a rehearsal, Walter mentioned a baptizing at a neighboring rural church on the following Sunday and asked if I would like to go. Since these events were big affairs in rural areas, I thought it would be a nice outing and accepted the invitation.

DOUBLE TROUBLE

Sunday dawned bright and warm, promising a lovely autumn day. Turner dropped by our house in the early morning and took a seat on the front porch, where he was joined shortly by some other men. I thought it a bit unusual for Miss Frances to have so many male visitors so early on an "off-Sunday" morning. Because of the nearness of her house to the church, it was customary to have a houseful of visitors on meeting Sundays (every other Sunday) but most unusual to have guests on Sundays when there were no services, or "off-Sundays" as they were called.

When Walter arrived and I started out toward the buggy, Turner ordered me not to get in.

"What do you mean, 'Don't get in'?"

"I just mean what I say. Stay out of that buggy!"

"You don't have anything to do with whose buggy I get in. You must be out of your mind," I retorted as Walter helped me in. And away we went.

We had an exciting day, arriving back at Pisgah near dark. Walter asked if I would like to stop by his house and meet his parents. "It's getting late," he said. "I would like to feed my horse and put him in the stable before it gets too dark. If you don't mind, I'll walk you home."

After a brief and pleasant visit with his parents, we started on the short walk to Miss Frances's house, strolling down the road a little way, then across the churchyard to my front gate. He saw me to the door but did not come in.

As Walter made his way back up the same path across the churchyard, Turner jumped out from behind some bushes where he'd been hiding, put a pistol in Walter's face, and pulled the trigger three times. The gun misfired each time.

Soon word spread through the community that two neighbors, distant cousins who had been lifelong friends, were feuding over the new teacher and that one had almost killed the other. The eighteen-year-old teacher was blamed for the entire situation, although I was completely unaware of what was happening.

Both Walter and Turner, I soon learned, had been boasting that I was his girlfriend. Walter boasted that he called on the new teacher every day and played baseball with her on the school playground. Turner, meanwhile, was recalling his visits to Miss Frances's house, where he and his brother Scoot frequently joined my landladies and the older girls around the kitchen stove on chilly nights, sipping homemade wine, telling tales, eating popcorn, and singing spirituals, folk songs, and our favorite popular numbers.

Now Turner was quoted as saying, "She has told me often that I had to see Mama every night or I couldn't see Mama at all," never mentioning that these were no more than the lyrics of one of the popular tunes included in our family sing-alongs.

Each young man carried his boasts a bit further by betting he would be the first to carry the teacher out (meaning, in effect, to take me on a date). The contest got out of hand when other men in the community got into it, placing bets on either Walter or Turner. I had never heard of such shenanigans and knew nothing about it.

On that Sunday morning, the other men had come to the house to see what happened and collect their bets. When Turner lost, they reportedly teased him unmercifully, and he threatened to "get Walter." He almost did.

The deacons got out a warrant for Turner's arrest for disorderly conduct and attempted murder on church property. Turner went into hiding and couldn't be found. While the sheriff was still looking for him, his father negotiated an out-of-court settlement and he was able to return home.

Gossipers in the community blamed me for what had happened, saying I was undoubtedly flirting with both boys, leading them on. The incident changed our entire living pattern in the Tutt household. There were no more family fireside chats and no more sing-alongs. I stayed in my room, lonely in the evenings, trying to entertain myself with a good book while the landladies reverted to their old custom of "going to bed with the chickens." I addressed both Turner and Scoot very coolly when they came to do their afternoon chores, for fear that common courtesy would once again be mistaken for flirtation. I hardly saw Walter anymore and greeted him with the same air of coolness whenever I did.

This incident may seem insignificant by today's standards, but in those days it could have ruined my entire future since a schoolteacher was supposed to be the very epitome of morality. Any "toe stub" on this path of righteousness could be a major calamity. With that constantly on my mind, I continued the school program with a few changes. Special occasions, including Christmas and Valentine's Day, were observed appropriately and with special programs but without music. When the February festivities were out of the way, I again focused my attention on preparing my eighth-grade class for the county exam. To my delight, all three girls came through with flying colors.

Commencement would be the first held at the school in anyone's memory, and we went to great lengths to assure its success. I even employed and paid out of my own pocket for a popular jazz combo from Clarksville, Tennessee, to accompany the student solos of such popular numbers of the day as "I'll Be Loving You Always," "Me and My Shadow," "Three Little Words," "My Buddy," "Danny Boy," and the like.

My family came down from Russellville to attend the big doings, and Reverend Bigbee came with them to deliver the commencement address. It was a great affair and raised a sizable amount of money for the PTA treasury.

I left for home with my parents immediately afterward, and neither they nor Reverend Bigbee ever knew of the near tragedy that almost cost one man his life, another man his freedom, and me my job and my future.

8

A PLUNGE INTO THE
SEA OF MATRIMONY

Life did not seem the same on the opening day of the
second term at Mount Pisgah. My father and brother
drove me down, dropping me at the same boarding-
house, where I was warmly welcomed by my landladies, Miss Frances and Miss Molly. My students of last
year greeted me with affectionate hugs and friendly
handshakes while the new ones stood back shyly, waiting for me to approach them, get acquainted, ease their
fears, and make them feel welcome and comfortable.

I was encouraged by the large enrollment of students and pleased with the good turnout of parents
who came to greet me. But somehow the enthusiasm
was not exactly the same. While any mention of the
unpleasant events of the previous year was carefully
avoided, I still felt that sidelong glances of disapproval
were sometimes aimed at me, or accusing fingers still
being pointed behind my back.

My schoolwork had been so well organized the
year before that it got off to a smooth running start,
and most of the improvements that could be made
to the physical plant had already been accomplished.
Having become familiar with the format of the final
county-conducted examination for the eighth grad-

ers, I was confident that my senior class would be adequately prepared to pass the test without extra time for special coaching.

Members of the PTA attending the opening session discussed activities for the upcoming year and endorsed plans for some type of social function on every holiday, just as in the previous year. But the real thrill of introducing any new ideas had vanished.

My youthful companions of last year had now graduated and gone their various ways. Miss Frances had limited the visitation of her young, vivacious nephews, Scoot and Turner, since the latter had been charged with initiating all the trouble the previous year. Walter also seldom came our way. My two landladies returned to their old habit of retiring at the first sign of darkness. I had no radio or television to keep me company, no telephone for communication, and no popular magazines or daily newspapers through which to keep abreast with the times.

My room was papered with newspaper but was spotlessly clean. The uncarpeted floor was scrubbed weekly with a lye-water solution until it dazzled with whiteness like chemically treated driftwood. The main feature in the room was a fat featherbed with its snow-white counterpane. The thick tick stuffed with goose feathers was undergirded with another deep, open-topped tick filled with freshly threshed wheat straw, which gave off a clean, fresh, outdoor aroma like freshly mown hay. The combined straw and feather ticks built the bed to such height that one almost had to climb on a stool or box to get on it. But once there, you could really relax in comfort. On that first night, I lay flat on my back, closed my eyes, and tried to sleep, but sleep wouldn't come. Instead, the whole panorama of my early childhood and a complete review of my desperate struggle for achievement kept passing before my eyes. But I had only a blurred vision of what the future held for me.

The PTA at its first business meeting of the year decided to use the money left in the treasury from last year's commencement exercise to build a coalhouse. This was agreeable to me because the school had never had a coalhouse and the county board of education refused to build one. When the coal was delivered to the premises, it was dumped in a heap on the school yard. This was quite a disadvantage, especially in wet weather.

Since the schoolteacher had to serve as janitor as well as instructor, it was my responsibility not only to clean the building after school at four o'clock but also to arrive early enough in the morning to make a fire in the heater and have the room warm when the children arrived to start classes at eight o'clock. It was difficult on rainy days to start a fire with wet coal. The students suffered, too, when they had to go out in the rain to shovel up scuttles of coal to keep the fire going all day. Snow obviously made the task even harder. So the building of a coalhouse was a welcome improvement.

WALTER

Halloween was celebrated with a community party but without music. Likewise, there was no musical program with the Thanksgiving box supper. On both occasions, my purpose was to avoid direct contact with Walter, but he still attended all of our affairs. Soon I discovered that I could not avoid him altogether. It was my duty as a teacher to participate in church services every meeting Sunday. As church organist, Walter was always there. He made it his business to speak politely and engage in some small talk.

One Sunday, Walter said, "I've got to go down to your house today. I want to see Cousin Frances on a business matter. Mind if I walk along with you?"

I couldn't very well object without a reasonable excuse, so we walked together. His visits to Cousin Frances became more frequent and our conversations less formal. He was good company, and I soon began looking forward to his visits. As our friendship expanded, I also found myself subconsciously conducting a discreet poll of community opinion of Walter and his family. I soon learned that the Dickinsons were considered honest, hardworking, upstanding, and one of the most outstanding families in the entire area, highly respected by everyone. Walter was described as a quiet, polite young man, sincerely dedicated to his family, his church, and his community.

As a result of this informal opinion poll, I accepted Walter's request for a regular weekly calling night. Our friendship became more closely knit, and soon word got around that Walter and the teacher were going steady. Then, as is customary in small communities, gossiping tongues began to wag. "He ought to have better sense than to fool with that teacher. She almost got him killed last year."

"Looks like he'd know that a town woman don't want no country hick."

"She's just making a fool out of him. He ought to know that."

"She's just going around with Walter to spite Turner."

"She's just pretending that she's interested in Walter to justify what happened last year."

We both heard and tried our best to ignore the remarks.

Eventually, Walter asked me to marry him. With a great deal of hesitation and perhaps reluctance, I finally accepted. Maybe I was trying to prove something—that the gossips were wrong—or to show my family that, contrary to their contentions, somebody did want me. Or maybe I was following my mother's advice that "if you must marry, pick a country boy—they make the best husbands."

No announcement was made of our engagement. On an agreed date, Walter and I drove to Hopkinsville, about twenty-five miles away, where we were quietly married in the home of a Baptist preacher. When we returned and showed the marriage certificate to his parents, they were completely shocked, as was the entire community when the news got around.

My parents were equally shocked and very deeply hurt. I thought they would be pleased that I had chosen a country boy for a husband, but they had an opposite reaction.

"Marrying a country boy is all right," my mother said, "but why would you marry somebody so far back in the country?"

"Why would you marry anybody at all before the end of your second term as a schoolteacher?" my father asked.

"Why would you marry so young?" they both chorused. "You're only nineteen."

"We thought you would teach awhile, have some freedom, and give us some financial help before tying yourself up in marriage," agreed every member of the family.

TRYING TO ADAPT

In time, the gossip died down, the community accepted me, and after I moved into the Dickinson home, my schoolwork and community activities went on as usual. Our marriage was moving along normally until I decided, with Walter's approval, to redecorate our bedroom, replacing the heavy brown storm paper that covered the ceiling and walls with a beautiful, blue-floral wallpaper. The woodwork and the margin of the floor around the edge of the rug got their first coat of paint. I bought shades for the windows, which until then had remained bare except for a sheet or blanket hung over them for privacy at night. Over each I hung neat cottage curtains of stiff white muslin with blue flowered borders to match the wallpaper. Finally I replaced odd pieces of furniture with a secondhand, more modern bedroom suite that I purchased in Clarksville, Tennessee, the nearest town of any size.

I did all of this at my own expense, which I didn't mind because our bridal chamber was then much more colorful, comfortable, and desirable, with but one exception. We had to place a cot in there for Walter's teenage brother, with whom we shared our little love nest until we moved away more than a year later.

All this redecorating gave the tongue waggers something else to talk about. "The schoolteacher thinks she's too good to use the furniture Miss Willie (Walter's mother) had. She's thrown it all out and bought new stuff."

"I knew Walter didn't know what he was doing."

"Walter married a parlor princess. Somebody to sit up in the parlor for his mother to wait on."

These comments bothered Walter and his family, and I tried to offset them by pitching in with the housework. But it was still Miss Willie's house and she insisted on running it as she had always done, including planning and preparing the meals. The only contribution I could make was washing dishes, cleaning our room, and doing our laundry. I also devoted my spare time to farmwork. At the end of the school day, I would change clothes and go to the barn to help with the tobacco stripping. As spring came on and the crops were being planted, I would go into the field where the men were working every afternoon and help with whatever they were doing, from planting tobacco to cutting it.

I knew how to do this because I had spent my childhood helping my father with his crops. In addition, I learned something new—how to pick cotton. We didn't raise cotton in my section of the state, and I had never seen it grow. But I soon learned, and on Saturdays I was assigned the task of supervising the cotton pickers, weighing and recording their sacks, and figuring out their wages. In other words, I was considered overseer of the cotton pickers.

As the school term neared an end, Walter and I began discussing whether I would go back to Frankfort to study during the spring and summer term. He flatly objected. But my teacher's certificate would expire at the end of this term, and a certain number of credits had to be earned before then in order for it to be renewed. I had earned some credits during the last spring and summer session but not enough for certificate renewal. A summer school session, however, would give me nearly enough hours. So Walter agreed for me to attend the six-week summer school but definitely not the twelve-week spring term. I made arrangements with the school administration to take some required subjects by correspondence—a most unusual request that was granted after much discussion. When all my credits were added together, I had enough hours at the end of the summer term of 1926 to complete my intermediate teacher training course and proudly received my four-year teacher's certificate.

I returned to my job, but the novelty had passed. I had no more challenges to meet, and things seemed to be getting into a rut. I continued helping with the crops in the field after school, rising around four in the morning and working until dark. When the men went to the barn to feed the stock, I would wash my tobacco-gummy hands in the meadow pond and milk the cow. Saturdays were spent washing clothes, a few of which I would iron each night until the week's laundry was finished. I didn't mind the work so much, but I saw no progress ahead. It seemed that I was retrogressing rather than improving my lot in life, and I became restless.

Although we worked hard, Walter and I got no benefits from the crop during the entire year except something to eat. Any other necessities had to be purchased with my earnings, since I was the only family member with cash income. Walter assured me that at the end of the year, when the crop was sold and the debts paid, his father would share the profits equally with him.

THE CAR

Since the lack of a car made it difficult for us to go into town on weekends to do any shopping, Papa John (Walter's father) made me a proposition. We would buy a car—a second-secondhand Model T Ford. He would borrow enough money on his (and Walter's) crop to pay half the cost, and I would pay the other half out of my individual earnings. Actually, that would mean that Walter and I would be paying three-fourths of the cost since Walter was supposed to have a half-interest in his father's crop from which his share was being borrowed. I agreed, even though Walter's father insisted that the car be bought in his name since he was the head of the family. There was nothing we could do about it a year later, when Walter and I moved away and his father kept the car, costing us my half-interest as well as Walter's half-interest in his father's portion.

The straw that actually broke the camel's back came when the crop was sold. Instead of having some profit to divide between father and son, the landlord said the crop did not bring enough money to pay the family debt. Since Mr. Dickinson, like most sharecroppers at the time, had no records to prove otherwise, he had to take the landlord's word. Thus we came out owing the landlord after a whole year's work of four people—two full-time adults (Mr. Dickinson and Walter) and two part-time workers (the youngest Dickinson son and me).

I had been talking to Walter all year about getting out on our own. I thought it was time for him to stop acting like a twelve-year-old, to grow up and take on the responsibilities of an adult. I had mentioned moving into town—some town, any town—where he could get a job on his own and we could improve our standard of living. At least we could have a private bedroom.

I wanted to be in a place where we could have modern conveniences, such as electricity and running water. He paid no heed to my request but enjoyed getting before a crowd of people—family and friends—and making me the butt of ridicule by saying, "Alice don't like the country. She wants to be somewhere where she can touch a button and flood the room with light." This was his choice statement because it always got a hilarious response at my expense.

The family thought it ridiculous to even think of buying new clothes until it was absolutely necessary to hide nakedness or keep the body warm. I tried going along with this practice until my clothes got so shabby that I could no longer maintain the dignity of a schoolteacher without something more decent to wear. I broke the family tradition by buying three patterns of gingham on one visit to Clarksville to make cotton dresses for school. The material cost no more than twenty-nine or maybe thirty-six cents per yard. It only takes three or four yards to make a dress, which I did myself, saving the cost of a seamstress. Nevertheless it was one venture I was never able to live down. Relatives and neighbors began talking again. "Walter's wife thinks she's rich. She bought three dresses at one time! Who does she think she is—Miss Ann?"

All of this criticism succeeded in making me feel guilty, even though my clothes had gotten so shabby that even my mother was ashamed of me. When I visited her one weekend, she said I couldn't go to church with her on Sunday unless I had a decent dress—an unusual comment from a woman who had never put any emphasis on clothes. Using her own money, she bought me a black satin dress with accordion pleated skirt (high fashion at the time), along with a wide black velvet belt and trimmings, so I would be presentable at church service. I adored that dress, and it remained my one "good dress" for a long time.

When the Dickinson's tobacco crop left us penniless and in debt, that was the end of my endurance. I told Walter that I was leaving that community to seek a better life. If he felt that he could cut the umbilical cord, well and good, but if not, I would have to go it alone. Finally we agreed upon a compromise.

9

A RUGGED VOYAGE ENDS

I tried to persuade my husband to move to Russellville, where I thought each of us might have a better chance to find employment since I knew many important people there and was quite well known myself. I even made a deposit on the down payment of a cute little white bungalow with a deep, green lawn located on one of the principal streets (at least two miles from my parents' home in the country). But Walter flatly stated that he would not live that near my folks—a stunning position since I was living in the same house with his family. This decision made me more determined than ever to move out.

After more back and forth, we agreed to move to another farm in the same community, about halfway between Trenton and Pisgah. Here he would hire himself out on a day-by-day basis, and I would continue teaching at Mount Pisgah. The house we moved into was a typical tenant shack, set some distance from the road in the middle of a meadow, behind the "white folks' big house."

Besides the landlord's family, there were no neighbors for miles around, and since school was out, the isolation almost drove me out of my mind. When I

started talking about going back to Russellville, Walter and I reached another compromise. He asked, if I must live in town, would I settle for
Hopkinsville, a nearby town of about ten thousand. We moved there and
rented a little yellow three-room shotgun cottage on a short, dead-end
street, quite an improvement from the farm cabin we left. The big problem
was that neither of us had a job, and we didn't know anyone who could
help us find one.

It was not easy for an unskilled, inexperienced farmhand to find a job
in a strange town, and Walter would return home every day after a morning of job hunting with the same story—"No luck." I applied for a job in
the county school system, but I knew success was not likely since there
was still a surplus of teachers and a long waiting list in every county board
of education.

Paying bills was my responsibility, and my little savings dwindled rapidly until I hit rock bottom. Now somebody had to do something. I took
a page from my mother's early life story and made a door-to-door canvass
in the white neighborhoods seeking work—any kind of work. I landed a
job as a nursemaid for a two-year-old baby whose mother worked. This
paid a very small wage, only a few dollars a week, but it helped to meet
some of our expenses. Finally the woman expanded my duties to doing
the family laundry and added a little to my regular wage.

An expert laundress, I did so well at this that the "boss lady" recommended me to several of her friends until I had so much laundry work
I gave up the babysitting and went into the home laundry business full
time. This kept us eating but also crushed my ego, lowered my dignity, and
deprived me of all self-respect.

Conditions were only slightly improved over my first experiences as a
laundress. I still had to do the washing by hand using an old-fashioned
scrub board, but at least we had a hydrant in the backyard so I didn't have
to carry water a long distance. And while the water still had to be heated
on the coal stove in the kitchen, it was better than having to drag brush
from the woods for a fire. We also had electricity and I could enjoy the
use of an electric iron. (At last I could "touch a button and flood the room
with light," a convenience Walter also enjoyed in spite of his previous,
sarcastic taunts.)

While I was toting the bundles of dirty clothes to our house and hand
carrying the little baskets of freshly laundered clothes back to their own-

ers, Walter would be relaxing in the shade of our front porch. When I suggested that he help me carry the laundry, I was hurt when he arrogantly replied, "I'm not packing no white folks' clothes up and down the street."

Although we used coal in the kitchen stove for heating wash water and cooking, we never had enough money to purchase it in large quantity, so we bought it by the bushel at a little kindling and coal shed down the street. Since I couldn't carry a bushel of coal alone, I would give a little boy across the street a quarter for the use of his little red wagon, which I would pull while he pushed. Walter would still be sitting leisurely on the porch, never offering to help.

I would get awful mad and disgusted with him, but as I look back now, I realize he was doing this purposely to humiliate me in retaliation for insisting on living in town. He believed that eventually I would become so unhappy I would give in and agree that rural life was best after all.

A NEW OPPORTUNITY

Trying to recoup some of my self-respect, I applied for employment at M&F College, a small junior college in Hopkinsville owned and supported by the Baptists of the state. The school's president was Dr. J. F. K. Moreland, and a top official was Professor E. Poston, father of journalist Ted Poston, who became a nationally known *New York Post* reporter. There were no vacancies on the staff, but I was given an unpaid position as field representative. My duty was to visit Baptist churches in the Little River and Cumberland Valley District every Sunday, making a pitch for the college, soliciting funds, and recruiting students. The churches would take up a special collection for the college, out of which I could deduct my expenses.

At the climax of my lectures about the college at the various churches, I read a poem I had written called "An Appeal to the West Kentucky Baptist," which I also sent to the *Rising Sun*, a Negro newspaper published in Hopkinsville. The editor published it and gave me a number of free copies of the issue in which it appeared to distribute to the congregation where I next spoke. He subtly suggested that should I interest people in taking a subscription, he would give me a small percentage of those sales. He also suggested that I contribute something to the paper each week, which he would publish under my byline and supply me with free copies for distribution on my Sunday church visits. A bylined article, he contended, would enhance my prestige throughout the vicinity. At the same time, I could introduce the newspaper in unfamiliar areas, increasing circulation and broadening its advertising base.

Since I didn't have time to dig up hard news (without pay) and lacked the social contacts for a society page, my pieces consisted of features, poems, or opinions for the editorial page. Nevertheless, I welcomed the opportunity to get my hand into the newspaper game again. And while it did nothing to lighten my financial burdens, my contacts were wonderful. But with winter approaching, when the cost of living would increase, I realized I would no longer be able to carry the burden alone. Besides needing more fuel for heating, I would encounter more difficulties in my work, not the least of which would be drying piles of wet clothes out of doors throughout the freezing, damp winter season. At this point, I had no alternative but to accept Walter's proposal to return to the country.

A STEP BACKWARD

Heading homeward, Walter made a trade as a sharecropper on a farm a few miles from Pembroke, a town with a population under a thousand, about halfway between Hopkinsville and Trenton. The shack we moved into was worse than the first one we'd lived in. It was almost comparable to the one occupied by Loweezy and Snuffy Smith, the moonshining hillbillies of comic-strip fame. Winter winds whipped through open cracks in the walls, creating such frigidity that we had to pull the bed across the hearth before the open fireplace and keep a roaring log fire burning all night.

We had no money for food, so Walter arranged for us to do certain chores to pay for our meals. He would go to the "big house" around four o'clock in the morning to help milk the several cows. I would go up around five and wash the separator and other milk utensils as well as the breakfast dishes. This would pay for our breakfast of leftovers. I would also help prepare the midday meal and wash those dishes, while he would chop wood or do whatever tasks were assigned to pay for our dinners and the leftover scraps we would be given to carry home for supper.

In addition to the plantation arrangement for food and shelter, we were treated as plantation wards (or slaves)—rebuffed, belittled, talked down to, ordered around like cattle. This I couldn't take.

One day I blurted out to the self-styled "missus," "I don't have to take this stuff. I don't have to cringe and bow in humble submissiveness to anybody. I don't have to live like this. After all, I'm a schoolteacher. I can have a better life than this."

"I don't believe it," she replied. "If you were a schoolteacher, you wouldn't be living like this."

I rushed off to the cabin, brought back my certificate, and showed it to her. She gasped in surprise and made no further comment. But what she had already said had driven home a lesson to me.

After much unpleasant discussion in which I put my foot down, Walter asked if I would like to move back to Trenton, the little town nearest his home and about the size of Pembroke. Trying desperately to save our marriage, I agreed to go back if we lived in the village and not in some country farmhouse. Finally we arranged to move onto a farm on the edge of town. It was still one of those tenant houses but a little better constructed than the one we'd just left.

As was customary, the house was made available without a set sum for rent. But since it was still winter and too early to plant crops, Walter had to do a certain amount of work to pay for our occupancy. Although the weather was cold and bad, he worked a few days a week doing such tasks as mending fences or cutting saplings to clear off new ground for cultivation. For this he was paid $1.25 per day, a certain portion of which was deducted for use of the house, and the balance given him to buy food.

JUST A PAIR OF SHOES

I became active in the community, but there was little to do besides church work. Much to my liking, I became a Sunday school teacher, which helped me regain some of my self-respect. But once again I had become practically threadbare. I had only one pair of shoes, which were scuffed, run-down, and badly worn. I told Walter how self-conscious I was standing before a Sunday school class in those horrible-looking shoes and asked if he could possibly spare enough from his meager earnings to buy me a pair of new ones, but he refused.

Finally, one day I said in desperation, "I am not going to Sunday school or church service anymore until I get some decent shoes. I'm just going to stay home all the time."

"Stay at home if you want to. I don't care!" was his curt reply. "I don't care if you never go anywhere again."

After staying home a few weeks, I tried another approach. "I'm going to Sunday school and church every meeting day wearing these same old shoes. I'm just going to let people know you won't buy me a pair of decent shoes."

"Go to church if you want to," he shrugged. "If you want to go to church looking like the devil, I don't care."

This attitude, I know now, was meant to punish me for dragging him away from his beloved family. But it made me realize that the only way I would ever get anywhere in life or do anything worthwhile would be to do it on my own.

Soon I found a job doing a family's laundry at their house every Monday morning. The people were our nearest neighbors, so there was little walking to do to get to my work. They had running water in the house, relieving me of the burden of drawing and heating the wash water, and an old-fashioned washing machine, which was somewhat better than the old scrub board. There was also a roller-wringer, operated by turning a crank, which was an improvement over having to wring the clothes by hand.

When I hung the clothes on the line, I was finished with the job. The wife would bring them in herself and do her own ironing. I received a dollar a week for this washing. Soon I bought a secondhand sewing machine (the old-fashioned foot treadle kind) from my employer for twelve dollars, paying for it in-kind with my laundry work, clearing the debt in three months. I compensated for the lack of income by taking in sewing, which I soon had more of than I could do. My specialty was making school clothes for the neighborhood children. Besides being enjoyable and creative, this work revived my dignity and brought me in contact with many interesting people, which gave me a new lease on life. It also provided financial means with which I could purchase some decent clothes and once again feel a part of the human race.

BACK TO THE CLASSROOM

With two good years left on my teacher's certificate, I pulled myself together and sent out applications to the boards of education of Todd and adjacent counties. A few weeks before the opening of schools, I was summoned to the superintendent's office in Elkton, the seat of Todd County, and assigned a teaching job at Allensville. This was another little town about the size of Trenton and thirty miles away. The only way to get there if you lacked a car was by train. I made arrangements to board during the week with an elderly couple in Allensville—Mr. and Mrs. Tyler—who lived near the school. I would go to my job by train on Monday mornings and return home every Friday.

This school, a fairly decent two-room building, was quite an improvement over the one at Mount Pisgah. The headmaster was Joe Henderson (a brother of the man I replaced at Mount Pisgah). He taught grades five through eight, while I was responsible for one through four. In addition to freeing up more teacher time for the students, the principal assumed responsibility for seeing that the fires were made every morning and the building cleaned every afternoon, relieving the teacher of janitorial duties.

The *Rising Sun* newspaper in Hopkinsville had by this time gone out of business and been replaced by the Hopkinsville *Globe,* the editor of which contacted me with a proposal that I use my new contacts to solicit subscriptions to the paper. I would be compensated not only by a small percentage of subscriptions sold but also with the honor of having my name on the masthead as circulation manager. I welcomed the opportunity even though there was little money to be gained, and for the two years I taught in Allensville, I used the position to get into print any newsworthy happenings of the community.

The only downside of my successful school year in this little village was the tirade I encountered every weekend when I returned home to an irate husband who constantly complained about my being away from home.

"You weren't satisfied until you got me away from my folks," Walter would say. "And now you're running off every week leaving me in this house alone to cook for myself and endure the loneliness. Guess you're satisfied now!"

After my second year at Allensville, my teacher's certificate expired, and I had earned credits for only one six-week summer session, which made renewal impossible. My only salvation was to spend a full term in school to earn sufficient college hours for certification renewal. To this proposal, Walter strenuously objected, saying, "I don't care if your certificate expired. As a matter of fact, I'm glad! Now maybe you can content yourself staying at home like any other farm wife to cook and keep house for me and help me in the field with the crops. If you need extra spending money, you can always pick up a little change doing housework or laundry work for some of these white folks around here."

I was fit to be tied. "If I were going to spend a lifetime cooking, cleaning, and washing dirty clothes for white folks, it wouldn't have behooved me to struggle through high school and sacrifice to continue my education through college. I've had a hard struggle and I don't need to stop here," I declared. "I'm going to college next year whether you like it or not."

"Go ahead!" he shouted. "But if you go, you can just stay!"

So I did just that. I went and I stayed. But after that five-year, rugged matrimonial voyage, I was clever enough not to depart until filing for divorce.

10

MOVING ON

When I applied for campus work at West Kentucky Industrial College, I was immediately offered a job as second cook, for which I was to receive full board but no cash. This didn't sound very glamorous on the surface, but it turned out to be a very satisfactory spot.

WKIC was founded by Dr. D. H. Anderson and his wife, Artelia, for the sole purpose of providing opportunity for underprivileged youth. This was a half-century before the government gave any thought to educational programs for less-privileged youngsters or paid any attention to the dropout problem. The school operated for nine years on contributions solicited door-to-door by Dr. Anderson himself, who welcomed any amount from ten cents up, and money earned by Mrs. Anderson as a rural schoolteacher. She commuted to her school daily by bicycle and turned her entire salary over to the operation of the new college.

It was said that Dr. Anderson picked up for campus use every loose brick he saw on the street and every lump of coal that had fallen from a coal truck. He constructed most of the first building with his own hands and built up the enrollment by combing the streets of every small town in that section of the state, recruiting dropouts from street corners, pool rooms, and every other type of dump and dive, appealing to them to return to school and offering them a job to pay their way. Nobody who applied for a job at that school was turned down. All of the work on campus was done by students, and most of the food we ate was grown on the school farm cultivated by students.

In 1912, after nine years of independent operation, Dr. Anderson did what no black man had ever dared to do. He made a personal appearance before the state legislature to argue for the appropriation of funds for a state-supported school for black children in an area where it was sorely needed. The bill to make this school into a state institution failed.

He made another unsuccessful attempt in 1914 and another in 1916. Finally, in 1918 the legislature passed a law making West Kentucky Industrial College a state school with the same rating as the one at Frankfort. By 1938 when the school merged with Kentucky State College, it was reported to be the third-largest Negro junior college in the United States. This growth was attributed to the fact that no prospective student who desired an education was denied an opportunity at WKIC.

CULINARY ADVENTURES

The kitchen staff, to which I was assigned, was headed by a paid worker, an adult who served as chief cook. Her duties were to prepare the meats and oversee the entire food-service operation. As second cook, I was in charge of bread and dessert. The third cook, another student, was responsible for cooking vegetables. The second and third cooks were also responsible for cleaning up all the cooking utensils. Two other students called vegetable girls prepared fresh vegetables for cooking as they came in from the farm.

My specific duties consisted of making corn bread every day for the noon meal (dinner) and biscuits every Sunday morning for breakfast. Dessert was served twice a week. I made fruit cobbler every Sunday from apples, peaches, cherries, or blackberries, and a cottage pudding was served every Wednesday. The latter was something I had become expert at making during my so-called home economics class at the Russellville high school many years before.

There had been no requests for a culinary course at WKIC, so none was included in the curriculum. My thinking was that such a course might be instrumental in preparing me to teach home economics one day if the opportunity arose. My roommate, Rosa James, and I went to the dean and requested it—in fact, insisted on it—since the state had equipped the school with a modern kitchen and all the necessary utensils, although there were no funds in the budget for food to use in classes. Rosa and I agreed to buy the food ourselves if we were permitted to eat what we cooked. This was agreeable to all, and Rosa and I set about learning nutrition, menu making, table setting, and proper methods of serving under the instruction of a faculty member, while also cooking only what we wanted to eat.

When the rest of the faculty learned of our expertise, we started getting invitations to help serve at some of their exclusive parties. This was most enjoyable because it gave us an opportunity to visit off campus, a privilege not often granted students during the day and practically never at night. At these functions, we met many interesting people—celebrities, socialites, and famous political and religious leaders. While we received no formal monetary compensation for this "practice work," we did get tips and a taste of food we would never have had in dormitory life. As our reputation expanded beyond the faculty, we moved up to serving receptions and banquets sponsored by churches and organizations. The experience and good reports for efficiency gained in this work reflected favorably in our grades.

A BIT OF EVERYTHING

I had missed so much time in school during the past four years that I decided to take every available course to try and make it up, regardless of whether or not I received credit for the overload. One of the additional courses I requested was typing, which was not yet on the curriculum, although the state board of education again had supplied the equipment. The president's wife, then serving as business manager for the school, arranged for me to learn typing without a tutor, charging me something like a dollar a month for the use of a typewriter. Office work for black women was still practically nonexistent in that section of the country, so I saw no possibility of obtaining a secretarial or typist job at the time. Still, I thought that someday the opportunity might come, and therefore I requested a course in shorthand as well, which was not in the curriculum either. For fifty cents a week, one of my regular teachers, who just happened to know shorthand, agreed to give me two private lessons a week.

I had just learned the Gregg characters when I had to drop the lessons because of my heavy workload and meager finances.

Another opportunity grew out of a special assignment from our English professor, who had the entire class write a short essay on a specific subject with the promise that the best one would be published in the *Lighthouse*, the town's Negro newspaper. My story was not only selected and published but the editor (the publisher's wife) was so impressed with my writing that she invited me to visit the office whenever I had spare time and help with the editing, proofreading, and layout as an unpaid apprentice. That experience really put printer's ink in my veins.

The busy year passed all too swiftly, and as a senior I expected to graduate with the class of 1931. To my disappointment, however, when the dean's office added up my scattershot credits, it was discovered that I lacked eight hours necessary for graduation. To soften the blow, the dean assured me that I had enough credits to receive another teacher's certificate, which would allow me to work the next school year, and then earn enough credits in the spring term to graduate with the class of 1932.

This was some consolation, but I still regretted not being able to sit on the platform with the class of 1931 and its distinguished commencement speaker, Congressman Oscar DePriest, the first Negro to sit in the Congress of the United States since Reconstruction. (An Illinois Republican, DePriest was elected to Congress in 1929 and served three terms before being defeated in 1935 by Arthur W. Mitchell, the first black Democratic congressman.) I was sitting in the back of the audience, rather despondent as I enviously watched my classmates walk across the stage and receive their diplomas. When the procession ended, I had a great surprise. My name was suddenly called, and I was invited to the platform. I had no idea what it was all about as I nervously walked all the way from the back of the auditorium to the front with all eyes on me. When I reached the stage, the dean stepped forward and, with quite a bit of pomp and ceremony, presented me with a home economics certificate, the first ever issued by the school and the only one of the year. I was the only student in the entire school who had taken every course offered in the field, including sewing, cooking, domestic art, and even basket weaving. So I was "it." The special attention focused on me beyond all the members of the graduating class, especially in front of the congressman, sufficiently compensated for my disappointment over not graduating.

A NEW AND BETTER JOB

When I returned home from WKIC, my father proudly informed me that I had a job waiting in a rural school called New Hope. This was a modern Rosenwald school. Located about eight miles from Russellville, it was one of more than five thousand Negro public and rural schools funded by philanthropist Julius Rosenwald in fifteen southern and Border States. The unique architectural structure of these modern buildings clearly identified them as Rosenwald schools.[1] Painted white, New Hope's was a well-constructed, relatively new building with one large classroom, two cloakrooms, and a kitchen, as well as a large front porch where the children could play games during recess on rainy days. There was no remodeling or redecorating necessary.

Since teaching jobs were still scarce throughout the South, with long waiting lists, and the number of surplus teachers was increasing, I wondered how I had been so fortunate to have a job waiting for me. Then I had my first realization of the power of politics.

My father, who was a highly respected and influential citizen of the county, had thrown his support to the powerful Rhea political machine. As a result, his request to county officials for a job for me was granted immediately, despite the protests of some who had long been on the waiting list.

Kentucky at that time was a forceful Democratic stronghold, and Logan County was fertile Democratic territory. Tom Rhea, the state Democratic boss, was a resident of Russellville in Logan County. He headed the nationally known Rhea machine, which was just as powerful in our state as the well-known Byrd machine was in Virginia, the Crump machine in Tennessee, or the Pendergast machine in Missouri. Whatever Tom Rhea and his followers said was law and gospel in the state of Kentucky and particularly in Logan County. Following my father's example, I aligned myself with the political machine and became active in the political life of the county, activities that over the years greatly influenced my entire career.

11

WADING THROUGH
THE DEPRESSION

Up until this time, I had been so busy with the challenges of my personal life that I had paid little attention to the problem of racial discrimination. But this issue hit me rather forcefully at the first countywide teachers meeting in Logan County, which I attended on Saturday prior to the opening day of schools.

Unlike in Todd County, where teachers never met the superintendent unless they took the initiative to visit his office, in Logan County it was the custom for all teachers of both races to attend a pre-opening meeting with school administrators, at which the teachers were informed of county policy and instructed in the method of operation of the schools. Other such meetings were called at intervals at the discretion of school authorities.

My first observation was that all white teachers were seated on one side of the aisle in the courthouse auditorium, while the blacks were seated on the other. I voluntarily seated myself with my own people but suggested before the meeting began that some of us should find seats among the whites. This brought a howl of protest from some of the older teachers, who reminded me that I was new to teaching in this county and there was no need for me to create confusion at my very first meeting. Some even commented, "She wants to be white so bad."

At every subsequent meeting, I tried to get someone to join me in breaking down the color-seating barrier, but to no avail. Finally one teacher agreed to join me in finding a seat in the "white section." There was no protest. No apparent resentment. Nobody said a word. Nothing happened. Once the ice was broken, others gradually moved over to the other side of the aisle until finally there were no discriminatory seating arrangements. The separation, I later learned, had been voluntary in the first place.[1]

The only restroom for women in the courthouse was still marked "White Ladies" as it had been in my childhood, and I still used it whenever necessary as I had done many years before. I secretly hoped someone would object so the matter could be brought out in the open and resolved. But nobody ever complained. The sign stayed there for several more decades, and it took an act of Congress to force its removal.

The county in those days sponsored an annual, one-day tobacco festival with a parade of floats and marching bands, and an outdoor program in the city square.[2] The participants were all white. One year when the festivities were in the planning stage, I offered to give a dramatic reading since I had become proficient in drama and public speaking. My offer was readily accepted without hesitancy or noticeable surprise. The festival programs were always amplified so that they could be heard throughout the village. I gave one of my favorite readings from the words of Paul Lawrence Dunbar. The reading turned out rather well, I thought, judging from the crowd's enthusiastic applause. But criticism came later from my own people, many of whom heard it from afar through the loudspeaker since blacks hardly ever bothered to attend the festivities. Some of my critics called me an Uncle Tom or Aunt Jane. Some charged me with being a "white folks' nigger" for butting into white folks' affairs. Others claimed that I was publicly belittling our own folks with a lot of "nigger talk." Apparently this group was completely unaware that dialectical vernacularism is an accepted poetic style of expression and that Dunbar's works were proclaimed classics by famous literary authorities. Even years later, famous poems written in dialect by such prominent poets as Langston Hughes won worldwide acclaim from outstanding intellectuals as well as common people.

After this occasion, there was never another festival held in Logan County without Negro participation. Black school children marched in the parade along with those from white schools (although the blacks were for a time placed at the back end of the march until this custom, too, eventually changed). Finally discrimination in Logan County's festivals completely vanished without public protest or unpleasant utterances from either side.

I had six successful years teaching at New Hope, and I was both highly respected in the community and admired by the students. I was pleased and surprised when the local white weekly newspaper did something that had never been done before. It published a feature article on a Negro school—our school. The article listed the number of prizes we had won over a given period, and it rated me the county's number-one rural teacher. This was a great credit to our community and a source of personal pride to me.

THE RETURN OF CHARLES DUNNIGAN

My personal—or more specifically, social—life had also changed with my return home from West Kentucky Industrial College. By some quirk of fate, Charles Dunnigan, that neighbor friend of my brother during my early childhood, returned home the same summer after fifteen years away. By this time, he was a handsome, well-dressed young widower of about thirty whose wife had recently died in Louisville. I was an energetic divorcée of twenty-five, fresh out of college and full of ambition to get ahead and build a good life. Charles dropped by to see me one day and we had a wonderful chat—talking about our childhood days, discussing mutual friends of the past, and swapping stories about more recent experiences. Charles's conversational ability, his knowledge of current events, his apparent dignity, and his graceful poise acquired through extensive travel "up North" and experience in big city living placed him head and shoulders, in my estimation, above other young men of my acquaintance.

He apparently felt the same way about me because his visits became more frequent, and soon we were seeing a lot of each other. He escorted me to movies, parties, concerts, and even to church. For the first time in my life, I also sat in prestigious, reserved seats with a boyfriend when the Silas Green show came to town. "Silas Green from New Orleans," a black tent show that toured the South, included a musical review, comedy, and minstrel acts. I felt like an adolescent since this was my first time to properly date a young man without interference from my family or critical comments from meddlesome neighbors.

Jobs were scarce during the Depression, so Charles, being a skilled cobbler (a trade learned from his late stepfather), went into business for himself. Using his father's equipment, he opened a shoe shop near the location where his father's shop used to be and established a very profitable business.

All was going well until my parents detected that our affection for each other was obviously increasing and our courtship was apparently taking on a more serious trend. For fear that marriage was in the making, they set out to drive a wedge between Charles and me.

As I see it now, they were looking out for my best interest. They were proud to have me home for the first time in several years and were pleased with my successful career. They were delighted that I had pulled myself out of the previous unpleasant position, and they were trying to prevent me from getting involved in a similar situation. Much as I hate to admit it, they were right in their desire to head off marriage, but they were going about it in the wrong way. My mother, for example, gave me long lectures on what she thought were Charles's most undesirable traits, as she remembered them.

"Charles has always been a sporting man," she warned. "He's a man about town. A woman's man." She continued that because he was good looking, an excellent baseball player, and a smooth talker, girls were attracted to him. "They throw themselves at him and he can't resist."

She kept telling me, "Charles has never loved any one woman. He likes to play the field. He'll never marry you—he's not the marrying kind. If he does marry you, he'll not stay with you. I dare say you'd be separated within a month," Mama predicted. She didn't believe me when I told her that he'd been married and that he lived with his wife until her death.

These charges only drove me closer to him. I wanted to triumph over all those admirers she had mentioned. I wanted to prove that Charles did love me, that he would marry me, and that we would stay together. But my mother was right to a great extent in her evaluation of Charles's personality. She had known him since birth and had watched him grow up. She had observed without bias his characteristics. Furthermore, she was older and wiser than I in the ways of the world and had a greater understanding and a clearer vision of life, not fogged by youthful infatuations or blinded by the illusions of love.

My parents could have handled the situation much more wisely by permitting us to continue our courtship while at the same time warning me of the pitfalls ahead and advising caution. But their blatant request that I break off the relationship without a definite cause was like snatching from me a whole lifetime of contentment and happiness and shoving my future existence into a deep, dark, damp dungeon of despair. I couldn't let this happen, so I didn't quit seeing him, which led them to devise another approach.

My father took the lead this time, confronting Charles with the observation, "You and my daughter are obviously becoming very seriously involved. I want you to know that our family disapproves of any consideration of marriage. So we have agreed that it might be best for you to stop seeing each other."

This broke up our social evenings together, but we didn't stop seeing each other. I would sometimes drop by his shoe shop in the afternoons on my way home from school, if only for five or ten minutes. Sometimes we would sit in the railroad station for a brief conversation. The station was always deserted since only two trains came through the town daily and seldom did anyone board them from that depot.

This went on for nearly a year. Although Charles had proposed to me months earlier, I had not definitely made up my mind. I wanted a little more time to find out more about him and to determine whether we would make a suitable pair. But Charles had gotten tired of our chance meetings, and one day he firmly put his foot down. "If we are going to get married, we should just as well go ahead and do it," he said. "If not, we might as well break it up. We are both grown, and it doesn't make sense for us to be slipping around to see each other like teenage schoolchildren. I'm tired of it."

TRYING MARRIAGE AGAIN

With this ultimatum, I gave my word because I didn't want to lose him. We agreed that the wedding should be secret. After the ceremony, we would each go our separate ways, continuing to see each other a bit more boldly. If my parents should see us together and raise an objection, we could proudly produce our marriage certificate and watch them squirm as Charles boastfully announced, "This is my wife."

We planned to get married quietly during Christmas week of 1931 in the home of a Baptist minister who lived around the corner from Charles. The first part of our scheme worked out as planned, but the latter part, pertaining to secrecy, did not. Word leaked from the parson's household that we were married. When the news hit the gossip grapevine, it spread quickly through the village, finally reaching my mother's ears. When she confronted me about the accuracy of the rumor and I proudly confirmed it, she ordered me out of the house.

"If you are married," she said, "you go on and live with your husband." When I told Charles, he arranged for me to move into his home with his mother and sister.

All went well for several months until Charles was given a political appointment on the staff of a mental institution in Hopkinsville, some twenty miles away. The job called for twenty-four-hour standby duty, which meant that he had to reside on the premises with only one day off a week and one weekend per month. With this arrangement, he couldn't come home very often, so he sold the shoe repair business.

TOUGH TIMES

The Depression was hitting America harder and harder during this period. The board of education arranged that year to open the rural schools in June, three months before the regular opening date. This was supposedly done to save fuel since schools could then close by Christmas, before the extreme cold weather set in.

The salary of seventy-nine dollars per month that teachers were then receiving was cut to fifty-six dollars per month, and we were informed that although we had an early opening date, we would not receive our salaries any earlier. The first paycheck would not be delivered until October. The state was not allocating the salary funds to the counties until the regular opening time in September, and the funds would not be matched with county funds and paid to teachers until the end of that month or really the first of the next month.

This arrangement imposed an extreme hardship on county teachers, including me. I had no means of transportation since I had sold my first car out of necessity when I was unable to keep up the payments. It was most difficult to find someone in a financial position to transport me to and from school for three months before I would receive any pay.

I finally succeeded in making favorable arrangements with an eighty-five-year-old veteran of the Spanish-American War, who had just purchased a new red Plymouth coupe and employed a younger man to drive it. The older man, Pete Helm, could afford to wait three months for his pay because he lived on an army pension.

Since Charles and I were now absent from each other for such long intervals, word began to drift back that my husband had found an outside interest in Hopkinsville, just as my mother had predicted. Whether it was true or not, his visits home became more and more infrequent.

I was only able to stay in the schoolroom three months that year, having to take off in September on maternity leave. I was still living with Charles's family, but his mother began to make me feel unwanted and uncomfortable after I was forced to give up my job temporarily. She constantly reminded me that Charles was doing nothing for me, nor was he sending her any money to help support my upkeep. Finally she bluntly told me that she was not able to feed me, so I would have to make some other arrangements, even though I was helping her with her daily household chores and her occupational laundry work.

I tucked my pride under my arm and went home to Mama and Papa. Being too independent to accept full support from them, I got a job cooking for the family of Tom Rhea and stayed with it until the baby was born. I became so heavy with the pregnancy that I was confined exclusively to the kitchen, doing only the cooking and helping with the dishes, while Rhea's chauffeur was assigned the duty of waiting tables, bussing dishes, and even helping me wash them. For this job I received only three dollars a week, but at least I got something to eat and didn't have to depend upon someone else to feed me.

It was at this point that trouble began between Charles and me, and it never entirely ended.

In December 1932, our son, Robert William, was born, about two weeks before our first wedding anniversary. His father was absent for his birth, which took place in my mother's home since there was no hospital in our town at the time. It was nearly three months later before Charles came home to see his son. I was still staying with my parents, who naturally resented his visit. But he claimed to be very proud of our beautiful little child and promised to come home and move us into a house of our own, where we could live together as a family should.

He gave up his job in Hopkinsville, came home, rented a house, and moved the baby and me into it. Work was still scarce, however, and Charles couldn't find another job. He became sullen and despondent. I soon realized that my husband, like many other men I knew, couldn't face responsibility and was unable or unwilling to meet hardships head-on. He tossed aside his fatherly responsibility just as a child would discard a broken toy, and he walked out on us just as the rent was due. His only explanation was that he couldn't live here without work. He had to go somewhere to find a job, but he didn't know where. So he walked out, leaving the baby and me without rent money, food, fuel, or a job.

With tears in my eyes, I had to humble myself and go to my mother for advice. I feared that she would gloat with satisfaction, saying, "I knew this would happen," or that old saw, "I told you so!"

But Mama spared me that hurt, perhaps because she felt sorry for me. She only expressed regret that this had happened and offered to keep the baby so I could work. So my parents took little Bobby when he was only four months old and carefully reared him, seeing that he finished elementary school and high school and then entered college with my assistance and a one-thousand-dollar scholarship from the Elks fraternity. He was a junior at Kentucky State College when my mother passed away in 1952.

Immediately after my parents relieved me of the care of the baby, I took a job with a milk dairy, washing bottles by hand for two hours in the morning from seven to nine o'clock, and two hours in the afternoon from five to seven. For this I was paid two dollars a week. I was given a free breakfast and a snack in the evening for supper.

A GOVERNMENT WORK PROGRAM

The Works Progress Administration eventually came into full swing nationwide as a means of providing employment for needy families.[3] The wpa paid no cash, instead giving workers a statement called "scrip" that verified their working time. Unlike a check, this scrip could not be converted into cash. It could only be exchanged for food at the grocery store or for fuel at the coal yard. In my hometown, the project was proceeding rather well in providing employment for poor white women. A number of

Robert Dunnigan with his
grandmother, Lena Pittman
Allison (Dunnigan Papers,
MARBL, Emory University)

black women had applied for jobs, but few, if any, had been hired. I put my application in for a WPA job and at the same time confronted one of my political contacts as to why more Negroes had not been employed. Since the project was financed with federal funds, I argued, it should be open to all needy families regardless of race.

I was told in confidence that this discriminatory hiring practice was not the idea of city officials administering the program. They were acting under pressure, I was told, brought by the middle-class white women of the town, who feared that if black women were employed on a public project at the rate of six dollars per week, then all of the cooks would leave their kitchens, where the work was more demanding and the pay considerably less, and take jobs with the WPA. The local WPA administrator agreed to honor their requests unless, or until, someone from the black community complained. They assured me that this injustice would be corrected. Soon a few Negro women, including myself, were called to work. Even then, women with an average-size family were allowed to work only one day a week at one dollar a day, while those with larger families could get two days' work per week.

I raised a ruckus about this arrangement but soon received the "quietus treatment" by being instructed that I would be allowed two days per week if I would keep my mouth closed, a deal I accepted. Some of my coworkers complained privately about my being given the maximum work time despite having only two people to support, myself and my baby, but since they never complained openly or publicly, nothing was changed.

This project, like most other federal projects controlled by county and municipal officials, was never operated fairly. The white women continued to work on one of the two job projects to which they had previously been assigned. One was a sewing project where dresses and shirts for needy children of all ages were made from material supplied by the federal government. The other was a job patching tattered and torn textbooks with Scotch tape in the office of the county school superintendent.

Jobs had to be created for black women. We were told from the beginning that our first job would be cleaning public buildings. In a town of that size, there were not very many public buildings. We were first assigned to clean the schoolhouses. There were four in the city. One was a combination elementary and high school for whites. The same type of school operated for the colored. There were two white colleges, one for boys and the other for girls.

Soon these buildings were thoroughly cleaned, windows washed, walls and floors scrubbed. The next task was cleaning the county courthouse in the same manner. Then came the jailhouse and finally the calaboose. The latter was a small workhouse occupied mainly by hobos or drunks picked up on vagrancy or other minor charges and made to break rock on a rock pile for a few days to pay their fines. We found this place infested with body lice and reported it to the authorities, who ordered all cots and blankets burned immediately. We were given the rest of the day off to go home, take hot baths, and wash or burn our clothing. This ended the cleaning of public buildings.

We were sent back to the white schools with picks, shovels, and garden forks to dig up the ground and transplant shrubbery in appropriate places on the lawns. When this was completed, we were all sent to the "colored cemetery," where we squatted around all day digging up wild onions with a spade.

The city dump was located near this cemetery. Every day, we would watch for the grocery trucks to dump their refuse, and then we'd take off to the dump to see what could be salvaged in the way of food. Often we would find such things as cabbage rotted on the outside. We would remove the rotten leaves and carry the cabbage home for cooking. Potatoes and apples half rotten would be picked up, the decaying parts cut off, and the good part kept for use. Moldy bologna and wieners were salvaged, the mold scraped off, and the meat soaked overnight in hot water and ready for eating the next day.

We worked faithfully at the cemetery until there were no more wild onions to dig. Then we were transferred to the Maplewood (white) cemetery. This lawn was so well kept that no wild onions had been allowed to grow, so we were ordered to wash the tombstones.

After a few weeks, this job was completed, and there was just nothing else for us to do. The supervisors said that the only thing left was to clean the city park, located in the center of the town square, sweep the streets surrounding it, and then sweep Main Street.

This was the limit for me. I had laid aside the dignity of a schoolteacher to do all of these other things, but I refused to sweep the streets like a common convict. So I gave up the WPA job, grateful that it was near time for school to open again.

While I was still working on the project, I had further supplemented my income by taking on a third job, that of cleaning up the residence of a white family and cooking the heavy midday meal (dinner) between the dairy hours on the five days that I was not working with WPA. For this I received $1.50 a week and a free dinner.

Even this would not take care of all of my expenses. Although my parents didn't charge for keeping the baby, I still had to buy food, furniture, and medical protection for him. So I added another $1.50 to my income by doing the laundry for the county attorney's family.[4] Both the washing and ironing had to be done at night since my days were entirely occupied with other jobs.

I now had a total weekly income of seven dollars, earned by doing four jobs. With this I managed to get by maintaining a home and supporting a baby until September, when I returned to my schoolteaching job.

12

SEEKING IDENTITY, EXPERIENCE, AND RECOGNITION

It was a relief to be back in a position of dignity, but I was faced with another immediate problem. I had no means of supporting myself until the first paycheck arrived, about six weeks after school began. I was fortunate to renew my previous arrangements for transportation to school, and the landlord was generous enough to wait until I received my paycheck before collecting rent. But there remained the problem of eating. There were no more free meals, or "thanky pans," from white folks' kitchens. (Cooks for white families were usually given all of the leftover scraps from meals to carry home for their families. These were customarily carried in little pans commonly known as "thanky pans.") Many days, there was not a bit of food in the house and no money to purchase any. No grocer would open credit accounts to new customers. The Depression was still upon us.

Often when I stepped into the car on my way to work, tears of hunger would well up in my eyes. Carvin Bibbs, the driver, was in the same shape. He had no steady employment and received no pay for driving Pete Helm's car—just the benefit of having a car at his disposal for his own convenience or to sometimes pick up a few quarters by transporting friends to their destinations. On seeing me hungry, tears would come to his eyes both out of sympathy for me and because he, too, was hungry. Sometimes he would drive by Miss Sity's restaurant and order breakfast for both of us, informing the proprietress that he would stop by after taking me to school and mop the floor, wash the dishes, or do any chore she wished to pay for the food.

Sometimes Carvin would park the car when no traffic was visible and, dashing into a farmer's cornfield, help himself to a dozen or so roasting ears. I would cook them when I got home and invite him to the feast, sometimes consisting only of fried corn and bread and sometimes only corn on the cob and no bread.

Whenever we saw a chicken crossing the road at a safe distance from any farmhouse and no traffic was in sight on the highway, Carvin would strike it with the car and pick it up, and we would have a scrumptious dinner of fried chicken, broiled chicken, or chicken and dumplings.

This had to be done with a great deal of caution because it was against the law to pick up a chicken that had been hit by a car. If it was accidentally hit and left on the road, nothing could be done about it because this did not constitute a crime. But if it was picked up and carried away, the driver would be charged with the same offense as if he had stolen the chicken. The penalty in Kentucky was one year in prison for every chicken stolen.[1]

A young couple who lived with the bride's grandmother across the street from me was caught up in the Depression squeeze when neither of them could find work. The husband found it impossible to cope with this situation and deserted his wife, leaving her to the constant nagging of her grandmother for marrying a "no-good man." Eventually the wife was ordered to get out and make a way for herself.

With nowhere to go and unable to find a job, she came to me in tears, relating the story. Although I had no money for food, I offered to share my home with her. She was most grateful and agreed to compensate by doing the housework, doing the laundry, and helping in some way to obtain food for both of us. Before long I was amazed, having left home in the mornings with no food in the house, to return home in the afternoon and find she had cooked a hot meal for us.

When the pressures of the Depression finally began to subside, she would look back over those lean years and laugh about how she had managed to secure food.

"I would walk down the street toward town with a big paper bag folded and neatly tucked in my bosom," she said. "When nobody was looking, I would sneak into a neighbor's garden, hide from view behind the tall corn, and gather a mess of butter beans or string beans, putting them in the paper bag. Then I'd walk straight back home past the neighbor's house as if I'd been to market and purchased vegetables for dinner."

She recalled that one of our neighbors raised chickens that roamed around freely in our backyard. She would spread grains of corn in a straight line from the backyard to the back door. A chicken would begin picking up the grains and follow the row right into the kitchen. She would close the door, trapping the chicken inside, and tap it on the back of the head with a poker. The chicken would keel over dead without making a sound. So we would enjoy a delicious chicken dinner. She also recalled that she used to get up early in the mornings before the neighbors arose and pick up apples from beneath their trees so we could have fried apples for breakfast when nothing else was in the house.

Finally my first paycheck arrived, and I was able to put in a supply of food and pay off some debts. Life at last became a little easier. For all of this time, I had not heard a word from my husband, who flew the coop at the first sign of hard times. Now, when our problems were beginning to iron themselves out and we were contentedly adjusting to a normal way of life, Charles unexpectedly returned home and insisted on rearranging our entire lifestyle.

His first move was to order my roommate to find another place to live. With her departure, the burden of housework once again fell upon me, along with my regular schoolwork. He never turned a hand to help me in any way although he still was not working. He was a specialist in building construction, having also learned that trade from his late stepfather. He was skilled in carpentry, plastering, painting, and cement finishing. But winter was upon us, and little of this type of work was available.

Charles spent his days hanging around the poolroom and the restaurant, dancing with available women to the tune of jukebox records. Sometimes he would spend all night at poker tables or some such endeavors, bearing out my mother's warning that he was "a sporting man."

He didn't even bother to have a fire made in the house when I arrived home after a cold ride from school. (Since there were no heaters in cars in those days, a long winter ride was indeed a cold one.) The house would be so cold sometimes that after making the fire in the grate, I would have to go to a neighbor's house and wait until the room got warm enough for cooking dinner or doing other chores.

At the end of the seven-month school term, I had no savings to tide me over the five months I was unemployed. When school was out and I was broke, my husband sneaked off again, leaving me penniless and jobless. There was no federal aid in those days. Welfare assistance, unemployment compensation, and Social Security were unheard of. Everybody lived by that old American standard rule: "If you don't work, you don't eat." Once again, I turned to domestic work for survival, managing to make $4.50 a week plus meals.

ANOTHER PRESS OPPORTUNITY

During the school term, I had managed to carry on my other three interests—speaking, writing, and politicking. My reputation as a politician, a speaker, and a writer had become rather widespread locally. R. L. Berry (former editor of the *Owensboro Enterprise* for whom I once worked) had become editor of the *Kentucky Reporter*, published in Louisville. He asked me to write a column for his paper. Since no compensation was involved, I used material I had prepared for other purposes, such as speeches I'd made on various occasions. The subject matter related to good health, motherhood, homemaking, environment, how to be a good wife, business and professional women, birth control (for which I was advocating at a time when this controversial subject was very unpopular), parental care, proper training of your child, youth, life, feeling, character, education, culture, cooperation, opportunity, and success. These essays were condensed into a series of articles that the *Reporter* published under the heading "Scribbles from Alice's Scrapbook."

In teaching American history at New Hope, I always included the role that the Negro played in the development of this country. The same was true for Kentucky history. I had found that these children had practically no knowledge of any prominent black Kentuckians past or present. Going beyond the regular teaching requirements, I prepared typed information sheets naming outstanding Kentuckians of color and their contributions to the founding and growth of the state.

Soon I realized that perhaps children throughout the state were as uninformed as those in my district. So I sent copies of these fact sheets to Frank Stanley, who had just recently established the *Louisville Defender*.

He published this information under my byline in a column called "The Achievements of the Kentucky Negro." People started sending me biographical sketches of other prominent people who historically had made outstanding contributions or who were now doing worthwhile things. This helped me to keep the column new and interesting while at the same time keeping my history class informed on contemporary history. The series went over so well that I. Willis Cole, the editor and publisher of the *Louisville Leader*, the city's oldest Negro newspaper, visited me during the school term of 1935 to inquire why I contributed this material to the *Defender* rather than to his paper since I had already done some work for the *Leader* several years earlier. When I replied that I'd had no special reason for choosing the *Defender*, he invited me to come to Louisville at the close of school and work in the *Leader* office.[2]

I welcomed the opportunity. Although Cole offered to pay me only five dollars a week, that was two dollars more than I would be earning in a cook-kitchen in Russellville. Furthermore the work would be dignified, the experience wonderful, and the contacts helpful. And this time I would beat Charles at his own game, leaving home this summer as soon as school closed. This worked out marvelously for me but was quite a surprise to him.

Although I had to operate on a tight budget, I learned a great deal about the newspaper game. I was assigned the position of women's editor, learned to proofread, did the paper's bookkeeping and banking, became familiar with layouts, composed headlines, and even helped with the mailing. In addition, I met many interesting people and was in daily contact with leaders in business, professional, political, and social life in Louisville.

I spent evenings taking classes in sociology and social service administration at Louisville Municipal College with the thought that an opportunity in this field might present itself one day. I also accepted an assignment as editor of the *Bulletin*, a quarterly publication of the Louisville YWCA, an uncompensated position but one that offered experience, identity, and recognition.

When I returned to teaching in the fall, I continued writing a column for the *Louisville Leader*. This one was called "Negro Women's Contribution to American History." At a state teachers' organization (Kentucky Negro Education Association) in Louisville, I met one of the great Negro historians of all time, Carter G. Woodson, founder of the Association for the Study of Negro Life and History. I became an early member of this organization and remained friends with Dr. Woodson until his death in 1950.[3] Another "great" whom I met through the Kansas National Education Association was Mary McLeod Bethune, founder of the National Council of Negro Women and a woman I had admired since childhood because of her work for the advancement of Negro people, women in particular.

In the spring of 1936, I enrolled at Tennessee Agricultural and Industrial State College (now Tennessee State University) to take some special training in journalism. This was the nearest Negro college with journalism courses in the curriculum. It would also be my way of getting out of the state for the first time. Once again, at the close of the school term I left home—this time for Nashville—before Charles could pack his things and beat me out the door. Since 1928, Tennessee A&I had been headed by a journalism pioneer, Dr. George Gore, author of an outstanding history of the Negro press. I excelled at Tennessee A&I, writing a term paper that was deemed the best of the class and was published in the school journal. The following spring, I returned to Nashville to study journalism and public speaking, this time adding classes in library science.

MOVING UP

After six years of teaching at Mount Hope, I began to feel that I had reached the peak of my usefulness in that community. Using my political contacts, I sought and was assigned to a better position, a teaching position in the Adairville consolidated high school—the only high school in the county for Negro children (besides the Russellville "city" school). It was the best the county had to offer. One small room at the school was converted into a library, the only one in the county, and because of my recent library science training, I became part-time librarian in addition to my regular assignment teaching grades three and four.

Because this was a consolidated school, children were bused from one end of the county to the other, a distance of at least fifty miles a day. Decades later, there would be great controversy about busing children to maintain racial balance in schools, but in those days, black children were bused for miles and miles to maintain racial segregation.

I had four wonderful years teaching in Adairville before the authorities devised a plan to save county money at the expense of black children's education. They abolished the high-school department at Adairville, consolidating grades nine through twelve with the Russellville high school. This added another twenty-five miles to the bus route and required many children to leave their homes before daylight and return after dark.

The termination of the high-school department also meant the elimination of a third of the faculty. Two elementary school teachers, including me, were let go, and two high-school teachers were demoted to the elementary level. I was fortunate enough to be reassigned to the county's largest one-room school at Keysburg, about eighteen miles from home—thanks to my political contacts and an outspoken confrontation before members of the school board.

Charles, meanwhile, over the three summers I'd spent away from home, had experienced the loneliness involved when one spouse deserts the other for an entire summer. So in 1938, following my first year of teaching in Adairville, he informed me that he was going to Louisville to work with a building contractor and he wanted me to go with him. I did, and I used the opportunity to take courses in English and French at Louisville Municipal College. The summer passed uneventfully, but I began to realize more and more that although my husband and I shared the same house, we were living in two entirely different worlds with different values and different goals in life. He seemed ill at ease with my friends, and I was equally uncomfortable with his. He seemed disinterested in the things I enjoyed, and I could not adjust to the things he liked.

In autumn, we returned to Russellville and I resumed my work as teacher at Adairville; then we returned to Louisville after the school term so that Charles could resume his summer trade with the builders. I accepted a job as feature writer for the *Derbytown Press*, a semimonthly magazine covering activities in Louisville's Negro business section. This magazine was short lived but was soon replaced by a leaflet called the *Shopping Guide*, for which I was offered the job of advertising manager. Out of this publication grew the *Informer*, a triweekly tabloid on which I worked as coeditor.

TRAVEL!

Then came another big moment in my life—the realization of a dream to travel. One day, Joe Bowles, a retired railroad man, came into our newspaper office and expressed a desire to appear on *Major Bowes Amateur Hour*, a radio show in New York.[4] He asked if I would write the major on his behalf requesting an audition. In time, his request was granted. Because of his age, his inability to read, and his lack of experience traveling in a big city, the elderly gentleman insisted that I accompany him on this trip, serving as his secretary and travel guide. I had no more travel experience than he, but at least I could read and find my way around. Eventually I agreed to accompany him on an expense-free trip with no salary attached.

The former railroad employee arranged transportation through passes issued by the L&N Railroad Company, to which he had given more than fifty years of service. The tickets called for stop-offs at Cincinnati, Pittsburgh, and Washington, D.C., then continuing on to New York. We had heard a great deal about equality "up North," so we were pleased when we encountered no racial difficulties in the first two cities visited. But it was a great shock when we were denied taxicab service at the railroad station in Washington, D.C. We were later informed that a certain cab company, which held the franchise to operate from Union Station, was reluctant to serve Negroes. We were told that the company's policy on discrimination was optional, with the practice left entirely to the discretion of the driver.

At any rate, when we tried to hail a cab, we were directed by the white driver to another cab with a black man in the driver's seat, parked almost a block away on the opposite side of the station plaza. Since we had such a brief stay in Washington, we hired this cab for a sightseeing tour of the city. Having a black driver turned out to our advantage because he showed us some things of special interest, such as the Howard University campus and the residential section of the black bourgeoisie, as well as the monuments and usual sights.

We journeyed on to New York, where we spent more than a week. Our first few days were occupied at the radio station for audition and rehearsals. Finally the big night came. Joe Bowles—age eighty-five; very dark complexioned; with white, woolly hair; wearing a white suit typical of Kentucky colonels (he is credited as being the first black man so commissioned); bent with age; leaning heavily on a cane—stepped upon the stage depicting a perfect image, both in name and physical appearance, of the character portrayed in the song "Ole Black Joe."

The audience went wild with applause, sending his rating to the top of the scales. He was declared winner of the evening and awarded the customary thirty-five-dollar top prize. Without opening the envelope, he handed it to me as a bonus for my patience and endurance.

With this mission accomplished, we had a few more days to see the sights of New York and attend the 1939 World's Fair. Our return trip carried us through Chicago for a brief stop before journeying homeward.

I kept a running account of the trip and used the material in sort of a travelogue column that was serialized for a number of weeks in the *Louisville Defender* under the title "Observations of the East." In evaluating my experience, I concluded that I had learned more in a few weeks of travel than I could learn in months from books, so I decided to spend more time and money traveling rather than attending summer school. The following summer took me to Michigan and across the river to Windsor, Canada. I returned through Chicago for a brief visit to the American Negro Exposition of 1940.[5] Next I traveled to Mound Bayou, Mississippi, to attend the fifty-sixth Founders' Day celebration of this historic all-Negro town in the Delta.[6] I was treated royally as guest of the city's mayor, Benjamin Green. Both of these trips were similarly chronicled in my travel column as "Observations of the North" and "Observations of the South," respectively. A planned trip to the west had to be postponed because of the war, which limited travel.

SEARCHING FOR A WAY OUT

Back in Russellville, I secretly longed for a job out of town. My life had become very unhappy in this complacent little village, not only because of marital problems but also because it offered no opportunity for growth, and I wanted desperately to get away.

I had also become very sensitive to racial discrimination, which prevailed in our town. Although we had been successful in breaking down the racial barriers in some instances, much of the policy of segregation still remained. I recall one incident that infuriated me terribly. It was a day when I came home from teaching with an awful migraine headache causing extreme nausea. I stopped at a drugstore to buy aspirin and ordered a bottle of Coca-Cola with which to take the pills. They sold me the aspirin but informed me that they could not sell me a Coke because they didn't serve colored people.

I assured the clerk that I didn't want to sit at a booth, I only wanted to stand in the aisle and take a few swallows to down the pills because I was very sick. When he still refused, I became so mad and so sick that I couldn't make it any further. I went outside, sat down on the curb, and regurgitated right on Main Street in the heart of downtown. Passersby gawked at me, appalled, as though they thought I was drunk or crazy. I even heard one remark as she looked back, "Ain't that the Adairville schoolteacher?" I wished later that I had stayed in the store and vomited in the middle of the floor.

I remember another incident that a chauffeur friend related about this same drugstore. One day, his boss ordered two fountain Cokes at curb service. When the waiter came for the glasses and discovered that the colored fellow had consumed one of the drinks, he threw the chauffeur's glass against the curb, breaking it into bits as he remarked, "This store will never serve a white person out of a glass that a nigger used."

Since no NAACP or Urban League chapters, labor unions, or any other type of civil rights organization existed in that town, my minister brother-in-law, the Reverend R. D. Langley, and I conceived of the idea of calling citizens together to form what we called a civic league to fight the injustices imposed upon black citizens.

At this meeting, we talked about the post office's refusal to deliver mail in certain black neighborhoods supposedly because there were no paved streets. We asked why the city did not pave the streets in those areas and why there were no gas lines there, either.

We mentioned segregation in the town's only motion-picture theater, where blacks were relegated to the buzzard roost (balcony). We also discussed the wages paid cooks in this town and recommended setting a certain wage floor below which no cook would work. If they would agree to a minimum wage and stick to it, the white people would be forced to pay better wages. The majority of attendees verbally agreed to our proposals.

But the next morning—Monday—many of them went back to their places of employment and told their "good white ladies" that the Reverend Langley and Alice Dunnigan were down in Black Bottom trying to stir up trouble. They claimed we were trying to turn the black folks against the white folks and trying to make them lose their jobs. As a result, I nearly lost mine!

With all of this in mind, I continued looking for a way out of this city and once again relied heavily on prayer for a solution. World War II had been in progress almost a year when I noticed a government poster in the local post office announcing positions for clerk typists. Postmaster Edward Coffman agreed to administer the civil service typing examination if

I furnished my own typewriter. I had an off-brand, broken-down, foreign-make portable typewriter that I'd ordered several years before through a magazine ad, and I brought it to the test. (There was no place in town to rent a typewriter.) While driving me to the post office, Charles launched into his usual tirade, lambasting me for my aspirations, starting an argument for no other reason than to make me so angry and nervous that I would be unable to pass the examination. He almost succeeded.

The exam papers had to be graded at the civil service regional office in Cincinnati. The results would be returned to my hometown postmaster. When the grades arrived, sure enough, I had failed the actual practice test. But I had made such a good showing on the written part of the exam that the postmaster agreed to allow me a second chance on the typing test. This time, I managed to control my nerves. Although my typewriter skipped spaces and some of the letters were out of line, I made the grade.

I completed the standard government application, stating that I would be available to work anywhere in the United States. In a short time, I received a telegram telling me to report for work at the Labor Department in Washington, D.C., the following Monday. The telegram arrived on the day before Thanksgiving in 1942, and I had just begun my second term as teacher at the Keysburg school. I immediately placed my resignation in the superintendent's office and hurriedly prepared to leave Russellville on Sunday in order to report for work in the nation's capital on Monday morning.

I went off happily to this strange and enchanting city, leaving my husband behind. I had not a single friend or acquaintance in Washington nor the slightest idea where I would reside. Whatever apprehension I might have felt, however, was soon overcome by the exotic fascination of exploring a great new world and the grateful realization that my prayers had been answered.

PART II
A GREAT NEW WORLD

13

CONVERGING ON WASHINGTON

One of my college professors often counseled her students to always find their way to the YWCA when in a strange city. "It's the best, cheapest, and safest place to stay," she'd advised. I learned she was right when I went to Louisville to work on a newspaper and again when I accompanied "Uncle Joe" Bowles on his New York adventure. So that's where I headed when I arrived in Washington.

The Phyllis Wheatley YWCA was a busy, crowded place during those early war years, with an influx of young women, like myself, converging upon the capital city for war work.[1] Like many other girls, I ran into a little difficulty attempting to register for an indefinite stay. The registrants were required to name three reputable persons as references. I had no difficulty naming prominent people back home, but that didn't suffice. The registrar required three Washington references.

I immediately named three Washington celebrities whom I had met quite formally when they were guest speakers on various occasions—Mary McLeod Bethune, Dr. Carter G. Woodson, and the Elks' grand exalted ruler, J. Finley Wilson. If any of these references had been checked, I'm confident not one would have remembered me. But it worked, and I was accepted as an indefinite resident. I lived there comfortably until the YWCA, through a special home placement committee, found a suitable furnished room for me with the wonderful Pratt family in the fourteen hundred block of "R" Street.

I spent the first few days of my government job in a typing pool. Then I was assigned to the filing section of the War Labor Board on what was known as the "swing shift," working from three until eleven o'clock at night. A number of Howard University students worked this same shift. I learned that the Howard men were all classified as grade CAF-3 clerks, earning an annual salary of $1,620 while still students, as compared with my CAF-2 grade and annual salary of $1,440, although I had a complete undergraduate education and fourteen years of working experience as a teacher, lecturer, journalist, and politician.

The $1,440 salary had sounded very good to me when I left my $623 per year teacher's salary in Kentucky (my top salary was $89 per month for a seven-month school term). I didn't realize, however, that a grade-two job was practically at the bottom of the federal service. When I found out, I did not hesitate to let my displeasure be known. A longtime believer in organized labor, I joined the United Federal Workers of America (UFWA),[2] and with its support I launched an all-out fight for a job more commensurate with my qualifications. Within a few months, this battle was won, and I received a grade-three rating as an assistant statistical clerk with the coding section of the War Labor Board at an annual salary of $1,620. Still working below my capabilities, I fought on and within a year received a second promotion to CAF-4 statistical clerk, earning $1,800 a year.

Still interested in newspaper work, I contacted Claude A. Barnett of Chicago, founder and director of the Associated Negro Press (ANP), a national news-gathering agency serving 112 Negro newspapers throughout the United States.[3] Although ANP had a Washington representative, Ernest Johnson, Mr. Barnett agreed to employ me on a space-rate basis covering national affairs that the regular correspondent missed. For this he offered me one-half cent per word for all material accepted. Although I didn't make much money, I could do this part-time while still working for the government. It was great fun, and my name became known as a national reporter.

I still believed that my grade-four rating as a government clerk was not commensurate with my academic record or sixteen years of prior professional experience. Grade four, however, was about the limit that black workers could reach at that time, and only a few (mainly lawyers) had pierced that ceiling. It was not until some two decades later that New York Congressman Adam Clayton Powell Jr. brought this unwritten policy to public attention, leading to its eventual crumbling. After taking evening classes at Howard in economics and statistics, I transferred to the Office of Price Administration (OPA), the most liberal of all wartime agencies, where a promotion would be more likely. Soon thereafter, I was promoted to my first federal professional grade (P-1), which at $2,000 a year seemed like a huge milestone. It also meant greater respect and prestige, perhaps the most immediate manifestation of which occurred on paydays, when checks were delivered to the professionals' desks while clerical workers from grade four down had to stand in line to receive their pay envelopes.

POSTWAR

When the war ended in 1945, OPA was no longer needed and was given a year to gradually terminate. Employees were let go as their particular section was abolished, but because of my tenure, I was shifted from section to section until the very end of the agency's existence in late December 1946. As providence would have it, the Washington correspondent for the Associated Negro Press was leaving his job about this time to accept employment in New York, leaving a vacancy. Since I had been doing part-time work for the ANP, I had no difficulty being hired on a trial basis for what the ANP termed chief of the Washington Bureau. But there was a hitch. Since the news agency was not sure how well I could handle such a big national assignment, it was not willing to set a salary and insisted that I continue working through the trial period on a space-rate basis of half a cent per word.

I agreed to try it for a month and sent in loads of copy each week. At the end of the month, I received a check for thirty dollars. "This is ridiculous," I argued. "No one can live on thirty dollars a month."

During this period, my husband joined me in Washington after much back-and-forth in letters in which he expressed a desire to seek federal employment. After considerable persuasion, I finally agreed, thinking and hoping that we could make a better life together in a different environment among new acquaintances. But after a fair trial, it still didn't work out—our values, aspirations, and goals were still very different. Finally Charles and I decided to part ways, and I continued to navigate on my own.

After some debate, ANP agreed to pay one cent per word, and I agreed to try it for two more months. The same amount of my copy was used, and my monthly checks came to sixty dollars each. I managed to survive these three months on a payout for unused leave from OPA and a refund of my federal retirement contributions. When this money was gone, I informed ANP that I must have a definite salary. The agency agreed to pay me twenty-five dollars per week as a base salary and gave me permission to pick up some extra money doing other jobs to supplement my ANP salary. Freelancing for magazines and doing some political work, I managed to make this arrangement work for fourteen years, and I was averaging more than eight thousand dollars annually when I left newspaper work to accept a political appointment in 1961. It was a rough ride at times but also a good one, and I wouldn't trade it for anything.

14

BREAKING DOWN RACE— AND GENDER—BARRIERS

I began my job as chief of the Washington Bureau for the Associated Negro Press on the first day of January 1947. My first assignment was to cover the potential ouster of Theodore Bilbo of Mississippi from the U.S. Senate for misconduct.[1] I was fairly familiar with legislative procedure and with the Capitol building, having often lobbied with a delegation from the Southern Conference for Human Welfare[2] for passage of anti-poll-tax legislation and an antilynching law, two bills of major concern to that organization. But I knew nothing of press operations on Capitol Hill.

On the opening day of Congress, I secured from my Kentucky senator a pass admitting me to the visitors' gallery. Upon arrival, I found a long line waiting for seats in the already overflowing gallery. For hours I stood in this line, which moved only when a few people left the gallery, making room for a few others. I became very disgusted and anxious to get inside so that I could get to work on my assignment. I was completely unaware that it was against Capitol rules for spectators to take notes in the visitors' gallery. When I discovered this, I realized that the visitors' gallery was not an appropriate place for reporters, anyway.

Liberals March In D. C., Seek Action

By ALICE DUNNIGAN

WASHINGTON—(ANP) — All roads led to Washington last week when groups of representative citizens from all over the nation gathered in the capital for the opening of the 80th Congress.

Still others, from various sections of the south, bent on accomplishing the same aims, began the eastward trek by all modes of transportation.

LEADERS SPEAK

The Robeson group had been engaged in an 100-day American

Blacks converged on Washington from all over the country for the opening of the Eightieth Congress, soon dubbed by Truman the "do-nothing" Congress. (*Atlanta Daily World*, January 5, 1947)

While standing in line, I noticed a number of newsmen entering and going up a back stairway that was securely roped off with the usual red velvet ropes so commonly seen in places of dignity around the nation's capital. This stairway was guarded by Capitol police. The reporters would step up, show their passes, and be admitted. I saw no reason why I shouldn't do that. So I stepped up to the stairway, only to be stopped by the guards and asked where I was going.

"I'm a newspaper reporter," I explained, "and I'm going wherever those newsmen are going."

"But this is reserved only for reporters of accredited newspapers," one policeman replied.

"I'm a reporter for an accredited news bureau," I argued, proudly producing my newly acquired ANP press pass for inspection.

"Even with that," the other guard chimed in, "I don't think you belong up there. But I'm going to let you through. If you have no business up there, they'll send you back, anyway." With this he unsnapped the rope and allowed me to pass.

At the top of the steps, I opened a door marked "Press Gallery" and walked in. To my surprise, I was in a large suite of rooms completely equipped with all types of apparatus needed by reporters. There were rows of typewriters and shelves filled with reference books, dictionaries, and congressional registers covering many years. A Western Union machine was ticking away in one corner of an adjoining room. One whole wall was lined with telephone booths. Through an open door, I could see another room full of radio and television equipment. Still another room was furnished with comfortable couches and easy chairs for relaxation.

Press releases were piled high on a little table, surrounded by stacks of copy paper, carbon paper, Western Union blanks, letterheads, and envelopes. The main door led into the gallery overlooking the Senate chamber. Rows of circular seats were provided for reporters to watch the Senate in action. This is indeed a reporter's haven, I thought, as I gazed around in awe. Suddenly I was facing a gallery official who politely asked if there was anything he could do for me.

I explained that I was a reporter assigned to the Bilbo hearing and wanted only to see what was going on inside the Senate chamber.

"No one can observe from the gallery except accredited Capitol reporters," the man explained.

"What does one have to do to become an accredited Capitol reporter?" I asked.

Without specifically answering my question, the official stated that they were not accrediting any more reporters because they already had more members than they could accommodate in that space.

"Are there any Negro reporters accredited?" I asked.

He gave a negative answer, explaining that there were certain qualifications. If a reporter met those qualifications, he could apply for membership. His application would be reviewed by the standing committee of the gallery, and if it met the requirements, his membership would be approved by the committee.

I asked for and received an application, which I later completed and submitted.

Weeks passed, and I received no word regarding my application. When I called about it, I was told that the standing committee had not yet acted on it. After more weeks passed, I called again and received the same answer. After a while, I began to make personal visits to the Capitol to inquire about the status of my application, probably making a nuisance of myself. Finally I was informed that I did not qualify for membership since applicants were required to represent daily papers.

To pacify me, I was given another application for membership in the Periodical Gallery. I submitted it and ultimately was notified that I did

He said that state, local and national governments must attack this problem now without waiting for "the slowest state" or the "most backward community" to catch up with the times. "It is my deep conviction," the chief executive said, "that we of all Americans. And again I mean all Americans."

Truman was forthright in his denunciation of discrimination. "If . . . freedom is to be more than a dream, each man must be guaranteed equality

(Continued on Page 4)

ADMITTED TO PRESS GALLERIES

ADMIT WOMAN TO PRESS GALLERIES

Washington, D.C. July 3—The standing committee of Correspondents voted Tuesday to admit Mrs. A. Dunnigan to the Senate and Congressional press galleries. Mrs. Dunnigan is a representative of the Associated Negro Press which services most Negro newspapers throughout the United States.

Before taking charge of the Washington bureau of the Associated Negro Press, Mrs. Dunnigan served as social editor of the Louisville Leader; columnist for the Louisville Defender and the Kentucky Reporter; reporter for the Owensboro Enterprise and Rising Sun; circulation manager of the Hopkinsville Globe; and co-editor of the Informer, a tri-weekly news-

paper published in Louisville.

Mrs. Dunnigan is the first Negro woman to be admitted to the senate press gallery, the only other Negro member being Louis Lautier of the National Negro Publishers' Association.

Aside from her journalistic experience, Mrs. Dunnigan served for a number of years as teacher in Kentucky, and spent four years in the employment of the federal government. Her federal service included work as a statistician in the wage stabilization division of the War Labor Board, business economist in the food rationing division of OPA and pricing analyst in the pricing division of OPA.

Editors Note: The Leader pub-

(Continued on Page 4)

Mrs. Alice A. Dunnigan
Who appears above on the steps of the nation's capitol at Washington, is the first colored woman and the second race press representative to be admitted to the Senate and Congressional press galleries. Mrs. Dunnigan is a Kentuckian and formerly served as social editor of the Leader. The publisher was the guest of the Dunnigans while in Washington last week as delegate to the National Convention of the N. A. A. C. P.

The Louisville Leader (July 5, 1947) was one of the half-dozen black Kentucky newspapers for which Dunnigan worked before moving to Washington and breaking through the first of many barriers to the black press as Washington bureau chief for ANP.

not qualify for membership there because that gallery, they said, was exclusively designed for magazine writers and I was representing weekly newspapers.

The fight for membership continued, with various organizations and the newspaper guild getting into the act. After a time, the Senate Rules Committee, chaired by Illinois Republican senator C. Wayland (Curley) Brooks, held hearings on the matter. The upshot was the committee ordering that the rules of the gallery be changed to admit representatives of news agencies.

A few weeks later, Louis Lautier, representing another news agency—the National Newspaper Publishers Association (NNPA)—was notified that he had been accepted in the Capitol press corps, thus making him the first Negro member. Percival L. Prattis was admitted to the Periodical Gallery a few days earlier as a representative of *Our World* magazine.

I was disturbed about Lautier being admitted before me since I had

The office of the Illinois senator sent this group picture of Senator Charles Wayland Brooks (second from right), chairman of the Senate Rules Committee; Griffing Bancroft, chairman of the Senate Press Gallery Standing Committee; Alice Dunnigan of ANP; and Louis Lautier of NNPA to Negro newspapers around the country, most of which gave the rules change a good play. (From Alice Allison Dunnigan, *A Black Woman's Experience—from Schoolhouse to White House*, [Philadelphia: Dorrance & Co., 1974])

vigorously carried the fight, but I never questioned it. Sometime later, however, I found out that action on my application had been delayed because ANP director Claude Barnett was a little slow in sending in a letter of recommendation.

When I had contacted Mr. Barnett regarding the need for such a letter, he was somewhat skeptical about recommending me because I was "daring to rush in where angels feared to tread." "For years," he wrote me, "we have been trying to get a man accredited to the Capitol Galleries and have not succeeded. What makes you think that you—a woman—can accomplish this feat?"

It was only after quite an exchange of correspondence and telephone conversations that Barnett reluctantly sent a letter of recommendation, and soon afterward, in June 1947, I became the first Negro woman to receive Capitol accreditation. My acceptance received widespread publicity, and the Republican-controlled Congress received credit for opening the Capitol Press Galleries to Negro reporters.

Lautier and I were the only Negroes holding accreditation to the regular galleries for a number of years, until Ethel Payne came to Washington in 1953 to represent the *Chicago Defender* and qualified for accreditation because of her affiliation with the new Chicago daily paper. (Roscoe Conkling Simmons, the first Negro writer on a daily newspaper in Washington, D.C., the *Times-Herald*, was accredited to the Capitol Press Galleries in January 1951 but died four months later.)

One of the people who took me under her wing and coached me on the do's and don'ts of Capitol reporters was one of the nation's best-known journalists and one of the nicest people I have ever met—May Craig, who represented several Maine newspapers. She gave me tips on how to win friends, introduced me to many of hers in the national press and Congress, and helped me immeasurably in winning acceptance and respect on the Hill. She was also instrumental in my becoming the first Negro member of the Women's National Press Club. Although it took eight years to happen, she had initiated and supported my membership from the start.

ON TO THE NEXT GOAL

After being credentialed at the Capitol, my next goal was accreditation to the White House to cover presidential press conferences. Lautier was already a White House correspondent—the only black one—having succeeded NNPA representative Harry McAlpin, who in February 1944 had become the first Negro in the White House press corps. I took on this fight alone, without assistance from my employer, by going to the White House to appeal for more Negro representation among the White House press. In a conversation with Charlie Ross, President Truman's press secretary,[3] I said, "The Republican Congress has lowered the barriers against Negro reporters in the Capitol Galleries. What is the Democratic administration going to do about admitting more Negroes to the White House press corps?" Ross's advice was to send a letter to the White House requesting accreditation. I did, and I received the coveted White House press pass in short order and without any problems. Later, without further effort, I became a member of the White House Correspondents Association.[4]

Next I sought membership in the State Department Press Association, of which my predecessor, Ernest Johnson, had been a member as well as James (Jimmy) Hicks and Louis Lautier, both of NNPA. In August 1947, I became the first woman of my race to receive membership in this group.

I had no further trouble receiving accreditation until I applied for a metropolitan police pass and was called in for an interview by the accrediting officer, who was connected with the Associated Press (AP). He informed me that an objection had been registered against my receiving credentials. The complaint came from a reporter for the Washington *Afro-American* newspaper, who contended that I had no need for a local police pass since I represented a national news agency. He assured the accreditor that one Negro police reporter was sufficient to assimilate news of interest to Negro readers. When the accrediting officer learned that I held a Capitol press pass, he issued my police credentials without further ado,

In the 1940s, it was not unusual for Dunnigan to be the only female reporter in an interview. Here, she is interviewing Illinois Republican Charles Wayland Brooks with Louis Lautier (NNPA), Al Sweeney (Washington *Afro-American*), and Chick Webb (*Pittsburgh Courier*) in 1948. (Dunnigan Papers, MARBL, Emory University)

making me one of the few women at the time to hold a Washington police press permit.

Another necessary pass for newswomen in those days was one that admitted the holder to the First Lady's press conferences, which were held in the East Wing of the White House. (The president's press conferences were held in the West Wing.) I had no difficulty obtaining this pass.

It didn't take me long to establish contacts in each of the executive departments whom I could depend on for news tips unavailable to the general press. This was especially true after top Negro executives (commonly known as the Black Cabinet) became confident that I would protect my sources. These few Negroes holding high-ranking government posts were serious about improving conditions for black people. When they were unsuccessful in their attempts to right a wrong in their respective departments through negotiations with superiors, they would discreetly leak the situation to the Negro press, even at the risk of losing their jobs if discovered doing so. I had many exclusives from these sources because I made it a practice to visit the agencies periodically, digging for information and usually getting it. The sources also realized that the story would get broad coverage in newspapers across the country, often leading to pressure on politicians from Negro communities to solve a problem to the satisfaction of black voters.

LONG DAYS FOR LITTLE PAY

My work days had no hourly limit, and my work weeks had no end. Day and night, Saturdays, Sundays, and holidays, I was on the job if there was the possibility of a news story breaking anywhere, from the upper chambers of the government to Embassy Row, the slums or city streets, sports arenas, social circles, or halls of justice. These efforts produced a vast number of exclusive stories that appeared under my byline in newspapers throughout the country. Soon ANP was said to be doing a better job than ever before of dispersing firsthand, on-the-spot news to its clients. Previously, it had been sending out so many rewrites from big city dailies such as the *Washington Post* and the *New York Times* that some of its clients had begun to refer to it as the "Associated Clip Service."

While some of ANP's clients expressed delight to see the service come alive, the accolades brought me no additional compensation, and I was still making difficult choices regarding living expenses, the cost of cabs around the city, and trying to make a good showing. Contemporary fashion trends created a challenge in the latter regard when hemlines suddenly dropped and I had no cash for new clothes. One of my contacts in a well-known women's organization told me later that I paid a price for that when some of its middle class, socialite members objected to my receiving an award from the organization on grounds that I wasn't representative of black women because I went to the White House in "those old short dresses" and wearing neither a hat nor gloves. I was cut deeply by those remarks because I'd done many hours of volunteer work for the organization, and I wondered how its members could take such an attitude toward someone who had worked so hard to pull herself up by her own bootstraps.

I told my confidant to go back and tell those women that since a presidential news conference is not a reception, one does not go there attired as if attending a reception but rather to work, and I would look pretty silly going there in anything but simple office clothing. I never had further confirmation of my informer's report, but neither did I ever receive any public recognition from this organization, although I was honored by other women's organizations, among many other groups.

15

A TRIP WITH THE PRESIDENT

I had only been an accredited White House reporter for a short time when I noticed an announcement on the bulletin board in the press room regarding President Truman's forthcoming "nonpolitical" whistle-stop trip to the West Coast. Reporters were requested to sign up immediately if they were interested in accompanying him.

I didn't know at the time how reporters were selected for such assignments. So once again I called on the president's press secretary, Charlie Ross, to inquire why Negro reporters had never been selected to accompany any president on political tours. I had in mind some strong points in favor of setting this precedent, but I never had a chance to present them. Mr. Ross immediately said, "Alice, you can go. We have estimated that the trip will cost each reporter around a thousand dollars." I was shocked and bewildered because somehow I thought the reporters were selected by the White House and the trip would be gratis since this was a special train provided for the president. But I didn't let my ignorance show and instead said, "Thank you. I'll try to go."

Dunnigan talks with Truman's press secretary, Charlie Ross, in 1948 about accompanying the president on a whistle-stop, cross-country train trip. (Dunnigan Papers, MARBL, Emory University)

Regardless of cost, I desperately wanted to go for many reasons, personal and otherwise. I had been active in politics back home and had supported the Democratic Party since the last days of Herbert Hoover, whom the nation held responsible for the Great Depression. The majority of Negro Republicans left the party of Abraham Lincoln during that period when so many people were out of work and almost starving.[1] I was concerned about seeing the Democrats remain in office but, like many other people, thought that Mr. Truman's chances for election were very slim. I thought the appearance of a Negro traveling with the presidential party would do much toward influencing the Negro vote. I also felt that this would be a breakthrough for Negro reporters. On a personal level, I had never been to the West Coast and so much wanted this experience. Finally, I thought the opportunity would show recognition of my competence as a qualified reporter.

I immediately called my boss by long distance at my own expense, explaining that I had been chosen by the White House to accompany the president on his West Coast trip, and I outlined the cost. In his usual slow, nonchalant manner, Mr. Barnett replied, "Women don't go on trips like this."

"That's why I am so anxious to go," I emphasized. "This is a new venture for women and a forward step for Negroes in general. It's a breakthrough, and that's important!"

"Do you think this trip is worth a thousand dollars to you?" Mr. Barnett asked. When I replied in the affirmative, he said, "Well, it isn't worth it either to me or my service. The daily papers will be recording every event of the trip, and we can pick it up from them."

Disgustedly but firmly, I stated, "Well, I'm going with your consent, even if I have to defray my own expenses."

I had no more than two hundred dollars in the bank and no idea where I could get more to finance the trip. Determined to go, I began to think of ways to raise the balance. I had some good friends among the top echelon of the Elks, and I knew that fraternity had money—lots of it. I contacted Judge William C. Hueston to ask if the Elks would lend me the money, every cent of which I promised to pay back.[2] The majority of the Elks officials were Republicans, however, and did not take kindly to this request, turning me down on the grounds that it was not a lending organization. Instead I was offered a fifty-dollar contribution on the theory that the trip would perhaps pave the way for future opportunities for Negro newspeople.

I turned next to my sorority, Sigma Gamma Rho, but it could offer no more than a ceremonial send-off and a corsage, which I also turned down, suggesting that they give me something useful instead since I needed either money or clothes. They responded with a lovely blouse, which was not only beautiful but practical and useful.

I had a confidential conversation with the assistant to the president for minority affairs, putting my cards on the table.[3] My bottom line was to ask whether the Democratic Party could quietly make a contribution to my trip. The aide responded that although the White House realized the political implications of my making the trip, they just couldn't afford to contribute anything toward my expenses.

"Think what the other reporters would say when they found out that we were contributing to your expenses while their newspapers had to bear the full cost for their representatives. And they would surely find out because somehow Drew Pearson [then a very well-known syndicated columnist] never misses a thing. Somehow he'll find out." Again I shot a blank.

I turned next to the National Council of Negro Women because I knew that its president, Mary McLeod Bethune, had political clout and maneuvering know-how, even though the organization had no money. I thought she might be able to use her influence in obtaining at least a loan for me through her many contacts.

Mrs. Bethune gave me a pep talk on how pleased she was that I had been chosen for this unprecedented experience and how proud she was to see "my beautiful black women" receive the recognition they had so long deserved. But she had no idea how the trip could be financed.

"I'll call Claude," she said, referring to my boss, "and impress upon him the importance of sending you on this trip. This would mean so much to black people everywhere. It would add a great deal to his business. So he should see that you go, even at the greatest sacrifice."

After having this telephone chat with Mr. Barnett, she turned to me and said, "Claude said he was not sending you because you are not qualified for such a big assignment. He is afraid that you can't do the job adequately."

This was more cutting than any of the excuses that had been offered by others. Subsequently, salt was rubbed in the wound when I was informed by Mrs. Bethune's confidante that the "great lady" had secretly agreed that my experience was inadequate to do a satisfactory job. According to this woman, Mrs. Bethune had openly expressed regret that this honor had not been granted to her friend Venice Spraggs, an excellent reporter for the *Chicago Defender* whose writing style I had long admired and tried to emulate. Mrs. Spraggs, however, had not qualified for credentials in the Capitol and White House. That placed me a step ahead of her in consideration for this trip.

Again I called Mr. Barnett, relating my feeling about his and Mrs. Bethune's mutual position on my qualifications, and I expressed a definite intention to go, no matter what. This time, he agreed to contact his four biggest newspapers to request that they contribute $250 each to the cost of my trip. "I'll call you back as soon as I get a decision on this suggestion," he said.

In a few days, he called to say that the *Chicago Defender* did not approve of his idea. If it had to contribute to a reporter's expense, it might as well send its own reporter and receive the prestige for its own paper. The *Defender* then contacted the White House and made arrangements to send a reporter—John Young III.[4]

The *Pittsburgh Courier* took the same position and arranged with the White House to send Stanley Roberts as its representative.

The *Afro-American* was willing to accept Mr. Barnett's offer if he would promise the paper exclusive stories, which as head of a syndicated news service, he could not do.

The *Norfolk Journal and Guide* was just not interested.

The deadline for travel plans was drawing near, and the White House was pressuring me for a definitive answer as to whether I was going or not. Later I learned that the pressure was because Doris Fleeson, a famous syndicated columnist, was the only female reporter signed up for the trip, and since space was limited, she had been asked if she would share her compartment with a Negro. She replied, I was told, "For Alice Dunnigan I will gladly share my compartment, but not for any other woman I know." As it turned out, there was sufficient space for each of us to have our own separate accommodations. At any rate, Doris left the train in Detroit for another assignment, leaving me the only woman reporter to continue through the entire trip.[5]

As a last resort, I turned to my friend Leslie Perry, legislative director for the NAACP, asking if he could use his influence to float a loan from the organization. He told me the NAACP constitution and bylaws would not allow that, but he agreed to personally recommend me for a loan from his bank. Such a loan would have been impossible on my own since I had no collateral. With Les's recommendation, however, I was successful in borrowing five hundred dollars on my signature alone. With this loan, along with my little personal savings and some careful planning, I had enough to cover the expenses of the trip.

ON MY WAY

On June 3, 1948, I boarded the Presidential Special with President and Mrs. Truman and their daughter, Margaret; the White House secretarial and press staffs; and sixty correspondents, photographers, and radio and television technicians. The group of correspondents for the first time included two women reporters and three Negroes.

The trip lasted fifteen days and covered more than nine thousand miles through eighteen western states. The two Negro male reporters stayed very much to themselves throughout the trip, spending scarcely any time with me except to speak in passing. They seemed to view the assignment as a pleasure trip rather than a working one. It was my impression during my years as a reporter that men didn't seem to take their work as seriously as women and that it was customary in our society for men not to have to work as hard as women to get recognition. A woman, it seemed, always had to work twice as hard when she was holding what was considered a man's job if she hoped to win public approval.

Several of the white reporters, on the other hand, seemed to almost bend over backward to be helpful and cooperative. The train was equipped with a mimeograph room, where the official press staff turned out reams and reams of paperwork daily—press releases, copies of the president's speeches, schedules, memos, and the like. At first, I tried to grab everything that came out.

It was Eddie Folliard of the *Washington Post* who took the time to explain to me how to cover this type of operation. (Folliard had covered presidents as far back as Calvin Coolidge. He won a Pulitzer Prize for Telegraphic Reporting—National in 1947.) "You don't need those 'canned' releases," he said. "The whole purpose of personal coverage on a trip like this is to pick up real, live color for your story. Get off the train at every stop. Mingle with the people. Pick up bits of conversation. Ask questions and get answers. Use as many quotes as possible. Get a line on the attitude of the crowd. Determine whether the president is favorably or unfavorably accepted. Get reactions of the people. Don't worry about the president's speeches; they will be published verbatim in many periodicals anyway, and people will have a chance to read them. Important portions will be repeated on radio and television programs."

I heeded his advice and was soon writing in true "Folliard style." But there was another challenge in writing for Negro newspapers in that all of our stories had to have a Negro lead or angle. This was hard to find in some of the western states where there were very few Negroes. No doubt that is why the two Negro male reporters didn't bother to hop off the train at every little whistle stop.

As for me, I never missed a beat. I jumped off the train at every stop and often created a lead for a story if anything of interest happened in a certain city. Sometimes the story would begin with a simple statement like: "Not a single Negro was seen in the crowd of hundreds of people assembled at 'such and such' when 'this or that' happened." Then it was on with the interesting details of the occasion. When hard news of interest to the Negro press was not available, I often searched for topics of interest among our fellow travelers that could be developed into feature articles. For example, I did a feature on "democracy at work" in which I described the different races and nationalities represented among the press corps aboard the "Rolling White House."

I also did in-depth interviews with service workers on the train, incorporating them into an informative piece on behind-the-scenes activities responsible for the smooth operation of the trip. This story, which included the duties of the president's valet, the mimeograph operators, the waiters, the bartenders, and the Pullman porters, was picked up by *Service* magazine, the official organ of Tuskegee Institute, as well as by our member newspapers. A special feature on Arthur Prettyman, the president's valet, who had interesting stories to tell about his work with President Roosevelt as well as President Truman, was published in the magazine section of the *Afro-American* newspaper.

A MIDNIGHT SCOOP

Civil rights was the most important subject to Negroes during the forties, but it was still so unpopular among many American voters that politicians usually shied away from it. For much of this trip, President Truman had made no mention of civil rights. The first big news break for the Negro press came around midnight at an unscheduled stop in Missoula, Montana. The president and many of the reporters had retired since no other stops were planned for the night. But as the train reached this little college town, hundreds of students had gathered along the railroad track to see the president. The train came to a halt, and President Truman, dressed in pajamas and robe, briefly addressed the young people from the back of the coach. After his remarks, the students began asking questions. One yelled out loudly and clearly, "Mr. President, what do you say about civil rights?"

The president quickly replied, "I'll say that civil rights is as old as the Constitution of the United States and as new as the Democratic platform of 1944." He then intimated that it would be renewed in the 1948 platform.

That was one of the first of my big western stories, headlined "Pajama Clad President Defends Civil Rights at Midnight." Stanley Roberts and John Young missed the story because they were not out by the platform. They tried to prevail upon me not to file my story because it would make them "look bad" to have missed it. I did not comply, and they probably filed stories anyway based on discussions with other members of the press.

At many of these whistle stops, the president addressed crowds from the back of the train, while at others, temporary platforms had been improvised for him. In some of the larger cities, the party stayed overnight at the most exquisite hotel in town, where we could enjoy a good bath and a night's rest in a real bed. In some state capitals, the president was entertained at the governor's mansion while the press partied elsewhere. Sometimes the entire entourage would leave the train for a long bus trip through the backcountry, picking up the train in another city a hundred or so miles away. I wasn't the only news reporter thrilled to see the snow-capped mountains of Idaho or shepherds watching their flocks graze on a mountainside. Once in a while you would glimpse a deer or an antelope scampering through the forest or hear the howls of wolves or coyotes in the distance. It must have been equally fascinating for the people of the little villages in the backcountry to see for the first time a president of the United States.

WASHINGTON STATE

When the party reached Olympia, Washington, the president was an overnight guest at the governor's mansion while some of the reporters stayed at a downtown hotel. As on some previous stops, I chose to sleep in one of the Pullman cars that had been left on the side track for the accommodation of those who wished to use them. However, I did attend a cocktail party for the press at a nearby hotel, where I was the only person of color in attendance. I must have been a curiosity to the townspeople, who regarded me strangely at first but eventually pulled up chairs close to mine, forming a semicircle around me. Then they began asking all kinds of questions regarding race problems, my experience on this trip, my background as a reporter, why I was chosen for the trip, and so on.

When the party finally ended, a handsome, dignified, middle-aged army officer walked me to the Pullman car on the railroad track.

Later, I was informed that the few cars had been sidetracked for the accommodation of the Negro reporters because there had been some question as to whether the hotel would willingly accept us as guests. The White House officials dared not suggest that Negro reporters use the Pullman cars but made the decision optional, hoping the blacks would choose to use them. My choice was based on my financial situation and certainly not to save face for either the hotel management or the White House staff.

OREGON FLOODS

We left Olympia for Oregon by plane because of terrible flood damage in that state, which the president would view by air. This was my first flight, but my colleagues said I took it like a veteran. While I did get airsick, they never knew it, and to this day, I am not sure whether my nausea was due to motion sickness or a hangover from the cocktail party the previous night. This unscheduled flight cost each of us an extra twenty-five dollars, but for those of us not in a position to pay on the spot, the airline graciously waited until we returned to our jobs before collecting.

My interest in the Oregon situation was the number of Negro families affected by the flood. I had another exclusive story for ANP after I arranged for an interview with Maurice Reddy, director of the Red Cross in the Portland area, who informed me that the organization was assisting some twenty-five hundred Negro families left homeless by the flood, many of whom were facing problems finding shelter.

WESTERN HOSPITALITY

The Washington stop also included a boat ride on the *Kalakala* across Puget Sound from Bremerton to Seattle, Washington.[6] An elaborate feast was served on this voyage, consisting of all kinds of seafood with many varieties of each, prepared in every conceivable way. It was feasts like this, in addition to the many buffets, banquets, and cocktail parties with trays of hors d'oeuvres, prepared for the press in different cities that helped me to

2,500 Families Homeless
Due To Flood In Oregon

BY ALICE A. DUNNIGAN
(En Route On The President's Train)

SOMEWHERE IN OREGON—(ANP)—President Truman and his party viewed with awe and pity the terrible disaster caused by high waters, as they flew over the flooded area of Oregon Friday

The 2,500 Negro families who lost their homes in this flood are creating quite a problem for the city of Portland, according to an official there.

Because the majority of Negro homes in that city have been washed out, it became necessary to house these flood victims in school houses, churches, halls and other public

The plight of Negro families who lost their homes in the Oregon flood was one of several exclusives Dunnigan reported for black newspapers during the Truman trip. (*Atlanta Daily World*, June 16, 1948)

save money on food and make the trip for less expense than originally estimated. Being a woman helped in this regard, too, when a reporter would join me as I ate alone in the dining car and pick up the tab. I made no objection since most of them were allowed an unlimited expense account.

As we traveled through Washington State, we were showered with bushels of big, red, juicy apples, enough to keep us supplied for the remainder of the trip. Many days, my lunch would consist of only an apple or two. The orange growers of California gave us the same courtesy. Stacks of red mesh bags filled with golden, sweet oranges were piled high between the coaches, and I breakfasted many mornings on orange juice alone.

Train service workers were so pleased to have Negro reporters aboard that they would take no tips from me. Every time I offered to leave a tip for a waiter or porter, he would say, "Keep your money. Whatever you have to give us, consider it our contribution to your trip." The Pullman porter, who had served several presidents, said this was his first opportunity to serve one of his own people on a Presidential Special. Even the great liberal Franklin D. Roosevelt never had a Negro reporter traveling with him.

Being the only female reporter on the train provided another special advantage—flowers. My compartment stayed full of fresh flowers throughout the trip. At each stop, Mrs. Truman would be presented with gorgeous bouquets. She received so many flowers that she had no space for them in the presidential car, so she would send them to me. The porter who brought them would always remind me that Mrs. Truman had said, "You have nothing to fear; there are no bombs in them. The Secret Service has carefully examined every leaf and bud."

Segregation was still rampant throughout the nation, and word had preceded us all along the way that a Negro was traveling in the Truman party, apparently to alert hotel management what to expect and thus avoid any unpleasantness. (They usually said "a" Negro, perhaps because the advance report had gone out from the White House before they were aware that there would be three Negroes.) This advance information became evident when I registered at the Fontenelle Hotel in Omaha. The clerk was cordial almost to the point of being condescending. "You must be Mrs. Dunnigan," he said politely. "We heard you were with the president's party. Welcome to the Fontenelle."

The manager then came to personally greet me and welcome me to the hotel. "While in the city, you are to be the special guest of Robert Hill II, a member of our staff," he said. "Mr. Hill has a special breakfast prepared for you, and it will be served in the private executive dining room."

He seemed surprised to meet the other two Negro reporters but invited them to be Mr. Hill's guests as well.

I was delighted, not because I am so naive but because I welcomed any free meal. We were all a little skeptical about whether this was truly hospitality or the hotel's method of herding us off into a Jim Crow setup. While I politely accepted the invitation, Stan Roberts was hostile, letting it be known that he was a member of the president's party and didn't intend to come all the way to Omaha to associate with a headwaiter. "I don't do that at home."

Only Arthur Prettyman, the president's valet, joined me in this delicious, well-planned breakfast in the exclusive and beautiful dining room. I tried to apologize for our group's behavior, explaining to Mr. Hill that all of us appreciated his hospitality but the arrangement placed us in a rather embarrassing position. We didn't want to seem ungrateful, but neither did we intend to accept any segregated setup, no matter how subtle.

Mr. Hill assured me that the hotel had no discriminatory policy. He merely wanted us to be his guests because he was so proud to see Negroes in the presidential party. As we soon learned, he was the maître d'hôtel, a graduate of Wilberforce University, and a very intelligent man. His father,

Robert Hill I, was a graduate of Tuskegee Institute and had been employed at this hotel for twenty-five years. He had served as personal waiter to the hotel chain's owner but had now been promoted to room service captain. He was assigned exclusively to President Truman's suite during the visit.

Robert Hill II's son, Robert Hill III, who had recently graduated from the eighth grade at the age of twelve with the highest honors in academics, athletics, and the arts, had just been honored by the Omaha Rotary Club for outstanding scholastic achievement. The story of this family was a natural for Tuskegee, and its publication opened the door for a long and profitable relationship with its *Service* magazine.

To test the hotel's policy, Young and Roberts had breakfast in the coffee shop, where they were served without difficulty. The hotel further confirmed its nondiscrimination when members of the press, including the three Negroes, received special invitations from the management to attend a Spanish fiesta given that evening in honor of the president.

Another interesting story for ANP was the discovery at Father Flanagan's Boys Town near Omaha that Eddie Dunn, a seventeen-year-old Negro youth, had been elected mayor. That was the first time a young man of color had ever been elected to the highest position in that integrated community for disadvantaged boys, where blacks composed no more than one-fifth of its population. The young mayor presented gifts to the president, Mrs. Truman, and Margaret—a picture painted by a nine-year-old boy, a piece of handmade pottery, and a miniature cedar chest.

A RACIAL INCIDENT

The situation was a little different at Cheyenne, Wyoming, where Mr. Truman was guest of the governor and was scheduled to make some remarks from the front veranda of the governor's mansion. He was driven from the railway station in an official limousine, as was customary for visiting dignitaries. But no transportation was provided for the press, who had to hoof it from the station. Streets had been blocked off along the way, and traffic had been rerouted. Throngs of people, as usual, lined the street, held at a safe distance by the customary red velvet ropes reinforced by a military cordon representing every branch of the service. Only the White House press corps was permitted to walk down the middle of the street behind the motorcade.

The only woman and the only Negro in the group, I marched along with the white male reporters. (The other two black reporters did not accompany the president on this leg of the trip.) Suddenly one of the military officers stepped out of rank, ordering me to "get back there behind those ropes." I kept walking without a word. He grabbed me by one shoulder and gave me a shove toward the observers. One of the reporters, Texas-born Lacey Reynolds of the Nashville *Tennessean*, came to my rescue.

"Watch out, there!" he said to the officer. "You're messing with the party of the president of the United States. You know Mrs. Dunnigan is with us. She has her badge and she has it on." (All of the presidential party wore large badges the size of the top of a teacup, lined in big, bold letters saying "Trip of the President." Underneath was the name of the reporter and the paper he—or she, in my case—represented.) After this civilian reprimand, the military officer stepped back in rank without a word, and the party moved on without further interference. As far as I was concerned, the incident was closed as the president and his group moved on according to schedule.

Our next off-the-train stop was at Sun Valley, Idaho, where the Trumans were guests of Averell Harriman, then a top executive of a prominent railroad company. A cocktail party was planned at this luxurious resort hotel for members of the presidential party. There was plenty of food and drinks but no companionship for me. My two Negro colleagues did not attend, leaving me with a group of white men. Charlie Ross noticed me standing all alone and invited me to sit at his table. We talked, laughed, ate, drank champagne, and even danced. Finally he asked me how I was getting along. "Fine!" I replied.

"Oh no, you're not!" he emphasized. "You had trouble in Cheyenne. The president heard about it and has personally lauded Lacey for the way he handled the situation. He wants you to know that anytime anybody does anything to you on this trip, you are to report it directly to the president's immediate party."

I was indeed flattered to know that the president had heard about the incident and had shown some personal concern. Now I would feel a greater sense of protection for the remainder of the trip, giving me a feeling of security I had never known before.

After a pleasant stay of about two days in Sun Valley, we moved on to the next scheduled stop. Late one afternoon while the train was sidetracked for a few hours in Tacoma and everything had quieted down for the evening, I made myself comfortable in my compartment by kicking off my shoes and stretching my bare feet up on the seat opposite where I was sitting. I placed a little table (much like those used for food service in sick rooms) across my lap for a typewriter stand and began writing my copy for the day.

Suddenly there was a light tap at the door, which slowly opened at the same time, and in stepped President Truman. I was so shocked at his visit, and also so flabbergasted at my appearance, that I didn't know what to do. I knew that one was supposed to stand anytime the president entered the room, but I couldn't rise with the typewriter across my lap. So there I sat with my naked toes sticking up as I bounced up and down on the seat, making a vain attempt to stand. No words would come except, "Oh, Mr. President! Mr. President!"

Mr. Truman smiled understandingly and asked if I was being treated all right on this trip. When I assured him I was, he said, "That's good. But if you have any further trouble, let me know." Needless to say, it boosted my ego to know the president of the United States would show personal interest in an insignificant newspaperwoman and would take time out to express this concern. This, to me, was a true indication of a great man. The experience also increased my self-confidence in the presence of anyone, no matter how high his position.

CALIFORNIA

As we moved into California, the president was greeted with a spirit of friendliness and goodwill by Republican governor Earl Warren (future chief justice of the United States), who boarded the train in Sacramento and accompanied Mr. Truman throughout the state. At one stop, the president joined a political caucus of delegates to the Democratic National Convention to be held later in Philadelphia along with other top ranking party leaders. The press was barred, but word leaked out that civil rights was one of the hottest issues discussed at the meeting.

James Roosevelt (son of the late president and a future congressman and representative to the United Nations) subsequently introduced me to the two California Negro delegates to the upcoming convention. Few, if any, Negroes had served as delegates to political conventions prior to this time.[7] One of the delegates, the Reverend Clayton Russell, pastor of the In-

Dunnigan with California delegates to the 1948 Democratic National
Convention James Roosevelt, Sylura Barron, and Rev. Clayton Russell in
Los Angeles, where Truman affirmed his stand on civil rights
(Dunnigan Papers, MARBL, Emory University)

dependent Church of Christ in Los Angeles, reportedly asked Mr. Truman
at the closed-door session what he planned to do about the civil rights
program.

The president was quoted as forthrightly reaffirming his stand. "Of
course I am going to stand by it. When I make a statement or a promise, I
always stand by it." He reminded the group that the Democratic platform
of 1944 had a strong civil rights plank that he had assisted in writing.

The other Negro delegate, Sylura Barron, then expressed confidence
that the black voters of her city, San Diego, would support Truman now
that he had made clear his views. Prior to this commitment, many Negroes in California and elsewhere were leaning heavily toward the third
party candidate, Henry Wallace, on the Progressive ticket.

Says Sentinel First Negro Paper At A Truman Visit in 50 Cities

By Alice A. Dunnigan

,Aboard the Presidential Spe cial Somewhere in New Mexico)

LeRoy S. Hart, managing editor of the Los Angeles Sentinel with a reporter, Albert C. Woolfolk, and a photographer, W. L. Blakeley, were on the spot at Fairmont hotel in Los Angeles where President Truman and his party were entertained Monday.

These Sentinel newsmen were taking pictures and interviewing Negro conferees, luncheon guests and White House reporters.

FIRST IN 50-ODD CITIES

By the time the Presidential Special reached California, Dunnigan was disgusted with the scant attention black newspapers along the route had given the president's tour, but she credited the *Los Angeles Sentinel* for its coverage. (June 24, 1948)

Two other Negro politicians attending the meeting, the Reverend M. Fredrick Mitchell, president of the Interdenominational Ministers' Alliance, and attorney Thomas Griffith Jr., president of the local branch of the NAACP, both expressed support for Truman. In addition to these comments, I got an exclusive interview by calling Academy Award winner Hattie McDaniel (from *Gone with the Wind*), one of the few Negroes in motion pictures in those days who was publicly supporting Truman. These and other comments provided good news copy for my papers.

Until we reached Los Angeles, I had seen no evidence of Negro newspapermen covering the president's visit to the many cities. In L.A., we were happy to find LeRoy Hart, managing editor of the *Los Angeles Sentinel*, along with reporter Albert C. Woolfolk and photographer W. L. Blakey attending the festivities at the hotel. I had been critical of the Negro press along our route for its failure to give firsthand coverage to the president's stops, and I included this criticism rather keenly in the final "wrap-up" of the trip.

HEADING HOME THROUGH THE HEARTLAND

Headed homeward, we encountered many more Negro politicians and newsmen among the hundreds of citizens who greeted the president as we passed through his home state of Missouri as well as Kansas, Illinois, and Indiana. At Union Station in Kansas City, Missouri, the president paused to shake hands with Lucile H. Bluford, managing editor of the Kansas City *Call* newspaper, while the paper's photographer, Alaska Howell, was among the photographers who flocked to the rear of the platform of the sixteen-coach Special to get shots of the president.

Dr. Sherman R. Scruggs, president of Lincoln University,[8] welcomed Mr. Truman to Jefferson City, Missouri, while William L. Watkins Jr., the school's photographer, was on hand to take pictures. Among the politicians who formed the reception committee at Indianapolis was Forrest W. Littlejohn, then the Democratic nominee for the state legislature from Marion County, Indiana.

This scattering of black politicians and reporters would not mean much today. Actually any reference to their presence would now be criticized as "token integration." But in those days, it was considered a foot in the door, which would hopefully mean a wider open door for future generations.

Two representatives of the *Indianapolis Recorder* newspaper[9] met us at the station in that city and requested that the president pose for a picture shaking hands with me. It was a gesture that had far-reaching political benefits since it was published in a number of Negro periodicals after being carried on the front page of the *Recorder* with the caption "President

Although no members of the ANP contributed to Dunnigan's trip, their front pages carried many of her articles as well as this photo by *Indianapolis Recorder* photographer Thom Ervin from the Presidential Special stop in Indiana's capital. (June 26, 1948)

Truman congratulating ANP newswoman, Alice Dunnigan, for her contribution to the success of his 9,000 mile tour." That was the last major stop before returning to Washington after more than two weeks of continuous travel.

Although I made the trip for less than the originally estimated thousand dollars, it was well worth several thousand to me because I made some invaluable contacts. The friends I cultivated represented the top journalists of this country and some foreign nations. Among them were Doris Fleeson, who has been described as one of the most successful women journalists in American newspaper history. We remained friends until her death in 1970. Others were Merriman Smith, the dean of the White House press corps, and Edward Folliard, who in 1970 was awarded a Medal of Freedom by President Richard Nixon for having "contributed greatly to the enlightenment of three generations of readers." Lacey Reynolds, who had come to my rescue in Cheyenne, Wyoming, became a friend, as did Bryson Rash, editorial director for Washington, D.C., television station WRC; W. B. Ragsdale, *U.S. News and World Report*; Robert Riggs, then with the Louisville *Courier-Journal*; and several other top reporters.

There was no brass band or confetti parade to welcome us back to Washington, D.C., after the Truman trip. For me, there was not even a smiling face or cordial handshake of a friend. But I needed no more than the satisfaction of having enjoyed an unforgettable experience, by far one of the highlights of my journalism career.[10]

16

THE CIVIL RIGHTS FIGHTS OF THE FORTIES

After the marathon tour on the Presidential Special, I set my sights on covering the political conventions. There would be three that year, all of them in Philadelphia, including the newly formed Progressive Party's.

Once again my news agency denied my request, and once again I demonstrated a determination to go, even at my own expense if necessary. The train fare from Washington was minimal, and a friend in Philadelphia invited me to be her houseguest at no cost. So on July 12, 1948, I took off for the City of Brotherly Love to attend the Democratic National Convention. Without the support of ANP, I was unable to secure press credentials but finally finagled a messenger's badge, which permitted me to move around freely on the convention floor but deprived me of many special privileges usually accorded the press, such as access to pressroom facilities and press conferences, press releases, copies of speeches, resolutions, committee reports, and other documents. I was able to obtain much of this material, however, through friends in the press corps.

THE DEMOCRATIC PARTY

It was at this convention that Hubert Humphrey (mayor of Minneapolis, who was elected that same year to the U.S. Senate) made his famous civil rights address, climaxing an all-night session of the Platform Committee, which had spent hours debating the strong civil rights plank that was finally adopted, as President Truman had promised. Heard around the world, the speech endeared him to so many Americans but at the same time split the Democratic Party wide open. When he concluded, the southern delegations from Alabama, Mississippi, and South Carolina marched out of the convention hall in a body and ultimately out of the Democratic Party. They established the States' Rights Party and selected South Carolina governor Strom Thurmond as their standard bearer.[1]

The Democratic Party was now split three ways. The extreme liberal wing (which disavowed the Democrats when President Roosevelt dropped Henry Wallace as his vice president and chose Senator Harry S. Truman as his running mate in 1944) left the regular party and formed a new Progressive Party. This party held its first convention in 1948, nominating the disgruntled Henry Wallace as its presidential candidate. Thus, 1948 became the first year in the memory of most living politicians that American voters had the choice of four presidential candidates—Truman, Wallace, Thurmond, and Tom Dewey.

Most people seemed to feel that Harry Truman, the regular Democratic candidate, didn't have a ghost of a chance to win against two strong, splintered, Democratic aggregations (liberal and conservative) and his Republican foe. A large number of Negro voters became strong supporters of Wallace because of his reputation as a great liberal who had proven to be a friend of the poor and underprivileged. Truman's open commitment to a strong civil rights plank, however, siphoned off much of that support.[2]

I had an interesting experience with Mr. Wallace while traveling by train through the southland, prior to his announcing his candidacy. This was in the days when dining cars were still segregated. Two tables reserved for Negro passengers were set aside from the rest of the diner by a brownish, woolen curtain much like the old khaki army blankets. I usually referred to this arrangement as having to eat behind the "wool curtain." When I went in for dinner, all of the tables in the white section of the diner were filled. People were lined up between the coaches waiting for vacant seats. The two tables reserved for black passengers were completely vacant.

After taking my seat at one of these vacant tables, I heard a familiar voice on the other side of the curtain and asked the waiter if that was the voice of the former vice president, Henry Wallace. The waiter looked surprised and answered, "Yes." I gave him my White House press pass, requesting that he show it to Mr. Wallace and ask if I could have an interview with him.

The waiter soon returned with this message: "Stay right where you are. I'll be there in a few minutes." Soon Mr. Wallace appeared from behind the wool curtain and took a seat at the table with me, and we had a nice, long interview. He said he was doing quite a bit of travel in those days and was en route to New Orleans to make a speech. He was thinking of announcing his candidacy for president on the Progressive ticket and was anxious to feel the pulse of the people before making his final decision. Apparently the people's pulses were beating pretty strongly in his favor because he soon announced his decision to run.[3] The incident made a good story for ANP, headlined "Former Vice-President Defies Jim Crow Law to Talk with Negro Reporter."

Fearing that losing the southern vote and a great slice of the minority vote would cost Mr. Truman the election, the Democratic National Committee (DNC) made every effort to woo the Negro vote. Familiar with my work on the Truman train, the committee asked me to serve on the Democratic Speakers Bureau. I agreed and was sent on a two-month tour of Kentucky, where it was believed I would have the greatest influence, visiting most of the towns of any size in the state. Kentucky senator Alben Barkley shared the ticket with Mr. Truman as the vice-presidential candidate.

BOSS DAWSON

When Truman won the presidency,[4] I applied for a political post. While I loved my work as a journalist, despite hard work my income as a reporter had improved very little, my twenty-five-dollar weekly salary having been increased to only forty dollars. My request got nothing but an offer of a post without pay on the Publicity Subcommittee of the Inaugural Committee. Finally I suggested creation of a position in the information office of the DNC, and this started to move forward. I was informed, however, that Chicago congressman William Dawson, vice chairman of the DNC, had requested that no Negroes be employed by the party without his consent. I thought I would have no trouble, as I considered Dawson one of my best friends, but I was wrong. Dawson told me point-blank that he would not endorse me for a national position because he didn't think I was sufficiently well-known.[5]

For a long time, I held that against the senior Negro member of Congress, but I later realized that he did me a favor, that it was a blessing in disguise. Had I taken the job in the DNC information office, I would have cut short my career and missed out on many opportunities. That year turned out to be a banner year for me. I was selected by the *Louisville Defender* as one of the ten most outstanding Kentuckians of 1948, along with Vice President Barkley and eight others. In midsummer, I was one of the few reporters invited to cover a meeting of fifteen of America's most outstanding Negro leaders with Army Secretary Kenneth Royall to discuss the army's segregation policy, a meeting that is believed to have laid the groundwork for President Truman's executive order prohibiting discrimination in the military service.

RACISM IN THE CAPITAL

One of the problems brought to the president as the capital prepared for the inauguration in 1948 was the difficulty that Negroes might have finding lodging since they were barred from downtown hotels. The president was also reminded that unless some provision was made to abolish segregation in eating places, Negroes would have problems finding places to dine as we were also banned from downtown restaurants. Several organizations urged the president to issue an order banning segregation in the District of Columbia so that the thousands of Negro visitors attending the inauguration would be treated with the same courtesies and accommodations that were accorded other American citizens.

The only response we received to that suggestion was assurance that families of both races who occupied large houses in Washington had agreed to open their homes to mixed delegations. We were told that rooms in the large home of one white family had been reserved for the interracial delegation from California.

The president declined to issue an order such as we suggested, but the idea, like a large stone tossed into a sea of calm, generated a huge ripple of discontent that never subsided until integration in Washington came to fruition years later. The New York delegation, however, could be credited for giving the Truman administration a preliminary start in civil rights, when it made reservations at the Roosevelt Hotel for its sixty-man delegation. When the racially mixed delegation arrived, hotel management refused to register the eighteen Negro delegates. The leader of the Tammany delegation, who was also president of the borough of Manhattan, flatly stated, "We all stay or we all go." When he demanded the refund of his certified check, the hotel management held a thirty-minute conference with delegation leaders, after which the hotel agreed to register the entire group.

Close to midnight, when all the delegates were settled in their rooms, a Negro member of the delegation reportedly received a telephone call from William Houston, a prominent black attorney,[6] urging him to prevail upon the Negroes to move from the Roosevelt to the Dunbar (Negro) Hotel to prevent Dixiecrats (the coalition of Republicans and southern Democrats who often joined forces to defeat civil rights legislation) from criticizing the president.

The New York delegates refused to budge, and when the black press put heat on Houston for his alleged "Uncle Tom" intervention, he denied having made the call but acknowledged that he had been requested to do so, presumably by someone high up in the party. Several members of the delegation stood by their colleague's account of the call.

The Truman administration suffered another embarrassment early in 1948 when the Democratic National Committee sponsored its annual Jefferson-Jackson hundred-dollar-a-plate fundraising dinner. My contacts with reporters from daily papers let me know that they always received free press passes to cover these affairs. I complained to the minority advisor at the White House that Negro reporters had never been admitted to these swank affairs. Attempting to assure me that these affairs were not discriminatory and looking for a way to prove his point, he said, "We are offering free tickets to the colored employees of the Democratic National Committee."

Knowing full well that all "colored employees" of the DNC at that time were janitors, messengers, or mail clerks, I shot back, "I'm not talking about menial workers; I'm talking about bona fide reporters for Negro newspapers."

The White House aide said they had no more press tickets, but he would give me a free pass to sit at the employees' table. "This is not a matter of racial segregation," he contended. "It's just a matter of seating together people holding free tickets."

Ordinarily I would have rejected this humiliating arrangement, but in those fighting days, I concluded that sometimes much can be accomplished by making a sacrifice or by entering a situation through the back door just to get inside and obtain an eyewitness view of what was happening.

Word soon got around among Democratic bigwigs that Negroes would be attending this dinner. White southerners protested by staging a boycott in the days when boycotts were practically unheard of. Southerners who had purchased tickets for two tables located directly in front of the head table at a thousand dollars per table deliberately stayed away from the dinner, making the two vacant tables right in front of the president very conspicuous.

Newspapers throughout the country carried pictures of the two vacant tables and reported why southern Democrats were so conspicuously absent. Pictures were also taken of the all-Negro table where I was seated. At least two Negro guests had such fair complexions that the photographer apparently thought this was an integrated table. A copy of this photo was published on the front page of a Jackson, Mississippi, daily on February 24, 1948, with a caption calling Negroes and whites eating together something too strong for southern stomachs and citing it as another reason Democrats in the South were refusing to follow party leaders in Washington.

My accounts of racial prejudice in the nation's capital were published by Negro newspapers throughout the country, bringing the administration in for widespread criticism for not doing anything about it.

The following year, another Negro reporter, Louis Lautier, and I were issued regular press tickets to the Jefferson-Jackson dinner and seated at the regular press table with other Capitol reporters. The year after that, a representative of each of the local Negro newspapers was invited. Finally press tickets were made available to any Negro newspaper that requested them.

COMING TOGETHER

Although the "Fair Deal" administration of President Truman gave great hopes for a brighter future for American minorities, all advances toward civil rights were initiated by pressure from Negroes, either individually or in groups, and kept before the public by the Negro press. One such event was a prayer service on the Capitol steps in 1948 at the beginning of the second session of the Eightieth Congress (later dubbed the "do-nothing" Congress by President Truman) when 131 ministers representing seventeen states and the District of Columbia assembled in Washington to proclaim a "National Prayer Day" for human rights. The delegation was headed by Dr. W. H. Jernagin, president of the Fraternal Council of Negro Churches of America, which was said to represent seven million Christians in eleven denominations.[7] The praying, hymn-singing demonstration was described as the first organized expression of religious leaders aimed at concentrating attention on the need for federal legislation dealing with human rights. The principal speaker was Howard University president Mordecai Johnson, who chided the ministers for their previous lack of political action and urged each of them to "politicalize just as he prays." His speech was aired on the radio immediately following the broadcast of President Truman's State of the Union message.

In June 1948, I covered another mass rally and picket line staged in the nation's capital by a vanguard of seventy-five hundred civil rights supporters led by famed concert singer Paul Robeson. Called the National Nonpartisan Delegation for Passage of Civil Rights Legislation, the delegates split into small groups to visit their representatives on Capitol Hill and later held a mass meeting at the Sylvan Theater at the foot of the Washington Monument. The day ended with picket lines at the White House and the headquarters of the Democratic and Republican national committees. The event was credited with arousing considerable awareness of the need for civil rights legislation.

Another pressure movement took place the following month, when a civil rights conference of representatives from twenty-five national organizations met in Washington to draw up a five-point program for civil rights legislation. Called together by the NAACP, the conferees recommended enactment of legislation for a permanent Fair Employment Practices Committee (FEPC),[8] abolition of the poll tax, punitive measures to suppress lynching and mob violence, a ban on segregation in interstate transportation, and revision of the Displaced Persons Act to permit immigration of classes discriminated against. The conference passed a resolution urging President Truman to issue an executive order banning discrimination and segregation in federal services, including the armed forces, and to provide administration leadership to the civil rights program in Congress. Again, the public support marshaled by the Negro press for these measures probably influenced the president's later decision to issue several civil rights orders.

SITTING IN

The sit-in movement of the 1960s also had precursors during the Truman administration. On one occasion in 1947, I covered an incident at a White Tower hamburger stand on Fourteenth Street NW. A small group of high-school boys from New York on a tour of Washington had stopped for hamburgers. The whites and Puerto Ricans in the group were served, but the two or three Negro boys were denied service. So the entire group, without preplanning, occupied all of the seats around the counter and sat there for the rest of the afternoon, preventing any further customer service.

Toward year-end, a group of thirty white and Negro citizens staged an organized sit-in demonstration at the Greyhound bus terminal in downtown Washington in an effort to break down the long-standing Jim Crow segregation policy in the restaurant. The integrated party occupied all of the tables and refused to move unless the Negroes were served. The restaurant, which usually stayed open all night, closed at midnight, but the prospective customers stayed. Employees emptied quart bottles of ammonia on the tables and sprayed the restaurant with DDT. But the "sit-downers" placed handkerchiefs over their faces to deflect the strong fumes and still refused to leave. Police were then called in to remove them, and the officers informed them that while they were within their rights to occupy the tables as long as the restaurant was open to the public, after it had closed they were technically trespassing. The group left shortly after one o'clock in the morning. It was a preview of scenes that would occur at lunch counters and in restaurants across the country a decade later.

Here in Washington, this movement was expanded to the restaurant at National Airport across the river in Virginia, resulting in the Civil Aeronautics Administration (CAA) issuing an order in late 1948 calling for a complete end to racial segregation at the capital's airport. The order specifically stated, "Henceforth there shall be no discrimination or segregation as to race, color or creed in any of the airport facilities." Prior to this, Negroes had not been admitted to the Terrace Restaurant or the airport coffee shop. They could eat, however, at a small snack bar located in the basement of the administration building. In spite of the CAA ruling, the Terrace Restaurant still refused to serve Negroes on the grounds that integration in eating places was a violation of Virginia laws and the manager doubted the CAA had the authority to trump a state statute. The upshot was a lawsuit filed in U.S. district court by six Negroes against Air Terminal Service, Inc., and a statement from the commonwealth attorney for Arlington County, Virginia, that he had no power to enforce Virginia's segregation laws at the airport, where the federal government had exclusive jurisdiction. With that, Jim Crow crashed at National Airport.

In 1960, when the sit-in movement was picking up steam, the Student Nonviolent Coordinating Committee (SNCC) gave me an award for "news writing (pertaining to) Northern Virginia lunch counter integration," the coverage of which had been one of my passions for more than a decade.

17

PROFILES OF INJUSTICE

My first assignment in the criminal-justice arena was the case of Rosa Lee Ingram, a forty-year-old widow and mother of twelve children who was sentenced to death by a Georgia court for the alleged murder of a white farmer named John Ethron Stratford.

The trouble started in November 1947, three months after the death of Mrs. Ingram's husband. According to testimony during the trial, when the widow was informed that her mule and some of her hogs had strayed onto the adjoining property farmed by Stratford, she and her two elder sons set out to retrieve the wandering stock. They encountered the farmer armed with a rifle and apparently intending to kill the trespassing animals.

When Mrs. Ingram protested, Stratford struck her down and began beating her with the butt of his rifle, inflicting bloody wounds about her head and body. Her sons, seventeen-year-old Wallace and fourteen-year-old Sammy, rushed to her rescue. In the struggle, Stratford was struck a fatal blow on the head with a hammer.

Mrs. Ingram and the two boys were arrested and held without bail for three months. On February 3,

1948, an all-white jury found them guilty of first-degree murder after a one-day trial. Less than three weeks later, all three were sentenced to execution in the Reidsville prison.

Those familiar with the case maintained that the court overlooked three important factors: (1) it was said to be common knowledge that the victim was not as much enraged about the trespassing livestock as he was about Mrs. Ingram's rejection of his advances; (2) it was never proven in court which of the three was responsible for the fatal blow, and no matter which one it was, it appeared to be self-defense; and (3) the court apparently gave no consideration to what many saw as an inhuman, coldblooded act on the part of local law officials in hauling Mrs. Ingram and the older boys off to jail, leaving all alone the younger children, ranging in age from seventeen months to eleven years.

The oldest daughter, age eighteen, who was married and the mother of two, was in Florida picking beets. She had to leave her migrant laborer's job to return home and care for the little ones.

NAACP lawyers entered the case and filed a motion for a new trial in March. A couple of weeks later, the judge changed his former death sentence to life imprisonment for the three Ingrams.

The case received wide publicity, and protests were registered from across the nation and around the world. In an effort to do something about it, a group of Negro and white women from Washington and New York, headed by Mary Church Terrell, one of America's outstanding civil rights leaders of the time, formed the National Committee to Free the Ingram Family. In April 1948, I joined several members of this committee on a visit to Georgia to see what, if anything, could be done to free Mrs. Ingram. Racial tension in Georgia was very high, and we received word in advance that such a visit might not be physically safe.

Unable to make the trip herself, and very concerned about our welfare, eighty-six-year-old Mrs. Terrell sent telegrams to President Truman and Attorney General Tom Clark asking that they assure the group federal protection. When she received no reply from either, she reportedly made personal visits to the White House and the Department of Justice requesting that the government take steps to guarantee our safety.

The tension was so high upon our arrival in Atlanta that the white and Negro members of the group agreed to split, with the Negroes registering in an all-black hotel and the whites finding shelter elsewhere. The following afternoon, we drove to Americus to visit the Ingram children and had a firsthand view of the deplorable conditions in which they were living. The NAACP had solicited funds and was building a new cottage for them.

That night, we sneaked out of Americus and headed for Macon, where we boarded a train for Augusta, arriving around midnight. By prearrangement, the Negro members of the delegation went to the home of a prominent physician whose name we were asked to withhold for safety reasons. We were greeted in whispering tones and ushered into the living room. This colorful room, which under ordinary circumstances would have provided a bright, cheerful, and pleasant atmosphere, was now enshrouded in semidarkness, silence, and fear as a result of a telephone call telling our host of rumors that he was housing an interracial delegation from the North and that city officials were "up in arms." It was also rumored that the Ku Klux Klan was planning to burn a cross in his yard and might even attempt to torch his house. The apprehension, which gripped both the host and his guests, grew even worse when someone reported seeing a white man lurking outside the house in the dark.

Literally a stormy night, the rain came down in torrents with flashes of lightening and cracks of thunder. The dreadful weather, coupled with the feelings of terror, gave the delegation an excuse for not leaving the house that night, despite previous arrangements for only two people to remain there, two to sleep with a family across the street, and two others at another location. Nobody budged from the house that night. We all slept on the floor, fearing that bullets might be fired through the windows.

The next morning when our host called his pastor to inquire how tense the situation was, he was told that since it was learned that all of his guests were Negroes, the resentment had subsided.

A call made to the prison to ask for an appointment to see Mrs. Ingram was received with courtesy, and a time was arranged for the visit. By the time our delegation was ready to depart, the white members of the group had rejoined us. Expecting more hostility to this move, we boarded our cars for the long drive to Reidsville with renewed trepidation, but nothing unpleasant happened along the way.

At Reidsville, we were received cordially by the prison guards, who made no attempt to overhear our hour-long conversation with Mrs. Ingram.

The three-car caravan rolled down a graveled driveway across a spacious, well-kept lawn fronting the white-frame buildings that formed the Richmond County Almshouse. When the cars stopped, the visitors were met by a dignified lady of medium height and weight, wearing a crisply starched, pink print cotton dress that accentuated her soft brown complexion and glossy black hair, becomingly arranged in a pompadour across the front with the back hanging in loose curls around the lobe of the ear and the nape of the neck. When she stepped forward with hand extended in welcome as they alighted from the automobiles, the group's spokesman introduced the visitors as a delegation from the National Committee to Free the Ingram Family and expressed their desire to see Mrs. Ingram.

Almost everyone gasped in amazement when the gracious lady calmly replied, "I'm Mrs. Ingram."

Although incarcerated, Mrs. Ingram was not kept behind bars but was at liberty to move from building to building on this county farm, where she was one of eighteen trusted inmates (fourteen women and four men) who'd been brought to the almshouse to care for the poor whites who were housed there.

With the aplomb of a perfect hostess, Mrs. Ingram moved the group toward a white plank bench beneath a spreading fig tree and invited them to sit while warning that the bench might be a little dirty. Sitting on the bench, the women left space in the middle for Mrs. Ingram, addressing her in turn about the history and purpose of the committee. After describing the efforts they were undertaking at the federal, state, and local levels as well as at the United Nations, they asked if there was anything they could do for her now. She replied that all she wanted was her freedom "so I can go home to my little children."

Because it was an extremely chilly day and Mrs. Ingram wore only a short-sleeve dress, one of the ladies asked if she wasn't cold. When she replied that she was but had no coat, one of the ladies wearing both a suit and a topcoat took off the latter and placed it around Mrs. Ingram's shoulders. "The prison supplies us with dresses, such as this one," the convict explained, "but they do not furnish a coat," although she had requested one because her duties required her to move between buildings in all kinds of weather.

Other than a sweater from her daughter that she'd been allowed to keep, the prison did not permit her to accept clothing from the outside, and when someone sent her some other garments, she had to return them. When she added that she was allowed to buy additional food when she had the money and that any medicine she might need also had to be purchased with her own money, the women immediately filled her hands with dollar bills.

Some of the visitors wiped tears from their faces as Mrs. Ingram, calm and composed, described her daily life. When they left, the lipstick marks on her cheek from their kisses left it looking like "a patchwork quilt."[1]

Back in Atlanta the next day, I was assigned to call the office of Governor Herman Talmadge to ask for an appointment for the group. His secretary graciously informed me that he would see us if we arrived before a scheduled luncheon, but we were late and he'd already left. His staff, however, was extremely courteous. In fact, the entire atmosphere among Georgia officials had changed since our arrival. It now seemed as if a peaceful balm had been poured over troubled waters. We later had confirmed reports that the prison guards had been advised by the warden to treat us with courtesy based on orders from the Georgia Prison Board, acting under instruction from the governor, who had received the word from the attorney general, carrying out the wishes of President Truman. We credited the efforts of Mrs. Terrell for all this.

Spurred on by letters, telegrams, and offers of assistance from around the nation, the National Committee to Free the Ingram Family launched a petition campaign in which thirty thousand signatures were presented to the White House by Mrs. Terrell, who said the committee hoped that "the plea of women throughout America would so arouse the Chief Executive that he would denounce the inhumanity which so flagrantly violated the United Nations Declaration on Human Rights to which the United States had pledged its support."

Several years later when President Truman, just prior to leaving office in 1952, announced at a press conference the names of several prisoners he had ordered be released, I reminded him of the Ingram case and asked if he had given any consideration to clemency for this unfortunate woman. Mr. Truman replied that there was nothing he could do in this case, and some time later the pardon attorney in the Justice Department sent me a note explaining that because Mrs. Ingram was convicted in a state court of an offense against the laws of Georgia, the president was not authorized to grant clemency as he would be had the offense been against the laws of the United States. Truman at least had asked the Justice Department to look into it.

After more years of efforts on her behalf, including a local Georgia effort headed by Georgia businessman Clayton R. Yates and supported by Senator (former governor) Herman Talmadge, Mrs. Ingram and her sons were released on parole in August 1959.

THE CASE OF WILLIE MCGEE

My next involvement in the fight against racial injustice was the case of Willie McGee, who had been sentenced to death in the electric chair in Laurel, Mississippi, for the alleged rape of a white woman.

McGee, a truck driver and father of four children, was arrested in November 1945, accused of assaulting Willette Hawkins as she lay in bed in her home with a sick child asleep at her side while her husband and other children slept in an adjoining room, unawakened during the attack.

The victim said she made no outcry because she did not wish to awaken her family. The rape took place in the dark, she reported, and she could only identify her alleged attacker as having "kinky hair" and wearing a T-shirt.

The McGee case dragged through the courts for about six years, coming before the Mississippi Supreme Court four times, according to my records, and the U.S. Supreme Court three times. I was assigned to cover the case after it reached the high court in Washington, which refused to review the decision of the highest state court each time it appeared on the docket.

Telegrams and letters had poured into the offices of federal and state officials on McGee's behalf. The U.S. Department of State even got into the act when it found that newspapers in many foreign countries were publishing stories concerning U.S. injustice against Negroes in the South and that Communists were using this case to enhance their propaganda. The State Department sent "investigators" to the scene of the crime and released counterstories to the U.S. Information Service offices in London and other world capitals in an attempt to refute Communist charges. Still, protests of the verdict in the McGee case continued to pour into the governor's office from all over the world.

During the last days of Willie McGee's life, a large delegation visited U.S. government officials, pleading for clemency for the accused man. They visited their senators, congressmen, State Department officials, the Justice Department, D.C. commissioners, and Supreme Court justices and even attempted to get an appointment at the White House—with a presidential aide if not the president himself. Since McGee was a veteran, about three hundred fellow veterans of World War II staged a demonstration at the Lincoln Memorial one Sunday afternoon. More than fifty of these ex-GIS, white and black, chained themselves to the pillars in front of Lincoln's huge statue. No one could recall another demonstration of this kind in Washington, D.C. Approximately 250 other persons kept up a protest march in front of the memorial for hours, chanting "Lincoln freed the slaves—Truman, free McGee."

A picket line in front of the White House held vigil throughout that Sunday and the following day until zero hour on that blue Monday, when McGee was scheduled to die at midnight.

At the eleventh hour, a last-minute appeal was made to Supreme Court justice Hugo Black for a stay of the execution, but this plea was denied. Chief Justice Fred Vinson later turned down a similar plea presented by former New York congressman Vito Marcantonio[2] and other attorneys in the case, including another fighter for civil and human rights, Bella Abzug, who was elected to Congress nearly twenty years later (1970).

As a last resort, the attorneys called one of President Truman's top aides asking that he request the president intervene in the case. The answer came back that the president would not intercede and there was no point in discussing the case any further.

Word reached us in Washington that eight hundred telegrams and tens of thousands of messages had been received by the Mississippi governor, Fielding Wright, on the day prior to the execution. At the same time, reporters, hearing that a mob had formed around the Mississippi courthouse to demand that the prisoner be put to death as scheduled, were on alert to be ready for anything in the event the execution was postponed.

In the end, all of the efforts on his behalf having failed, Willie McGee died in the electric chair within five minutes of Mississippi's state executioner throwing the switch at 12:05 a.m., May 8, 1951.

MARTINSVILLE SEVEN

Another criminal case in which I became deeply involved as a reporter is known as the Martinsville Seven case, in which seven young black men were tried, convicted, and sentenced to die in the electric chair for the alleged rape of Ruby Floyd, a thirty-two-year-old white woman. The Capital Press Club became so interested in digging out the facts of the case that it sent a committee of three members to the scene, including Sherman Briscoe, Department of Agriculture; Oscar Haynes, *Afro-American* newspapers; and me. We spent several days in Martinsville interviewing family members of the accused men; city leaders; defense attorney Martin A. Martin of Richmond, Virginia; and other citizens. Sentiment was strong that the men were innocent.

The facts as we gathered them revealed that on the evening of January 8, 1949, while walking down the railroad track, the victim (described as a former mental patient who now made her living selling magazines and secondhand clothes in the Negro community) met this group of black men. Apparently stopping for conversation, she allegedly told them how nice looking they were and hinted that she needed five dollars. It was then that the action supposedly began.

According to her testimony, the attacks continued in spite of her struggles and resistance until she finally managed to get away and go to the home of a Negro woman. Together they walked to a nearby store and called the police and an ambulance. Mrs. Floyd was said to have been admitted to the hospital and released forty-five minutes later.

It was reported that police then swarmed over East Martinsville, arresting every black male over fourteen who had mud on his shoes. Later it was announced that confessions had been secured from seven men who were being held on the charge.

The men were tried during the latter part of April and early May. Testimony indicated that Joe Henry Hampton, age nineteen, had been drinking wine on that night but couldn't remember attacking any woman, no matter what was in the confession he was said to have signed.

Frank Hairston Jr., nineteen, testified that the woman offered no resistance because she understood that she was to receive some money for her act. Booker T. Miller, nineteen, denied he had any relationship with her. The woman asked him not to, he said, and he didn't touch her.

Howard Lee Hairston, nineteen, claimed that he was physically unable to have relations with her. John C. Taylor, twenty, claimed to have been afraid to have relations with a white woman. James Luther Hairston, twenty, said the accuser offered no resistance, nor did she make any complaint.

The only married man in the group was thirty-seven-year-old Francis DeSales Grayson, the father of five children. He denied attacking the woman and claimed a confession had been wrung from him by police.

In spite of this testimony, all seven men were found guilty and sentenced to death in the electric chair. Four were to be executed on July 15 and the other three on July 22, 1949.

After the verdicts, the NAACP and the Civil Rights Congress stepped into the case to appeal the death sentences.[3] The state supreme court upheld the decision of the lower court. Shortly thereafter, the CRC dropped out of the defense, and the case was handled by NAACP legal staff headed by Martin A. Martin.

After two years and several stays of execution to allow appeals in the case, all legal recourse had failed. At this time, a group of humanitarians gathered in Washington for a mass protest. With them was Josephine Grayson, wife of one of the doomed men, with their five children, ranging in age from four to nine. The group trudged through the streets of the capital in snow and subfreezing weather trying in vain to help these men. Mrs. Grayson tried to see the president but was told he was out of town. She then tried to see Vice President Alben W. Barkley but was told by Secret Service officers that he could not be disturbed. Neither marches nor prayer meetings did any good. The governor of Virginia could not be moved into an act of clemency.

I stayed on the case from beginning to end, reporting on every action and every step, including a series of human-interest features describing the environment where these men lived, the heartbreak of their families, and their hopes and prayers for justice. The deep-seated prejudice against Negroes in the South could not be shaken by public opinion aroused by the press, by nationwide pleas from the general public, or by sincere persuasion from fair-minded people that the courts of law make some effort to see that simple justice was fairly administered. America suffered for it overseas, as NAACP executive secretary Walter White pointed out later in a message to Virginia governor John Battle: "This execution was exploited throughout the Orient and Africa as another demonstration of American color prejudice."

LEGAL LYNCHING

President Truman had received widespread publicity for his pledge to see that all citizens received civil rights protection guaranteed by the Constitution. He had taken one of his first steps in that direction back in December 1946, when he appointed a committee to investigate and report on the status of civil rights in America. In its report to the president in October 1947, the fifteen-member committee—which included only two Negroes, attorney Sadie T. Alexander of Philadelphia and Dr. Channing Tobias of New York—listed ten important recommendations on how to "Secure These Rights." In his State of the Union message the following February, President Truman urged Congress to enact these recommendations into law. One of them dealt with the need for federal protection against lynching.

An antilynching law would not only make it a federal crime when a person was lynched at the hands of a mob but would also have an adverse effect on "legal lynching," that is, a court-imposed death sentence apparently based more upon the defendant's race than his guilt or the seriousness of the crime. Truman, the first U.S. president to take such a stand, proposed legislation that would give the federal government the power to intervene where justice was denied because of race, creed, or color:[4]

> The federal government has a clear duty to see that constitutional guarantees of individual liberties and of equal protection under the laws are not denied or abridged anywhere in our nation . . . [this] can be fulfilled only if the Congress enacts modern comprehensive civil rights laws, adequate to meet the needs of the day.[5]

The proposal for a strong antilynching law was only one of ten such requests outlined by the president. The other nine included legislation to strengthen existing civil rights statutes, the establishment of a permanent civil rights commission, the prohibition of discrimination in interstate transportation, home rule for the District of Columbia, statehood for Hawaii and Alaska, the equalization of opportunities for residents of the United States to become naturalized citizens, and a settlement of evacuation claims of Japanese Americans.[6] Not only were many members of Congress not of a mind to agree with these proposals but some made the debate a painful experience for participants as well as reporters.

18

THE PRESIDENT PROPOSES;
THE CONGRESS DEBATES

From the Capitol Press Gallery, I listened enthusiastically to President Truman's strong plea for civil rights legislation and followed the Congress through its entire eightieth session as it failed to adopt any of these proposals, leaving it to the executive branch to take the lead. In addition to creating a civil rights committee to study the problem of segregation, President Truman in July 1948 issued an executive order abolishing segregation in military establishments, and he later appointed a seven-man advisory committee known as the President's Committee on Equality of Treatment in the Armed Forces to see that his desegregation order was carried out. The two Negro members of this committee were Lester Granger, executive secretary of the National Urban League, and John H. Sengstacke, publisher of the *Chicago Defender*.

In another executive order issued in July 1948, the president established a federal fair employment board charged with responsibility for overseeing the end of racial and religious discrimination in all federal agencies. Industrial Bank of Washington president Jesse Mitchell and Eugene Kinckle Jones, then an executive of the Urban League, were the two Negro members of this seven-man board.[1]

The failure of the Eightieth Congress to take action on any of President Truman's proposals brought him right back to the legislature's next session with the same agenda. Again, I was in the press gallery when he said:

> The Civil Rights proposals I made the Eightieth Congress, I now repeat to the Eighty-first Congress. . . . They should be enacted in order that the federal government may assume the leadership and discharge the obligations clearly placed upon it by the Constitution. I stand squarely behind those principles.[2]

During this session of Congress, black reporters often found themselves swallowing insults and humiliating racial remarks—sometimes even witnessing fist fights—and sitting through filibusters that often lasted for days as bills based on the president's proposals were debated on the floors of the Senate and the House or in committees. I recall one filibuster in March 1949 that lasted eighteen days while senators were debating a motion to change Senate Rule No. 22 to allow a simple majority vote to invoke cloture, a term meaning the right to shut off debate on any issue before the body. The rule as it originally stood required two-thirds of the entire Senate to enforce cloture. After all the talk, the motion was defeated anyway by the Dixiecrats.

As for fisticuffs, I recall an incident in midsummer of 1949 during a congressional debate on an administration bill calling for the construction of federal housing for low-income families. Tempers flared between the "gentlemen" from the North and those from the Southland to such a boiling point that Congressman E. E. Cox, a sixty-nine-year-old Democrat from Georgia actually struck Adolph J. Sabath, an eighty-three-year-old Illinois Democrat, sending the eyeglasses flying from the face of the white-haired dean of the House of Representatives. The stocky, aged gentleman from Chicago came back with a hard left and right to the jaw of the lanky Georgian, leaving him holding the side of his painful face.

In 1950, I was covering a hearing of the House Committee on Lobbying Activities, which had subpoenaed William L. Patterson, executive secretary of the Civil Rights Congress, to answer questions on the CRC's programs and sources of funds. Congressman Henderson Lanham (D-Ga.), acting chairman at the hearing, questioned Patterson as to whether

POLL TAX MEASURE FACES TRADITIONAL SENATE IRE

Booker Washington Called "Greatest Nigger" By Southern Congressman

The Black Dispatch

NATIONAL EDITION

VOLUME 34—NUMBER 32.   OKLAHOMA CITY, OKLAHOMA, AUGUST 6, 1949   PRICE 5 CENTS

POLL TAX BILL SKIDS BY IN HOUSE BUT FATE LIES IN COLD SENATE

Stubborn Dixiecrats Force Seven Long Roll Calls in Effort to Defeat Measure

35 REPUBLICANS TO VOTE FOR CLOTURE

(By Alice A. Dunnigan)

WASHINGTON — (ANP) — Having survived two days of bitter battling, the anti-poll tax measure finally passed the House of Representatives by a vote of 273 to 116.

The bill which is the first of the President's civil rights measures to be acted on in this session of Congress, has now been sent to the Senate where on-▶

"BOOKER T. WASHINGTON WAS GREATEST NIGGER OF THEM ALL," SAYS SOUTHERN CONGRESSMAN

Poll Tax Fight Brings Assault Upon NAACP And American Council on Human Rights

DR. CLARK FOREMAN CALLED AN "INGLORIOUS PINK" MISS

WASHINGTON — (ANP) — The American Council on Human Rights and the NAACP were among the national organizations attacked by southern representatives on the house floor last Tuesday.

Dunnigan had the two top stories in Oklahoma City's *Black Dispatch* (August 6, 1949), when debate on a bill to abolish the poll tax left no illusions about racial progress in the Eighty-First Congress.

he was a member of the Communist Party or whether his organization was a Communist front. An argument seesawed back and forth until Patterson proclaimed, "If you claim our organization is undemocratic, then you contend that the defense of the Negroes' rights in this country is undemocratic."

Patterson proceeded to mention the "legalized lynching" that was taking place all over America and the role CRC had played in defending defenseless people, particularly in the southern states. When he mentioned Georgia as one of the lynch states, Lanham called him a liar.

"Blacks have no rights in Georgia that a white man is bound to respect," Patterson countered.

The Georgia congressman again called him a liar.

Patterson snapped back, "If you contend that Georgia is not a state noted for its lynching—then you're a liar."

At this point, the infuriated southerner rushed from his chair on the dais, mumbling, "You black son-of-a-bitch!" and plunged toward Patterson, obviously intending to attack him physically.

I was seated at the press table directly behind Patterson. When I saw

Civil Rights Dead In This Congress

By ALICE A. DUNNIGAN

WASHINGTON (ANP) — Vice President Alben W. Barkley stated' last week that he saw no possibility of accomplishing any part of the civil rights program in this session and probably not in this Congress. In an interview with reporters,

The chances for passage of any civil rights legislation remained at zero through the Eighty-Second Congress, as Dunnigan reported in the *Philadelphia Tribune*, September 1, 1951.

this big man, face red with anger, right hand in pocket, making a leap toward the witness, I thought there might be a shooting, so I jumped up quickly, knocking over my chair with a loud crash that frightened other spectators. Patterson sat quietly, unperturbed while Capitol police quickly subdued the aggressor.

Later I asked the witness how he could have remained so calm in the face of apparent danger. He answered with a smile, "Had the Congressman attempted to strike me, I intended to crown him with that pitcher of water sitting on the table."

Another historic conflict—this one in 1955—was not witnessed by the press because it reportedly occurred in an executive session of the House Committee on Education and Labor after New York congressman Adam Clayton Powell Jr. strongly denounced opposition to his amendment to deny federal funds to schools maintaining segregation and in so doing provoked a physical attack upon himself by Representative Cleveland Bailey, Democrat of West Virginia. According to reports leaked to reporters, Bailey charged Powell with seeking to destroy federal school aid legislation by insisting on an antisegregation amendment. When Powell replied in rather strong (perhaps unprintable) language, Bailey reportedly jumped up and swung at the tall New York legislator, landing a blow or two before other congressmen could separate them. Accounts from other committee members reported that chairs were overturned in the melee and that Powell was partially knocked off balance before the other members could assist him. The chairman then gaveled the meeting to order, and business continued as usual after members were warned to keep their passions in check.

Another incident related to a Powell bill—this one to establish a Fair Employment Practices Commission—is illustrative of the racial slurs black reporters encountered from southern lawmakers on Capitol Hill. One of the opponents of the measure, Congressman James Patrick ("Pat") Sutton (D-Tenn.), displayed before the crowded congressional chamber an enlarged stereotypical photograph of a little black boy with snaggle-teeth and short-clipped hair, grinning over a huge, half-eaten slice of watermelon.

"This," said Sutton, "is an example of Negroes in my home state of Tennessee. These colored people are perfectly happy and contented. They are satisfied with conditions in Tennessee and they don't want no FEPC law. Show me a person who is happier than this boy, and I will give you a suit of clothes."

As insulting as this was to any black person present, it was sanctioned and accepted, even considered comical, by the highest political body in the land.

At another hearing before the House Committee on Un-American Activities, where a number of Hollywood writers, producers, and actors were being questioned about their loyalty, Eric Johnston, then president of the Motion Picture Association of America, was asked about the censorship of some of his films by local boards. Johnston replied that his pictures had occasionally been rejected by local boards for silly reasons, such as the one the Memphis board refused to show because it had a black boy playing with white children as an equal.

To this, Congressman Richard B. Vail (R.-Ill.) remarked in a wisecracking tone, "He wasn't in the woodpile, was he?" (This was an unsubtle reference to the old slur about "a nigger in the woodpile.") The committee seemed so stunned at this remark that nobody inquired any further about the arbitrary and un-American action of the board in Memphis.

Another unpleasant scene took place during a congressional hearing before a House District of Columbia subcommittee on a bill introduced by Representative James C. Davis of Georgia[3] designed to resegregate the district's fire department. Davis set the stage for action with an introductory statement on the circumstances surrounding the desegregation of the fire department during the previous summer.

First of all, he contended that the integration order was invalid since it was issued after Congress had adjourned. Next he claimed that Washington firemen disapproved of integration because they had to spend nights

Racial Insults Ring Out In House Debate

By ALICE A. DUNNIGAN

Neither aspirins, cokes, nor cig- arettes would keep down the blood pressure of this reporter as she sat in the press gallery of the House of Representatives Monday and heard insults imposed upon

brothers to "search your hearts, search your souls" before you vote on this legislation which is inspired by the Communists.

Small of stature, as well as of mind, this little Georgian raised himself to tip-toe, beat on the

South in spite of the fact that he was beaten up by white people.

John Bell Williams, Representa- tive of Mississippi, took the floor at this point and injected what he has previously stated in a com- mittee hearing, that King Cole had sense enough not to allow him-

Dunnigan used her column in the *Chicago Daily Defender* (July 19, 1956) to describe the racial ranting that made Congress a difficult beat for a black reporter in the mid-1950s.

in the firehouse. White firemen objected to sleeping on the same cots that "niggers" have used, he explained, adding, "White people don't mind working with niggers, but they don't want to socialize with them."

Taking their cue from the committee chairman, the segregationist witnesses, including the fire chief, constantly referred to the colored firemen as "niggers." Supporters in the hostile audience yelled and applauded at any scurrilous remark made about black people. At the same time, they heckled and agitated the black reporters present into action.

One newswoman was so annoyed, she left the hearing room for Congressman Powell's office, where she reported the whole episode. Powell immediately sent a wire to the district commissioners demanding an investigation of the fire chief for his "flagrant and anti-Negro attitude" before the subcommittee. The commissioners were told that the chief repeatedly used the word "nigger" even after he had been corrected by Representative Arthur Klein of New York.

I had been around the Capitol so long and heard these epithets so often that I had become somewhat hardened. However, I had not heard the word used so profusely since the days of Rankin and Bilbo.[4] I clenched my fist, gritted my teeth, wrestled with my blood pressure, and stuck it out until the hearing ended. Then I carried a complaint to William L. Dawson of Chicago, the senior Negro congressman. In his usual quiet, calm manner, he showed little emotion but his expression at least showed some concern. Because he was an expert politician, his take on the incident was from a political perspective.

"This was only a political move on the part of Congressman Davis and

John Bell Williams [of Mississippi]," he said. "They are seeking headlines for their papers back home. They know this piece of legislation will get nowhere. It will never get out of the full committee. So don't worry. Let them rant and rave and have their field day. Nothing will come of it."

While little could be done about racist slurs on the floor, around the halls of Congress and elsewhere I found that even southern lawmakers treated me with respect as an individual. At social gatherings at the Capitol, it was usually people like North Carolina's Senator Sam Ervin who would make a point to join me for a brief chat. Even those with whom I almost always disagreed properly recognized my work as being accurate and fair. This was all I expected.

JIM CROW AT WORK ABROAD

At a summer party in 1948, a group of young men from the Panama Canal Zone gave me a tip about a system of discrimination against colored workers in the U.S.-controlled zone that had prevailed for almost a half-century. The young men were members of an organization calling itself "The National Committee to End Jim Crow 'Silver-Gold' System in the Panama Canal."

The name derived from the original practice of paying the wages of colored workers on the canal—Negroes, West Indians, and Panamanians—in silver while paying the white workers in gold coins. Although this method of payment, in effect when the United States took over construction of the canal from the French in 1904, had since been abolished, the reference to the colored as silver workers and the whites as gold workers continued to exist. Silver workers were still receiving only a fraction of the wages paid gold workers, although the cost of living was the same for both groups, according to the committee. The silver workers, out of necessity, lived in primitive barracks and were forced to accept inadequate educational and recreational facilities, while the government was said to have maintained excellent facilities for the gold workers.

The newly formed organization, aimed at equalizing the pay of persons engaged in the same type of work, petitioned President Truman to issue an executive order outlawing the segregated treatment of twenty million colored workers who were employees of the United States. The petition pointed out that "although the system grew out of the original method of paying wages, it had, through the years, degenerated into a complete pattern of discrimination against colored workers and continued to operate as if it were fashioned by the most violent southern racists."

Reporting on this group's plea for justice for colored workers on the Panama Canal, I included a letter written to President Truman on August 30, 1948, by former secretary of the interior Harold Ickes urging him to abolish the silver-gold system. Mr. Ickes told the president, "You need no act of Congress. You have the power to put an end to a situation in which the United States Government, in a department directly under your control, sponsors an economic-social pattern of race discrimination which, were he still alive, would undoubtedly win the approval of Hitler. Both the responsibility and the opportunity are yours. The occasion calls for no words, but action."

The former interior secretary further suggested that while doing away with race discrimination in the Panama Canal Zone, the president might well sign another order instructing the navy to stop treating the natives of Guam and American Samoa as if they had no civil rights. "It is not a question of restoring civil rights to these subject peoples," wrote Ickes. "It is one of giving them their rights."

Situations such as these, linked with discriminatory employment policy within the continental United States, highlighted ever more keenly the need for fair employment legislation protecting employment rights of all American citizens, whether residing on the mainland or in U.S. territories. President Truman had previously recommended such a measure to Congress in his State of the Union message.

The idea was not an original one. President Roosevelt had created a committee on fair employment practices by executive order (8802) in 1941 as a result of a protest raised by Negro workers denied jobs in certain categories in the federal government and private industry. The protest was led by A. Philip Randolph of New York, president of the Brotherhood of Sleeping Car Porters, who staged mass meetings in various cities to plan a massive "March on Washington." As a result, Roosevelt called Randolph and a few other leaders to the White House for a conference. The outgrowth of this discussion was an executive order establishing the first FEPC.

At the close of World War II and the end of the Roosevelt New Deal era, Congress cut off appropriations for the wartime FEPC, causing its immediate termination. When President Truman came into office, he asked Congress to pass a law demanding that all Americans be given an equal opportunity for employment. For many years, this was the most controversial issue before the lawmaking body. Scores of bills were introduced. Thousands of pages of debate were recorded in the Congressional Record and millions of words uttered in congressional committees for and against such a measure.

When the debate failed to produce legislation, President Truman issued an executive order in December 1951 establishing a Committee on Government Contract Compliance. This committee was not very effective since it had no enforcement powers, but it operated as best it could until the president left office in January 1953.

After the change in administrations, Truman's contract compliance committee was apparently forgotten and lay dormant for eight months. It was at a presidential news conference during this period that I reminded his successor, President Eisenhower, of the committee's inactivity and asked if he had any plans to reactivate it.

Mr. Eisenhower gave no definite answer, but later, after much needling from the press, he apparently gave the idea some consideration. In August 1953, he issued his own executive order, completely abolishing the Truman Committee and replacing it with a new Government Contract Compliance Committee, which functioned until he left office.

During this entire period when the White House was attempting to provide equal employment opportunity by executive order, the Congress was still debating, year after year, proposed legislation to establish a permanent FEPC with teeth—enforcement power. But Eisenhower did not feel as strongly as his predecessor about accomplishing equal opportunity through the legislative process. He contended that civil rights could not be legislated—"It must come about in the hearts of men."

His theory was made clear in a March 3, 1954, press conference when I reminded him that his secretary of labor, James P. Mitchell, had sent a letter to a congressional committee endorsing a fair employment practices bill with enforcement powers introduced by New York Republican senator Irving Ives. I asked if this letter represented the administration's position on such legislation. The president snapped back that he had made his position clear a dozen times. He felt that there were certain things that were not best handled by punitive or compulsory federal law. Secretary

Mitchell and all other cabinet members were allowed to have views different from his on certain particular details of government activities, the president continued. He didn't consider this a matter of disloyalty to him. Rather he respected Mitchell for expressing his personal views because he didn't want a bunch of "yes men" around him.

One of President Kennedy's first important acts after taking office was to issue another executive order in March 1961 creating a Committee on Equal Employment Opportunity, which existed until Congress finally passed the Civil Rights Act of 1964, abolishing the temporary committee and replacing it with the Equal Employment Opportunity Commission (EEOC).

I'd reported on efforts to guarantee equal employment opportunity for all citizens from conception of the idea in the Roosevelt administration until creation of this government agency under Johnson's Great Society, and as early as 1948, I had been recognized for my contribution to the campaign by the National Council for a Permanent Fair Employment Practices Committee. The group's executive secretary, Elmer Henderson, sent a letter to ANP director Claude Barnett expressing deep appreciation for the "fine cooperation we received from the Associated Negro Press, and especially from your Washington Correspondent, Mrs. Alice Dunnigan, in our efforts to have Congress pass the Fair Employment Practices Bill." It took a decade and a half, but Congress eventually adopted the legislation.[5]

19

ALMOST PUSHING
THE PANIC BUTTON

Inadequate revenue was the perennial plight of most Negro publications. Since circulation was limited almost exclusively to the black community, advertising sales were very low. The big national companies and chain stores refused to buy space in these periodicals, which had to depend chiefly on subscriptions and operate on a shoestring.

Not able to place reporters on the scene in the nation's capital or other major cities, local editors depended on news supplied by ANP, which they bought for a minimum fee. Very often, they were not able to meet these subscription payments on time, and the news service, having no outlet for the sale of advertising space, had to limp along on whatever it could collect from other subscribers. Ultimately ANP seemed to be supplying copy to newspapers more as a crusading cause than as a high-powered, profit-making business.

Despite the thousands of words and countless exclusives I filed, working day and night seven days a week, often paying my own expenses to get these stories, the news service insisted on holding my wage to a bare minimum. Fifty dollars per week was the highest salary I ever earned from ANP. Thus it was a big surprise when Mr. Barnett once rewarded me for an extra-good job with a bonus check and a note reading, "You know our limitations as well as we do, but we really want you to prosper and be happy, which we will promote to the best of our ability." It rankled, however, that the company defended its position to the government's wage-hour office by claiming that I was employed part time and paid on that basis.

I'm not sure how editors of all Negro newspapers operated during those years, but I know that ANP expected reporters to "pick up" extra money from news makers—publicity seekers—just as waitresses paid the lowest possible basic wage were expected to make up the difference in tips. My agency, for instance, stressed the writing of profiles based on personal interviews of individuals rather than general political news. "Write more stories about people and fewer about issues," ANP advised. It was even suggested that a reporter representing a national news outlet should have no compunctions about proposing to prominent people that, for an under-the-table handout, she could get their picture published in newspapers all around the country, provided they supplied the photograph and paid for the mats and postage. In other words, it was implied that ANP furnished a vehicle that could be used to the reporter's advantage if she showed a little initiative. Emphasis was even placed on the logic of collecting an annual retainer from national organizations as an assurance that their activities would be given priority in the press on a national level. Or perhaps arrangements could be made with fight promoters to give advance publicity about an upcoming bout for a fee or an offer made to a trainer to "build up this boy" in the press.

This practice was commonly known in the trade as a "hustle." Such hustles might have worked out for reporters who had the brass to request, or even demand, some compensation for their favors. But it didn't meet my approval. I considered it not only unprofessional and unethical but dishonest as well. I refused to degrade the professional standing I had worked so hard to attain. There were rules, furthermore, that applied to Capitol and White House accredited reporters—foremost among them being accuracy, honesty, and reliability. So throughout my career, I preferred to suffer dire poverty rather than play this hustle.

And dire poverty was at times the only way to accurately describe my circumstances. Besides being meager, my weekly checks never arrived on time. I constantly requested that the home office in Chicago post my check via airmail, special delivery on Thursday, in time to reach me before the banks closed on Friday. But they were always mailed on Saturday and would not reach me until Monday. Since there was never enough money to carry me from one payday to another, I usually found myself broke every weekend, without even money for food.

Out of necessity, I established the humiliating practice of putting an old scarf on my head every Saturday night and strolling through the Seventh Street slum area, passing dumps and dives, bootleg and gambling joints, practically stumbling over winos and junkies, ignoring insulting remarks from the riffraff, and making my way to a pawn shop to put my watch (my most valuable possession) in hock. Since it was an inexpensive item, I was never allowed more than five dollars on it, just enough for Sunday dinner. On Monday when my check arrived, I would go down and redeem my prize possession by paying an extra dollar and a half for interest. This happened practically every week.

I was fortunate enough to maintain residence in Brookland, a highly respectable Washington neighborhood surrounded by many first families of Washington (FFW), who composed the cream of the district's social and professional sets. Included among the educators, doctors, dentists, and other black professionals on my block were people like Ralph Bunche (chairman of the Department of Political Studies at Howard University, and future Nobel Peace Prize winner). I was not ashamed to give my address to anyone or to point out the neatly kept townhouse with its well-manicured front lawn, but I was definitely ashamed to invite anybody inside. I occupied a one-room basement apartment in the home of Dr. Samuel Thompson, a dentist. The house had a huge, old-fashioned coal furnace in the center of the kitchen, and I received a considerable reduction in rent for shoveling coal into the furnace to heat the entire three-family unit and pulling out the ashes.

Even with the low-rent arrangement, I was always behind in paying and was occasionally threatened with eviction. Since it was important to me to live up to a certain standard and keep up a decent appearance while at the same time struggling to keep my son in college, I finally concluded that I would have to find a second job—one that would still allow me to do my usual amount of newspaper work.

HUNTING FOR WORK

Jobs in Washington were scarce and had been since the end of the war and the closing of a number of war agencies, leaving so many Washington newcomers unemployed. Opportunities were even more scarce for Negroes and women, and I combed the want ads daily for leads. One day, I found an ad for a typist at an embassy. There was no name given—only a telephone number, which I called and was given an appointment for an interview. It turned out to be the embassy of Thailand. Upon my arrival, I was met by a white American male who looked me over and asked, "Are you a Negro?" When I emphatically replied in the affirmative, he said, "Oh, I'm sorry. I didn't know you were Negro or I could have saved you a trip. This embassy does not employ Negroes."

I was so shocked and amazed I repeated his statement, "Doesn't hire Negroes? I can't conceive of that. Why would they be prejudiced? They're as dark as we are. What's the pitch?"

"That's just it," he replied. "It is because they're dark that they do not want to associate with colored people for fear that they will be mistaken for American Negroes. They try hard to avoid them."

Then the man went on to explain that he was from Virginia but he liked Negroes. He often attended plays at Howard University, he said, and had some friends who worked there. "This is not my idea," he continued. "It's just the policy of the embassy. I'm just a hired man here."

I was so thoroughly disgusted that I left without further protest and let the matter drop.

Since I still needed money desperately, I went to the local bank, where I did my limited banking transactions and asked about borrowing $150. The bank executive inquired as to why I needed the money, and I answered truthfully, "To pay my son's college tuition."

"This bank doesn't lend money for luxuries!" he snapped. "College is a luxury. If you're not able to send your son to college, then keep him home."

I almost broke down on the spot, so brutal and unexpected was this racial sting. My first thought was that he'd never make such a statement to a white mother struggling to educate her child.

BOOTLEGGING

I was so determined to find a way to make some extra money that I even considered driving a taxicab, but friends talked me out of it, citing not only the danger but the damage it would do to my prestige as a journalist, which I'd worked so hard to establish.

Then one day, a man whom I'd met casually in my political activities, who perhaps recognized my financial straits, asked for an appointment to discuss a business deal. We met, and he told me right away that he was a hip-pocket bootlegger. I had never heard this expression.

He explained that his job was to hang around a certain location with all of his pockets filled with half pints of liquor, which he sold after hours and on Sundays to people who wanted a drink after liquor stores were closed. He was now interested in expanding his territory to include another hotel that was located near where I lived. He wanted to know if he could arrange with me to stash his whiskey at my place until needed.

He had already arranged for a liquor store to supply the stuff. He would retail it. All they needed now was a cache. He would pick it up as needed and deliver it to the desired customer at a given location, and I needed not get personally involved at all. He explained, however, that there was a third factor needed for safety's sake—police protection, which had already been arranged. The profits, he continued, would be split three ways among the supplier, the peddler, and the stasher, each of whom would ante up to pay for the protection.

I had never been involved in anything illegal, and the very idea sounded fierce and frightening, though he did his best to make it sound easy and safe as well as innocent and rewarding. No one would ever suspect, he added, that the stuff was hidden in the basement apartment of a prominent newspaperwoman in a building housing a distinguished dentist's office in an exclusive VIP residential neighborhood.

The proposition was tempting given my financial straits, about which I was sure my employer did not give a hoot, and the feeling that nobody else even cared whether I ate, starved, or was evicted, much less whether I had any money for transportation to do my job. Fortunately, however, while I rolled the opportunity around in my despairing mind, word spread that the government had launched an all-out campaign against corruption among law enforcement officers. Investigations of bribery began within the police department, and the bootlegger's protection deal was canceled. The anticipated protector went undercover and warned his contact to get off the street and find himself a job. When the bootlegger objected that he had nowhere to go because he couldn't find a job, the protector was said to have found a job for him as a "super" in an apartment building. Luckily for me, I had never become involved!

MAGAZINE WRITING

I was complaining to a friend one day about my financial difficulties when he apparently tired of my squawks and said sarcastically, "If you're the hot reporter you think you are, why don't you write and sell some magazine articles?" I had been thinking about this for some time, and his taunt actually prompted me to accept the challenge.

Since Tuskegee's *Service* magazine had already used some of my articles, I had no problem putting together a two-part feature that it readily accepted on the U.S. Capitol, describing everything from its structure and daily operations to the part played by Negroes in day-by-day activities. I interviewed all the Negro employees I could find, including the library assistant, employees in the docket room and cloakroom, barbers, messengers, waiters, and the Senate's only black doorkeeper. The first installment was published in November 1949, and afterwards a Tuskegee official wrote the editor that the articles were "so packed with historical matter" that he was asking that they be used as a supplementary history text.

After writing a number of other articles for *Service* magazine, I was employed on a regular basis to supply the magazine with one story each month dealing with some aspect of the food business since Tuskegee was interested in encouraging more students to enroll in its newly organized dietetic department. Although this magazine paid only twenty-five dollars for the monthly feature, it gave me an opportunity to broaden my reputation as a writer, especially since my name headed the list of contributing editors on the magazine's masthead. I held this position along with my regular ANP reporting until the magazine finally folded many years later, and I had a lot of fun doing it. It also led to other magazine opportunities, which I welcomed as a means of expanding my experience as well as my reputation and, at least somewhat, my income.

In 1952, I followed a long, continuous hearing before a Senate Rackets Committee on racketeering and police corruption in the District of Columbia, reporting on the fascinating stories told by underworld characters known to the public only as Catfish, Bucklejaws, Jim Yellow, Pudden Head, White Top, and other such monikers. As a result of my crime reports for ANP, I was requested by a national magazine in 1953 to do an article on crime in D.C. The magazine wanted an "inside" story complete with photographs of numbers writers jotting down figures in their little black books, hip-pocket bootleggers sneaking a bottle of booze to a buyer, and gamblers engaged in a crap game in an alley.

I realized this was an impossible assignment if I wished to keep healthy. Since I was around the streets quite a lot and frequently circulating through the slum areas, I had met, by chance, many underworld characters and had a pretty fair knowledge of what was happening. While I felt free to write about it, I dared not reveal names or take pictures of these lawbreakers if I wanted to live.

The upshot was an agreement that I would do the story using young male amateur models for the pictures, which the magazine's editor would identify as such in the publication. It was a great embarrassment to all concerned, therefore, when the magazine failed to do that, and the young men, well known around town, were recognized by the magazine's readers. For a brief time, it appeared that both I and the magazine might be sued, but the matter died with time when nothing came of the article anyway.

TIES THAT BIND

ANP and I continued to disagree (through the mail) on an appropriate salary, knowing that neither would dare to cut the other loose. Through my hard work, Mr. Barnett had built up a satisfied clientele, and his subscriptions were increasing. He knew full well it would be impossible to get another person to turn out the vast amount of copy I did for the measly amount of money he was paying me.

On the other hand, I dared not cut myself off from ANP because it would cost me my White House and Capitol credentials, drying up my sources of fresh, interesting, behind-the-scenes material that was the lifeblood of my success. There was no other employment where I could keep these accreditations because only reporters for daily papers or news services were eligible for them. There was only one other Negro news service in existence at the time, and it was already well covered. There were only two Negro dailies: the *Atlanta Daily World*, which either was not interested in national coverage or was not in a financial position to employ a full-time Washington reporter; and the *Chicago Daily Defender*, which was already covered. No Negro reporters were being employed at that time on white dailies or other media such as radio or television. So ANP and I stuck it out and fussed it out together for fourteen years.

In all fairness to the ANP, however, I am grateful to the company, despite our financial conflict, for affording me an opportunity I could never have obtained elsewhere. I wept bitter tears at Claude Barnett's passing in 1967, and although I was no longer associated with ANP by then, I was deeply grieved when the great news agency he'd founded in 1919 gradually faded out soon after his death.

20

FREEDOM FIGHTS
OF THE FIFTIES

Monday, March 1, 1954, started out as a quiet—indeed dull—day on Capitol Hill. I was just one of the reporters and columnists roving the Capitol corridors in search of any tidbit of choice news around which to build some copy.

Then all of a sudden—"Boom! Boom!"—the fireworks started. Blazes burst forth from the southeast corner of the visitors' gallery, where a woman stood waving a Puerto Rican flag in one hand and shooting a gun with the other as she shouted something that sounded like "Vive Puerto Rico!" She was flanked by two men who were also firing pistols, sending bullets flying wildly through the chamber. Some hit the ceiling, while others found a target among the congressmen who at that moment were taking a standing vote on a resolution to permit debate on a bill authorizing continuation of a program admitting Mexican farm laborers to enter this country for temporary employment.

When the shooting ended, five congressmen lay wounded, one seriously, in pools of blood on the House floor. Reporters rushed from the press gallery down to the floor for a closer view. All were permitted except me. I was stopped by Capitol police until I fumbled in my purse and found my press pass. Later, my colleagues laughed that because of my complexion, "they thought you were one of the Puerto Ricans!" With that, I acquired from the gallery the nickname "Miss Puerto Rico."

Despite being delayed, I rushed to the telephone immediately following the shooting and called my home office in Chicago to report the incident. In his usual slow, unperturbed manner, Mr. Barnett calmly asked if either Dawson or Powell (the only two Negro congressmen at that time) had been shot. When I said no, he asked, "Then why are you calling here? You've got no story."

His attitude deflated my ego beyond imagination. I thought I did have a story—the story that both Negro congressmen escaped injury when the Puerto Ricans shot up the Congress. There was also another story, one regarding William Belcher, the Negro doorman at the House Gallery who actually captured one of the gunmen and was injured in the scuffle. After collapsing with a heart attack, he was rushed to the hospital for treatment.

A few months later, I covered the nine-day trial. The woman and her three male companions were found guilty of assault with intent to kill, although they denied any attempt to murder. They claimed that their only purpose was to stage a demonstration that would obligate the United States to end the colonial system existing in Puerto Rico and grant the island independence. All were sentenced to long—effectively life—terms.[1]

President Truman understood perhaps better than anyone the importance of the question of Puerto Rican independence. Two Puerto Rican Nationalists planning to assassinate him had tried to shoot their way into Blair House, where the president was staying during White House renovations, on November 1, 1950. A police officer was killed in the attack, as was one of the Nationalists. The other was sentenced to prison.[2]

Listening to the testimony of the defendants, I recalled the Panama Canal Zone history of color discrimination imposed by Americans on territories outside of the continental United States. Puerto Rico's Nationalist Party had grown out of discrimination that penetrated the island during World War I, when the U.S. Army assigned fair-skinned Puerto Ricans to all-white units while their darker-skinned brothers were relegated to all-black units.

As the story was told, a mulatto, a Harvard Law School graduate who was the son of a white father and colored mother, became so embittered at this arrangement that he formed the Nationalist Part early in the 1920s for the purpose of liberating Puerto Rico from U.S. domination.

The Capitol shooting, followed by the lengthy trial, was probably the most exciting as well as tragic incident I covered during my entire journalism career.

IN THE COURTS

By the mid-1950s, the movement of civil rights cases through the federal circuits and up to the Supreme Court necessitated the expansion of my news beat and additional credentials. Once again, the ANP director took a dim view of my application for accreditation to the highest court. Mr. Barnett took the position that I would do well to cultivate a closer relationship with court messengers and persuade them to sneak out to me advance copies of the decisions. This, he felt, would be more advantageous than spending hours in the official press box listening to extended arguments on specific cases.

I was enraged at this suggestion since Negro reporters had fought so hard and long for the same opportunities offered white reporters on these most important news beats. I devoted an entire column to blasting some Negro newspaper executives for insisting on holding onto that "old-fashioned, back-door" method of reporting to which we had for so long been relegated. I didn't think the papers would publish this scathing column—but they did.

Despite ANP's lack of enthusiasm for the idea, I had no problem obtaining a Supreme Court press pass and again took my place alongside some of the leading reporters in the country. But I did find it to be the most difficult assignment in my entire press career. Decisions were sent down to the press office every Monday. Sometimes they would be several pages long and others just a single sentence. In order to report on these decisions, one had to know the background of the case. For this, a reporter had to find the appropriate briefs on the library shelves of the pressroom and learn to quickly locate the specific paragraph that outlined concisely the facts of the case. Then the reporter had to translate any legalese into language understandable to the average reader. Since I had no legal training, that job never became a simple routine for as long as I covered the Supreme Court. The experience, however, came with the privilege of being on the spot when some of the most famous lawyers of that day argued some of the most significant cases of our times before some of the nation's most distinguished jurists.

It was the era of such giants of civil rights litigation as Thurgood Marshall, who eventually became an associate justice (appointed by President Johnson in 1967); James Nabrit, later president of Howard University; renowned constitutional lawyer Charles Houston; and Robert Carter of the NAACP. It was also the decade of landmark school desegregation decisions that, along with the courage of thousands of black men, women, and even children, such as the Little Rock Nine, who put their bodies on the line, led to an enormous change in race relations in this country.

I covered every case involving Negroes that reached the Supreme Court as well as others in the district court, Washington's federal trial court. It was there that I saw the tears stream from the eyes of Dr. W. E. B. DuBois's wife, Shirley, as her husband was escorted from a courthouse elevator in handcuffs. It was 1951, and the celebrated eighty-three-year-old socialist, historian, and civil rights activist had been charged with being an agent of a foreign power. Tears welled in the eyes of sympathetic reporters as well, as Shirley described how this grand old gentleman had been fingerprinted and searched for concealed weapons as if a common criminal.

Dr. DuBois was being prosecuted because he spoke out against the use of nuclear weapons and criticized the U.S. government for backing colonial powers at the San Francisco Conference, which established the charter of the United Nations. He had appeared before the House Committee on Foreign Relations in 1949 to urge Congress to vote down the payment of a billion and a half dollars for military assistance to the North Atlantic Treaty Alliance countries, arguing, "This country claims not to have enough money to spend fighting ignorance, disease, waste, or for old age security for its workers, but it is asking for a huge sum to be spent to murder, blind, and cripple men, women, and children abroad and destroy their property by fire and flood."

After that, the government tried without success to silence Dr. DuBois. In 1951, the government withdrew his passport, denying him the right to travel abroad. Still he continued to lead a group of citizens who claimed to be seeking peace in the world at the time when Senator Joseph McCarthy's anticommunist campaign was at its peak. This was what almost placed him behind bars. However, widespread publicity, primarily through the press, aroused citizens of the United States and around the world to protest against the prosecution of Dr. DuBois, and finally it was dropped.[3]

> **REPORT KKK CHASED FLORIDA A & M PRESIDENT FROM STATE**
>
> **WEEK-END CHATS** By James A. Hamlett, Jr.
>
> # BRAND ROBESON A RED
>
> **The Plaindealer** 10¢ PER COPY EVERYWHERE
>
> The Only Negro Newspaper Published In the State of Kansas · FOUNDED 1899
>
> THE OLDEST NEGRO NEWSPAPER IN THE SOUTHWEST — WE MOULD SENTIMENT
>
> VOLUME 51, NUMBER 29 · KANSAS CITY, KANSAS, FRIDAY JULY 22, 1949 · ASSOCIATED NEGRO PRESS NEWS
>
> **Un-American Committee Is Told Paul Robeson A Communist** By ALICE DUNNIGAN

Dunnigan had the lead article in many ANP newspapers when concert star Paul Robeson was denounced as a Communist. (Kansas City *Plaindealer*, July 22, 1949)

For years, I also followed the trials of another prominent American whose passport was revoked because of his political activities and statements. I wrote a running account of theatrical and concert artist Paul Robeson's conflict with the government from the very beginning (1948) when he was threatened with a jail sentence for refusing to tell a Senate committee whether he was a card-carrying Communist. Robeson sued in district court in 1950 for validation of his passport, but the court upheld the State Department's action, and the following year the court of appeals refused to review the case on the grounds that since the passport had expired, the case was moot.

After four subsequent applications for a passport to enable him to fulfill concert engagements abroad were denied, another lawsuit in 1955 brought results, and two years later his passport was reinstated. In the meantime, however, Robeson's income had suffered and his health had drastically declined. While some of the press coverage of Robeson's plight had ranged from hostile to at best ambivalent, his wife of forty-four years, Eslanda ("Essie"), an anthropologist, author, and journalist, took some solace in my stories, writing me, "It is such a pleasure to read a dignified story about the Robesons these days. We are sick and tired and angry about the malicious, wholly untrue, deliberately misleading stuff which the press keeps printing about us. I was delighted that it was the Negro press that saw fit to print the truth."

ON MILITARY BASES

President Truman's Executive Order No. 9981, issued on July 26, 1948, calling for equality of treatment and opportunity in the armed forces, also ordered desegregation of schools for children of personnel stationed on military bases. This latter provision, however, had met with resistance from some southern state officials as well as some high-ranking officials in the federal government. I brought this to the attention of President Eisenhower at a press conference on March 19, 1953, shortly after he took office, asking what he proposed to do about segregated schools on military bases. In reply, he made this famous statement:

> I have said it again and again: wherever federal funds are expended, I do not see how any American can justify—legally, logically, or morally—discrimination in the expenditure of those funds as among our citizens. All are taxed to provide those funds. If there is any benefit to be derived from them, I think they all must share, regardless of such inconsequential factors as race and religion.[4]

The president promised to look into this situation and give me a definite reply later. Months passed and nothing more was heard about this matter. Later that year, at the president's September 30, 1953, press conference, I again reminded him of this situation, pointing out that the Department of Defense had issued a statement that the integration of schools on military posts might be delayed until 1955, and asked for his comment on the proposal. Eisenhower denied any knowledge of this development and again said he'd have his press secretary, James Hagerty, look into it and let me know.

Soon afterward, the president announced that the Department of Defense had set September 1955 as the target date for ending segregation in all schools on military bases. However, all major posts except Fort Benning, Georgia, were reported to have integrated their schools peacefully and successfully long before the two-year deadline, after months of work by the NAACP, Senator Hubert H. Humphrey, Congressman Adam Clayton Powell Jr., and parents on the bases who objected to sending their children to segregated schools.

WASHINGTON LIFE

Halfway through the twentieth century, the nation's capital was still a very segregated city. Some of the many places from which Negroes continued to be barred in the late 1940s were downtown theaters. The National Theatre, the city's only legitimate playhouse, was closed to both black entertainers and black patrons of the arts. Washington residents rejected the policy and staged picket lines around the theater for months, and in 1947 the Actors Equity Association, the union representing stage actors and managers, stopped its members from appearing at the National Theatre unless it changed its policy. Rather than change, the management in 1948 converted the theater into a movie house. The Department of State found the lack of a legitimate theater in the nation's capital a source of some embarrassment when noted by foreign visitors. But that was about to change.

In 1950 when the Rock Creek Park amphitheater that became known as Carter Barron Theatre opened to the public, it was on a nonsegregated basis, and President and Mrs. Truman and their daughter Margaret were guests of honor on opening night. The president pushed the button that signaled the start of a beautiful pageant entitled "Faith of Our Fathers," starring an integrated cast of performers.

During this decade, segregation—at least overt, sanctioned segregation—in public places, including places of entertainment, was finally prohibited in the nation's capital after a three-year court battle. This Supreme Court decision grew out of a lawsuit brought against Thompson's Cafeteria in 1950 by three Negroes—Mary Church Terrell, the Reverend W. H. Jernagin, and Geneva Brown—and one white man, David Scull.

Central to the case was the validity of two old antisegregation laws passed in the District of Columbia in 1872 and 1873, respectively. The National Lawyers Guild claimed that these so-called lost laws were still valid, although they had not been enforced since the legislative assembly in D.C. was abolished in 1874. I followed the case from the Office of the Corporation Counsel (the city's attorney), which concluded that the seventy-seven-year-old laws had never been repealed, through the municipal court, which dismissed the case on the grounds that the laws had been "repealed by implication." The suit then went to the court of appeals, which reversed the lower court decision. Finally, the case reached the Supreme Court, which in June 1953 upheld the ruling of the court of appeals declaring the "lost laws" still valid.

The decision called for the immediate abolition of segregation in restaurants, hotels, bathing houses, soda fountains, theaters, and other places of amusement. Not more than two hours after the Supreme Court announced its ruling, I was privileged to accompany the plaintiffs to the same Thompson's Cafeteria for lunch, where we were all served with no problem.

I had been following Mrs. Terrell's actions since she accepted chairmanship of the Coordinating Committee for the Enforcement of the D.C. Anti-Discrimination Laws in 1949. I saw her in her ripe old age lead the fight to break down discrimination against Negro membership in the American Association of University Women. I watched her march in countless picket lines and make innumerable speeches against discriminatory hiring practices in downtown businesses until her efforts bore fruit and Negroes were finally employed as salespeople in department, shoe, drug, and variety stores.

One store in particular showed its commitment to racial equality by training and employing young Negro women as models for its fashion shows in downtown hotels and other venues. In 1968, I was pleased to see the Hecht Company receive an award for this service, upon my recommendation, from the President's Committee on Youth Opportunities.[5]

Mrs. Terrell, who deserves considerable credit for the progress made in D.C. during this era, was born in 1863, the year President Lincoln signed the Emancipation Proclamation, and died in 1954, after the Supreme Court's decision in *Brown*. In an interview after that historic ruling, she said, "Thank God! I can now die in peace. I have seen the last

Dunnigan was inspired by the great civil rights leader Mary Church Terrell. (From Dunnigan, *Black Woman's Experience*)

vestige of segregation wiped from our great nation—in transportation, hotels, and restaurants, in employment and recreation, and now in education." This grand old lady died a few months later without knowing the struggle, the pain, and the bloodshed that still loomed ahead before black Americans would finally enjoy the harvest of these seminal decisions of the high court. Her life and beautiful work, however, continued to inspire many others who followed in her footsteps. I thought of her as an idol and pledged to help continue the fight she had begun to advance the cause for a better America in the only way I knew how—with the pen, realizing full well the truth of the saying that it is mightier than the sword.

I met many firsts on the road to freedom as I used that power to report on both progress and problems along the way. I saw the first Negro employed as an elevator operator in the Capitol complex, the first black man appointed to the Capitol police force, the first African American chef assigned to the Capitol kitchen, the first black man appointed doorman to the Senate chambers (and later another to the House Gallery).[6] I interviewed the first black pageboy on Capitol Hill,[7] and I covered the commencement ceremony at the U.S. Naval Academy in Annapolis, Maryland, in 1949 when Wesley A. Brown earned the honor of being the academy's first Negro graduate. Some people today might scoff at my calling these breakthroughs or milestones, but they provided the shoulders on which future giants would stand to wage the battle for true equality.

ON THE FRONT LINES

One of the most distressing situations I ever covered unfolded at the end of the decade in Fayette County, Tennessee, when a small group of blacks, spurred by the voting rights provisions of the Civil Rights Act of 1957, attempted to vote in the 1959 primaries for state and local officials. When news of their effort spread, the whites in the county initiated an economic "squeeze" against those Negroes who dared challenge an eighty-year-old tradition by demanding to vote in what had been commonly known as a "white primary" since Reconstruction.[8]

The situation worsened after Negroes filed and won a suit against the Democratic Committee in the county, charging that blacks had been illegally barred from exercising their franchise. After this victory, blacks flocked from the farms to the courthouse in Somerville to register.

Irate white landlords became so embittered that they began ordering the sharecroppers off their farms. Merchants refused to sell them food or other goods. Banks declined loans to farmers for seed or fertilizer. Filling stations also denied them gasoline to operate their tractors. Wholesalers and distributors withheld produce from Negro merchants, practically forcing them out of business. Oil companies snatched their gasoline tanks from Negro owners of filling stations. A number of leaders of the voter registration drive or members of their families were fired from their jobs, ranging from cafeteria workers to schoolteachers.

White landowners who refused to join the economic squeeze against Negro voters were subjected to economic reprisal and ostracism by members of their own race. White journalists trying to get the facts about the situation were questioned and harassed by law officers.

Shepherd Towles, one of the few Negro farmers who owned his own land, permitted tents to be placed on his land to house the homeless sharecroppers. The site became known throughout the nation as Tent City, or as some writers dubbed it, Freedom Village.

News of these events and pleas from many organizations, spearheaded by the NAACP, brought shipments of food and clothing from around the country and abroad for the homeless, evicted blacks.

This was another story where I waded in without ANP support, since Mr. Barnett did not agree with my venturing beyond Washington for news. Nevertheless, I gave our clients a series of articles on the entire situation at no cost to the news service, which never asked how the trip was financed. Now I can tell. The tab was picked up by a prominent public relations firm that had as a client one of the nation's leading oil companies, which was sympathetic to the black farmers' cause in Fayette County and wanted to come to their rescue but was fearful of reprisals from the other boycotting companies. After getting a firsthand look, the company quietly began to supply gasoline to a Negro filling station owner with the understanding that he would tell no one how, when, or where he was obtaining it.

When the retailer's tank was filled with gasoline, it greatly relieved the black farmers who owned tractors and trucks. The white landowners were puzzled as to how and from where the gasoline was coming. My mission was to "case" the situation and especially to explore whether the whites had any inkling as to who was supplying the gasoline and whether the black retailer was keeping his pledge to secrecy. As it turned out, the retailer was mum. When I asked him how he got the gas, he replied, "It is delivered on dark, country roads, late at night, in unmarked trucks." When I attempted to catch him off guard by asking what kind of gas he sold, he quickly replied, "I sell 'independent' gasoline. But my friends say I should call it 'Tennessee squeeze' gas."

Shortly afterward, at President John F. Kennedy's first press conference (also the first presidential news conference telecast live) on January 25, 1961, I asked the new president whether his administration planned to take steps to solve the problem of the people in Tennessee who had been evicted from their homes because they dared to vote in the last election and were now forced to live in tents.

The president replied, referring to the Civil Rights Act of 1960, "Congress, of course, enacted legislation which placed very clear responsibility on the executive branch to protect the right of voting. I supported that legislation." He continued, "I am extremely interested in making sure that every American is given the right to cast his vote without prejudice to his rights as a citizen, and therefore I can state that this administration will pursue the problem of providing that protection with all vigor."[9]

While Department of Justice actions in Tennessee in the ensuing months brought some relief to black voters, it wasn't until passage of the Voting Rights Act of 1965 that the voting rights of blacks in Fayette and neighboring Haywood County were enforced.

IN THE FRONT ROW

By the 1950s, black athletes were being accepted in all professional sports—including baseball, basketball, and football. They were employed so rapidly after the field was opened that their induction into formerly all-white teams was no longer of special news value to the minority press. ANP's clients were particularly interested in boxing, which had many nationally known personalities. Although the fame of the mighty Joe Louis was beginning to decline, Joe Wolcott was in his heyday. I had the opportunity to see these great heavyweights in action as well as to interview them on various occasions.

I ran into a wall, however, when I attempted to crash what had previously been considered by sportswriters to be an exclusively male domain. I was barred from the front row seats reserved for reporters. The D.C.

After breaking through the sports world's gender barriers one by one, Dunnigan had no trouble interviewing such superstars as Boxing Hall of Famer Jack Dempsey, World Heavyweight Champion from 1919 to 1926. (From Dunnigan, *Black Woman's Experience*)

With Harlem Globetrotters (From Dunnigan, *Black Woman's Experience*)

Boxing Commission informed me that it was against the rules for women to sit at ringside. With that, I began waging a battle for equal rights for women sportswriters that lasted several months.

I had several Negro sportswriters in my corner. Foremost among them were Fred Leigh and Art Carter of the *Afro-American* and Chick Webb and Ric Roberts of the *Pittsburgh Courier*. Leading the fight on my behalf was Michael (Casey) Jones, a prominent boxing promoter. Jones thought of a scheme that he thought would do the trick. He formed an organization known as the Negro Boxing Writers Association and became its first president. Roberts was named executive vice president and Webb correspondence secretary. Carter was elected chairman of the executive committee, and Leigh was appointed historian. Other officers included Sam Lacey, treasurer; Van Nixon, secretary; and me, librarian.

The organization sent a delegation to the Boxing Commission demanding that I, a sportswriter and an officer of the Negro Boxing Writers Association, be allowed to cover fights from ringside like all other sportswriters. The scheme worked, and I became Washington's first and only woman sportswriter.[10]

As a representative of the Negro Boxing Writers Association, Casey Jones was invited to appear before the District Boxing Commission in 1949 to verify a statement he had earlier made before a congressional hearing regarding the appointment of a Negro to the Boxing Commission. Pointing out that the majority of fighters were Negroes and 85 percent of the fans were Negroes, Jones said his association would lead a boycott against the fights unless his request was given some consideration.

"Negro newspapers represent the articulate voice of the Negro people," declared Jones. "And they are advocating the infiltration of Negroes all down the line from Commissioners to referees and inspectors. Unless they get some favorable action, Negro fans will boycott the fights."

Through continuing conferences and negotiations with boxing officials, Jones and his association finally succeeded in having Dr. Joe Trigg, medical advisor for the commission, elevated to boxing commissioner. Continuing his fight for more Negro participation, Jones finally succeeded in getting Sam Barnes, instructor of athletics at Howard University, and Fred Leigh, former *Afro-American* sportswriter, appointed judges.

When I moved into football coverage, I was welcomed by local sportswriters who had become accustomed to seeing me around and had learned to respect my work.

Fellow Kentuckian "Happy" Chandler, a former senator and the state's forty-fourth and forty-ninth governor, was commissioner of baseball from 1945 to 1951. His approval of Jackie Robinson's contract with the Brooklyn Dodgers opened the major league to black players. (Dunnigan Papers, MARBL, Emory University)

Baseball was my next venture, although there was no client interest in Washington's American League team since, like all the others in the league, it had no Negro players. Jackie Robinson had broken the color barrier in the National League when he was signed by the Brooklyn Dodgers in 1947, and although I never got to see him play, I covered him on many visits to Washington, including several for civil rights causes.

One time, I attempted to cover a Major League Baseball game from the press box at Washington's Griffith Stadium but was denied entrance.[11] I was very upset because I thought I was being barred because of race. I let a male reporter use my press pass just to see what would happen. Although the pass bore my name, the reporter was admitted to the press box without question. Then I realized that the discrimination was not based on race but sex.

I still attempted to cover games in the Negro league, even if I had to do it from the bleachers. Once I tried to get an interview with Satchel Paige when he played in Washington with the Philadelphia Stars against the

Homestead Grays. Not being able to talk with him either in the press box or the locker room, I sauntered down to the dugout before the game. The superstitious players were furious, contending that a woman in the dugout would bring bad luck. The irate pitcher tried to control his anger and answer my questions with civility if not courtesy. He closed the interview with the curt remark, "I know we're going to lose this game. A woman sashaying around the dugout will surely put the jinx on us."

"The famous Satchel Paige will never lose a game," I replied cheerfully.

Paige was the starting pitcher but was relieved after three innings. And sure enough, to my regret, his team did lose the game. The manager of the Philadelphia Stars sadly lamented that this was the first game they had lost since Satchel had been on the team.

21

EISENHOWER'S PIQUE

During my regular news coverage, I seldom missed
a press conference held by top government officials,
and I never missed an opportunity to raise questions
regarding problems within their respective agencies
of concern to black people. Inevitably, I became sort
of a "flea in the collar" of many of these officials.

My routine questions regarding segregation in
swimming pools and on playgrounds in Washington,
D.C., were welcomed by Truman's interior secretary,
Oscar Chapman, who favored the abolition of discrimination, but the problem continued many years
before it was finally resolved.

There were marches on the D.C. Recreation Department, sidewalk polls, countless letters of protest, and
unpublicized negotiations and conferences before the
Washington Recreation Board in 1949 announced a
policy for gradual desegregation. The Interior Department, however, declared that all of its land should be
operated on an integrated basis and opened its swimming pools under the oversight of park police specially
trained to see that the integration order was carried out
quickly and with the least possible trouble. The D.C.
Recreation Board finally abandoned its plan to deseg-

regate playgrounds one by one over an unspecified period of time when the Supreme Court announced its school desegregation decision in 1954.

Another issue constantly raised by the black press was the need for clarification of government policy on the operation of federally supported health centers. When Surgeon General Thomas Parran Jr. told a press conference in 1947 that more young women were needed in the nursing profession, I asked about opportunities for Negro nurses. He quickly replied that this was left up to local authorities. He explained that while federal law required each state receiving federal funds for hospitals to make all facilities available to all people of the state, this dealt only with physical facilities, and the federal government had no jurisdiction over the employment of personnel.

The policy of allowing the states to decide how federally supported hospitals were operated with regard to racial segregation was reiterated in 1948 by Parran's successor as surgeon general, Dr. Leonard Scheele, who demurred in response to my question on the issue that he was not familiar enough with the text of a hospital construction bill pending before Congress "to express an opinion on the segregation policy to be practiced at prospective medical facilities" but that he assumed it would be left to the states. The black press, as before, blasted this position because African Americans were consistently denied a fair share of jobs and other federal benefits in most instances where funds were administered by state or local officials.

Finally, in July 1948, reporters heard a different response from Federal Security Administrator Oscar R. Ewing, who replied immediately and unequivocally that a proposed thirteen-story clinical research center in Bethesda, Maryland (the future National Institutes of Health) would hire the two thousand employees—professional and general—needed to staff the center on an interracial basis and would admit patients without regard to race. A few months later, Ewing recommended to President Truman that the government adopt a definite policy guaranteeing the availability of adequate medical services for all, regardless of race, stating, "We can no longer tolerate in our society a system of medical care under which Negro physicians and Negro patients are discriminated against."

Because federal law made no stipulation concerning discriminatory practices that barred members of minority groups from serving on the staff of hospitals, the FSA recommended that "all maintenance subsidies to hospitals be assured only on condition that professional personnel should be accepted as staff members, or as other workers, in the underwritten hospitals without discrimination as to race, religion, or sex."

In October 1948, one month after Ewing's recommendations to the president, Gallinger Hospital opened its doors to interns and medical training students of Howard University.[1] Prior to this time, Freedmen's Hospital[2] was the only place in Washington for training of interns from Howard's Medical School. Under the new arrangement, Howard was allotted a yearly quota of one-fourth of the total number of interns admitted, while the city's two white medical schools—Georgetown and George Washington—each was allotted a quarter of the slots, with the balance reserved for interns recommended by the District Health Department. Even then, however, the policy of segregation of physicians and nurses on the hospital staff remained status quo. I raised the issue in an early press conference of Oveta Culp Hobby soon after she took office as secretary of health, education, and welfare (HEW). She appeared a bit stunned by the question and passed it on to one of her associates, who gave a long, rambling but indefinite answer. Nevertheless the exchange served as the basis for a good news story and set wheels in motion that eventually brought results, although complete integration in medical institutions was not accomplished until passage of the Civil Rights Act of 1964, which (in Title VI) barred discrimination in programs supported by federal funds.

The integration of public schools, barely in its early stages during Eisenhower's first administration, was having the ironic effect of eliminating jobs for Negro teachers as they were replaced with whites. Therefore, when U.S. Commissioner of Education Samuel M. Brownell told a news conference that there were not enough teachers available to fill existing job vacancies, I called to his attention the fact that there was a surplus of Negro teachers in the country, many of whom were then unemployed.

"If the school systems throughout the country would employ teachers on the basis of qualifications rather than race, this problem could easily be solved, could it not?" I asked.

His face flushed and he gave no answer except to say something like, "I suppose so."

Commissioner Brownell was put on the grill again in early 1955, when he appeared before the Senate Committee on Labor and Public Welfare, along with HEW Secretary Hobby. Mrs. Hobby was appearing on behalf of President Eisenhower's aid to education bill aimed at relieving classroom shortages. The bill seemed to represent an apparent shift in previous administration reluctance to aid education. During the five- or six-hour grilling, Commissioner Brownell offered that by authorizing the purchase of bonds issued by state school building agencies, matched by federal grants, the bill would give the states "self-determination" rather than federal interference in how they operated. Throughout the hearing, the question of supplying federal funds to aid segregated school districts kept coming up with no clear answers, although Mrs. Hobby did deny the charge that this plan was devised as a way of avoiding the Supreme Court's desegregation order. My reports as well as those in the black press in general described the legislation as an attempt to circumvent the Supreme Court ruling by placing policy-making power in the hands of the states. At the close of the first day of Senate hearings, George Meany, president of the American Federation of Labor, put his union on record as supporting an amendment to the school aid legislation to deny federal aid to states that abolished their public school system in an attempt to nullify the Supreme Court decision.

It was common knowledge around Washington that Jane Spaulding, one of Eisenhower's top black appointees as HEW assistant secretary, lost her job after less than a year because she opposed Secretary Hobby's position on school desegregation. She took her case to the NAACP, and after much adverse publicity in the Negro press and a threatened investigation by the civil rights organization, the administration gave her an office at the Foreign Claims Settlement Commission, which she retained until public sentiment died down.

The greatest advantage of black reporters being accredited to the White House was the opportunity to raise questions of interest to the black population in order to get a face-to-face reply on important issues and the president's personal opinion on various subjects, as well as a promise as to what he intended to do about existing problems. This theory worked very well under the Truman administration. Whenever a question was raised with him, the reporter would either get a direct, concise answer or a curt "no comment." Either way, the reporter would have a story. But this theory didn't work so well with President Eisenhower.

It appeared that Mr. Eisenhower was not familiar with many questions raised on civil rights issues. Either he was not concerned enough to alert himself on these controversial matters or his advisors didn't bother to brief him sufficiently on this all-important subject. In any case, he would become very annoyed whenever such questions were raised.

The president was not in favor of any legislation aimed at wiping segregation from American society. As this question continued to arise at press conferences, the president once replied to the effect that it was his prerogative not to talk about segregation or discrimination. He said it was his job to support any federal court order that had been properly issued under the Constitution and to intervene where compliance was prevented by unlawful action. He had to do that, he said, but it was an entirely different matter for him to instigate new methods or new laws relating to this problem, which he contended could not be solved except by understanding and reason.

In spite of his acknowledged opposition to new legislation prohibiting segregation and discrimination, the National Newspaper Publishers Association (NNPA) in 1954 presented President Eisenhower with the coveted Russwurm Award, the highest honor offered by the nation's Negro publishers. The annual award is presented in honor of John B. Russwurm, founder of the Negro press in America, for outstanding contributions to human relations and racial understanding. According to the publishers, they gave the award in recognition of the president's order to eliminate separate schools on army posts, for strengthening the (Truman) policy of integration in the armed forces, and for the abolition of segregation in public facilities of the District of Columbia (as required by the Supreme Court) during his administration.[3]

Ethel Payne came to Washington in late 1953 as a reporter for the daily and weekly *Chicago Defender*, and because she represented one of the two Negro daily newspapers in the country (the other being the *Atlanta Daily World*), she qualified for immediate membership in the Capitol Press Galleries and the White House press corps. As I did, she raised direct and pointed questions at presidential press conferences.[4] On one occasion, she asked the president a question regarding discrimination in housing. Mr. Eisenhower became furious, either because he did not know the answer or did not wish to commit himself on the subject.

A few weeks later at his April 29, 1954, conference, I posed a question on discrimination in the Bureau of Engraving and Printing. This was a question that had been on the minds of many people for a long time. I had

Ethel Payne, who began reporting from Washington, D.C., for the *Chicago Defender* in 1954, often covered stories with Dunnigan, her friend and mentor. They jointly interviewed W. Averell Harriman, who held many high posts in Democratic administrations, including ambassador, peace negotiator, and cabinet secretary, and who was governor of New York from 1954 to 1958. (Photo by Sorrell; Dunnigan Papers, MARBL, Emory University)

continuously followed this fight led by the federal workers' union and was concerned about the climax. In order to bring the president up to date on the problem, I explained that the bureau had been charged with defying the recommendation of the Fair Employment Practices Committee (FEPC) by refusing to employ Negroes as apprentice plate printers. The FEPC had agreed six months earlier that the applicants for the apprentice plate printers jobs at the bureau were victims of racial discrimination. These findings reportedly had been made known to the U.S. Civil Service Commission but had never been released publicly. With this explanation, I asked Mr. Eisenhower if he planned to take any steps to have the FEPC's recommendations and decisions made public and to force the Bureau of Engraving to fulfill its obligations under the Servicemen's Readjustment Act.

President Eisenhower was infuriated. He asked why I had not gone to

the proper departments of government to ask this question and specifically whether I had raised the matter with the Bureau of Engraving or the
Civil Service Commission. He added that he liked to come to these press
conferences completely prepared to answer as well as he could any questions that came up. But he couldn't be expected to know details on how
a particular thing could be handled. Then, a bit calmer, he added that he
didn't know too much about this but he would have Mr. Hagerty (his press
secretary) look up this particular question and give an answer in time.[5]

Another time, Ethel asked the president if the administration was lending its support to proposed legislation to bar segregation in interstate
travel. In clipped words, the president replied that he did not know by
what right the reporter should say that legislation would have to have administration support. He added that the administration was not trying to
support any particular or special group of any kind but was trying to do
what it believed to be decent and just.[6]

On one bright morning in midsummer of 1959, the president cheerfully
faced the regular press corps with perhaps no thought of being badgered
with a race question, since no burning civil rights issues were in the news
at that moment. That is probably why he seemed so startled when a reporter hit him right between the eyes with a direct question as to whether
he felt that "racial segregation is morally wrong."[7]

"Myself?" asked the president, appearing a bit stunned.

"Yes, sir," replied the reporter.

After some hesitation, Mr. Eisenhower managed to say that there are
several phases of segregation but he assumed the reporter meant that
phase which deprived citizens of their economic and political rights. He
thought that phase was "morally wrong." The reporter pursued the question no further and the president, probably thinking he had handled it
well, went on with the conference, recognizing another reporter with
a different line of questioning. He was probably surprised (if he saw it)
when the reporter wrote, "President Eisenhower admitted that political
and economic segregation is wrong, but he tactfully avoided any comment on social or educational equality."

In an obvious attempt to intimidate Ethel and me, Louis Lautier, a
staunch Republican, ardent conservative, and absolute male chauvinist,
took a crack at us in his syndicated column. (Although we had no proof
of his motive, we felt confident that it was instigated by the White House.)

Dunnigan interviewed National Bar Association president (and future D.C. superior court judge) William S. "Turk" Thompson and keynote speaker Rev. Martin Luther King Jr. at the NBA's 1959 convention. King had repeatedly asked President Eisenhower to call segregation "morally wrong," and the president finally did a few days after the civil rights leader called his failure to do so "tragic." (Photo by Stitt; from Dunnigan, *Black Woman's Experience*)

He wrote a critical analysis of the questions we raised, saying, among other things, "The two gal reporters are hell bent on competing with each other to see which one can ask President Eisenhower the longest questions."

Lautier's criticism brought immediate protest from Clarence Mitchell Jr., then chief of the NAACP Washington Bureau. In a letter to the editor of the *Afro-American* dated May 25, 1954, Mitchell expressed great concern about this attack.

"The NAACP has had deep interest in both of the questions raised by these reporters," Mitchell wrote. "We were delighted when the queries were put to the President at his press conferences." He noted that Ethel's question regarded top officials at the Housing Agency having done nothing to implement a promise made by Eisenhower four months earlier that certain corrective steps would be taken in the field of government-assisted housing programs. Since the president had made the promise, Mitchell opined, he should be asked to explain the delay.

Regarding my question about discrimination in the Bureau of Printing and Engraving, Mitchell described the situation as "a conflict between top officials which the President must settle." In closing, he expressed the hope that we would continue asking questions because, "after all, that is what a press conference is for."

Using Lautier's phraseology, I might say the White House seemed "hell-bent" on gagging me, as far as questions on civil rights were concerned. This became evident at an embassy party, where I was approached by Max Rabb, the president's special advisor on minority affairs. Over cocktails, in a very pleasant manner, he made a proposition that went something like this:

"Alice, you're always asking the boss questions on some subject with which he is not familiar. This is very embarrassing to him. Why don't you check out your questions with me before going to the conferences? Then I will brief him on the situation and he will have a ready answer. All you want is an answer anyway, isn't it? This way you'll be sure to get your answer."

This sounded all right at the moment, and I agreed, but when I gave it more thought, I was enraged because out of the five hundred or more reporters, I was the only one, to my knowledge, who was asked to check her questions with the White House beforehand. But since I had already agreed, I felt I had to go along with it.

Before the next press conference, I called Rabb to tell him I intended to ask the president a question about the FEPC bill pending before Congress.

"Oh, no, no!" he exclaimed. "Don't ask that question." Then he went on to explain something about "the boss" working on this measure, and if it were brought to public attention, the southerners on the Hill would take reverse action and throw a roadblock in the president's plans.

This was exactly what I was afraid would happen. I was hurt as well as mad. I sat through the conference "all stuffed up," watching the white reporters jumping up all around me and asking questions of interest to their readers, none of which provided anything of interest to our publications. It seemed to me that it would have been a breach of journalistic ethics to ask my question despite Rabb's advising against it. So I left the press conference with nothing of special interest to our readers. I might as well not have been there.

I vowed to myself that I would never do it again—never check my questions in advance with anybody on the White House staff—but instead get up like everybody else and ask whatever I pleased.

But it didn't happen that way. Mr. Eisenhower had a different idea. He apparently had made up his mind never to recognize me again—and he didn't! I would go to every press conference and jump to my feet between every question, shouting for attention like all the other reporters, "Mr. President! Mr. President!" But Mr. President ignored me. He would recognize people all around me, in front of me, in back of me, on either side, but he always left me standing like the invisible man. The white reporters began to notice the snub, and one day one of them asked, "Do you realize how many times you were on your feet today asking for recognition?" When I replied that I hadn't counted, he replied, "Fifteen times."

Another white reporter wrote a story for a chain of newspapers in his state on the Eisenhower snub of a Negro reporter, and Drew Pearson, the nationally syndicated columnist, made note of it in his column. The *Afro-American* also picked up the story, and a New York radio station called me for a telephone interview. The *New York Post* called it an attempt by the president to dodge an issue as well as to pigeonhole two women reporters. *Labor's Daily*, May 21, 1957, ran a long article on the controversy, stating that I had not been recognized by the president in more than a year and a half, while Ethel Payne had been ignored as well.[8]

In a column in the *Daily Worker* headed "The Presidential Gag on Civil Rights," Abner W. Berry called the president's snub "censorship" and "an insult to the representatives of the Negro press," noting that it came "as these [reporters] became more persistent in seeking the President's thoughts on the role of the Executive in enforcing" civil rights decisions. Until the snub, Abner added, "newspaper readers at least got the fumblingly illiterate Eisenhower reactions to the issue of civil rights."[9]

The popular black weekly *Jet* magazine's "Ticker Tape" column observed, "Alice, the most regular attendant [at the press conferences] of the D.C. Sepia correspondents, hasn't gotten a word in edgewise in over a year and is trying to make a racial issue of the matter."[10]

Actually, I was not trying to imply that this issue was based on either race or sex discrimination, as it seemed more likely a move on the part of the president and his advisors to dodge controversial questions on which he was either unable or unwilling to take a definite stand.

When the 112 ANP newspapers picked up the story, it became widespread around the nation. But the story did not meet the approval of ANP Director Claude Barnett. He chided me for all the adverse publicity the president had been receiving regarding my questions and instructed me

President Kennedy recognized the importance of the black press when he called on Alice Dunnigan at the first live, televised presidential press conference on January 25, 1961, departing from Eisenhower's practice of ducking civil rights issues. The White House also assigned a regular seat at the news conferences to a reporter for black publications, *Jet* and *Ebony* magazines' Simeon Booker (second row, second from left, in bowtie). (Abbie Rowe, White House/John F. Kennedy Presidential Library and Museum)

in a letter that I shouldn't "lean too hard on the president." I had no as-surance, he wrote, that Eisenhower's motive was racial, and it could be personal. Barnett's letter concluded that the president might have been informed that I leaned toward the Democratic Party, and his action might be due to my partisanship, which the ANP did not condone.[11]

One White House staffer suggested that the controversy had something to do with professional jealousy on the part of male columnists and called it an "unprecedented professional battle-of-the-sexes."

There was so much notoriety around the situation that presidential as-sistant Rabb took to the air to deny that he had requested of certain re-porters that questions to be raised at the press conference be submitted in advance for White House approval. In an interview with Tomlinson D. Todd, director of the *Americans-All* radio program on Washington's WOOK, Rabb maintained that all questions raised at these conferences were spontaneous and that the president never knew in advance what he was going to be asked.[12]

After all this publicity on the Eisenhower controversy, when I was rec-ognized by President John F. Kennedy at his first press conference in 1961, the newspapers did stories to the effect that after several years of operat-ing under a gag rule, Alice Dunnigan's silence at last has been broken.

A *Jet* headline read, "Kennedy In, Negro Reporter Gets First Answer in Two Years." The article led with the observation that at "his first nationally televised press conference in Washington, President John F. Kennedy qui-etly scrapped a long standing White House policy," which was "to ignore veteran correspondent Alice Dunnigan at press conferences."

For two years, grandmother Dunnigan bobbed up and down at press con-ferences to get the eye of ex-President Eisenhower. She was skipped, passed over, and ignored. Even reporters noticed the snubbing and jokingly told her "to save her strength." She was regarded as an agitator by conservative newsmen.

. . . The ex-teacher and native of Russellville, Ky., got in Ike's hair twice on civil rights matters—revitalizing the Contract Compliance Committee and ending segregation at schools on military bases. Following Mrs. Dun-nigan's pinpointing of the conditions, the administration took action—in each case. Recalled Mrs. Dunnigan: "Colleagues told me that I got more action than anyone. Just ask the question."[13]

After this news conference, letters and telegrams came from people around the country who had seen it on television. Some complimented me for being the first black reporter to ask President Kennedy a question. Members of the Women's National Press Club lauded me for being the first female reporter to do so.

Thus, the controversy with presidents had ended for me, and I continued my normal routine of covering the White House press conferences.

EPILOGUE

Alice Dunnigan took leave from journalism in 1960 to work on the Kennedy-Johnson presidential election campaign, where her primary focus was to keep before the public all of the activities of the vice-presidential candidate favorable to blacks and other minorities. Toward this end, she turned out numerous press releases slanted toward Negro newspapers. Still included on the Democratic National Committee's mailing list herself, she soon noticed that none of this material about Johnson was being released. Taking her fury up the chain of command, she learned that certain black workers on the Kennedy side of the campaign, believing that Johnson as a southerner was "unpopular" among Negro voters, had suggested that no releases about him be sent out.

"You can't do that!" she blasted. "Whether you like it or not, Johnson is on the ticket, win, lose, or draw. Kennedy can't win without him. So the wisest thing is to familiarize minority voters with the good qualities of the man and what he actually stands for."[1]

Then she added a quintessential Dunnigan bottom line: "The black press is going to get this type of information whether or not it meets the approval of certain black campaign workers, because I'm going to send it out myself and it will be up to the editors whether or not they use it." With that understood, she proceeded to send out press releases directly from her desk.

Soon after the inauguration, Dunnigan left journalism to embark on her third career—in politics—becoming the first black woman appointed to

On leave from ANP in 1960, Dunnigan went straight to Senator Kennedy when necessary to do her job as a Kennedy/Johnson campaign press aide. (From Dunnigan, *Black Woman's Experience*)

Alice Dunnigan and son, Robert, say their good-byes to President Johnson at a farewell reception in 1968. (Over LBJ's right shoulder is special assistant and deputy counsel Clifford Alexander, later secretary of the army in the Carter administration.) (From Dunnigan, *Black Woman's Experience*)

a prominent position in the new administration. Vice President Johnson, director of the newly created President's Committee on Equal Employment Opportunity, appointed her education consultant to the committee staff. Ahead lay a rough-and-tumble road, during which her political or personal convictions would at times run head-on into positions taken by others in the party or the government. They were years that included, as she later recalled, both pleasant and unpleasant moments, during which she nevertheless added other "firsts" to her long list of accomplishments. All in all, the miles she logged during those years in the federal government were undoubtedly a lot easier than those she'd trod before.

In 1970, after serving nine years collectively as an education consultant on the staff of the EEOC and then the President's Council on Youth Opportunity, she walked "out of the federal government, out of the political arena, out of journalism, out of that mad, mad, mad world of work, and into the serenity of a quiet, comfortable home-life where there is peace, contentment and happiness." There, she observed, she could "reflect on a life well spent, and record these memoirs for the benefit of future generations."[2]

From the very beginning of her career, she'd had to fight prejudice based on both race and sex. Through her early working years, she had to overcome the additional obstacles of youth and inexperience. In her final working years, she strived to bridge the generation gap and overcome discrimination against the aging. Through it all, she hung in there, working hard and moving along slowly but steadily. In the words of the old spiritual, she just kept "inching along."

After publishing her autobiography, she wrote another book, *The Fascinating Story of Black Kentuckians: Their Heritage and Tradition*, published in 1979 by the Association for the Study of African American Life and History.

Dunnigan's son, Robert (whom she called "Bob"), lived near her in the Washington area for most of his adult life. After graduating from Kentucky State College in 1953 and a four-year stint in the U.S. Marine Corps, he worked in both private industry and the D.C. government in social work, education, and administrative positions. He also purchased a race horse farm in rural Maryland, where he enjoyed "raising winners." In his mother's later life, he escorted her to social functions, including a farewell reception for President Johnson in 1968.

Alice Dunnigan died in Washington, D.C., of an abdominal disease at the age of seventy-seven on May 6, 1983. It was nine years after completing her autobiography, which she dedicated to her son, whose inspiration and encouragement, she wrote, had made it possible, and to her grandchildren, Alicia, Suzette, Kevin, and Soraya, whose interest and enthusiasm kept her going. Her posthumous induction into the National Association of Black Journalists Hall of Fame on January 17, 2013, was the capstone of innumerable honors, accolades, tributes, and commendations she received as Washington bureau chief for the ANP. She had been inducted previously into Kentucky's Hall of Fame for both journalism and human rights.

During three successive careers, in teaching, journalism, and politics, Alice Dunnigan saw enormous social changes in America, not the least of which were changes in race relations carved into the social landscape by pioneers such as herself in the 1940s and 1950s. More than any other reporter of her time, she chronicled these events for the readership of more than one hundred black newspapers across the country and others in the emerging nations of Africa, documenting the dawn of a movement that would change America forever. Accepting the honor in his mother's memory, Robert Dunnigan said it was his hope that the story of her life would inspire a new generation, because "that's what she wanted."

ACKNOWLEDGMENTS

I begin by thanking the dedicated staff of the Library of Congress, where my acquaintance with Alice Allison Dunnigan began in the Jefferson Building's superb Main Reading Room. There, over several days, I read her meticulously compiled and documented account of an incredible life. Opening the three-inch-thick volume for the first time, I found it inscribed by the author to her friend and colleague *Chicago Defender* reporter Ethel Payne, who joined her in the Washington press corps in 1953 and with whom she remained friends thereafter. This copy itself was a piece of history. My later exploration of historic newspapers and magazines was facilitated by the LOC's always helpful personnel in the Periodicals and Microform Reading Rooms.

Special thanks are also due the staffs of other libraries and historical research centers that assisted in my quest for documents and photographs. Most notably: the Moorland-Spingarn Research Center at Howard University in Washington, D.C., repository of the papers of Alice Dunnigan most germane to this volume; the Harry S. Truman Presidential Library; the Dwight D. Eisenhower Presidential Library; the John F. Kennedy Presidential Library; the Lyndon B. Johnson Presidential Library; the Kentucky Historical Society; the Chicago History Museum (repository of the papers of Claude Barnett); the Manuscript, Archives, and Rare Book Library (MARBL) at Emory University (repository of the papers of Alice Dunnigan germane to her later political career and many of her photographs). Special thanks to researcher Jenny C. Bledsoe for digital reproductions of the photographs in the Emory collection. In addition, Indiana University–Purdue University Indianapolis (IU-PUI) Library, site of the archives of the *Indianapolis Recorder*, led me to the black weekly's front page photograph of Dunnigan shaking hands with President Truman during his whistle stop in that city in 1948.

I am also indebted to the friends and colleagues who read the manuscript and shared my enthusiasm for Alice Dunnigan's story as well as their astute editorial insights.

I would not have completed this project without the staunch support of my husband, Simeon Booker, who met Alice Dunnigan when he came to D.C. to work for the *Washington Post* in 1951 as its first black staff reporter. He frequently reminded me, as I followed Alice's coverage of a capital city still kowtowing to Jim Crow even in the late 1940s and 1950s, that she did it all alone—without an office, a secretary, or a teletype running even one of the wire services.

Finally, I am grateful to Lisa Bayer and the University of Georgia Press for sharing not only my enthusiasm for this book but also Alice Dunnigan's vision of her life's story as a source of inspiration for young women to see that even against formidable odds, with grit and perseverance, all kinds of things—even "firsts"—can be accomplished.

NOTES

EDITOR'S NOTE

1. "Pioneering no 'bed of roses,' Mrs. Dunnigan tells Iotas," ANP release, dateline Washington, D.C. (undated), Dunnigan Papers, Moorland-Spingarn Research Center, Howard University (hereafter Dunnigan Papers), box 186.

2. ANP correspondents were usually stringers or part-time contributors, but the Washington, D.C., bureau chief position was an exception. Lawrence D. Hogan, *A Black National News Service: The Associated Negro Press and Claude Barnett* (Haworth, N.J.: St. Johann Press, 2002), 93.

3. Barnett was not unique among editors in his gender bias. In 1949, *Mademoiselle* magazine surveyed twenty-seven daily papers and fifteen university journalism schools to learn who had gotten jobs the preceding year. The answer was that twice as many men had been hired (and fewer than one "girl" per paper); few of the women were offered the same type of assignments as men, and their average starting salary was 20 percent less than a man's. "Getting on a paper: 1949," *Mademoiselle*, August 1949, 308–12. Barnett, who also had offered higher starting salaries to men than to Dunnigan, was not at all out of step with the industry. Barnett correspondence with James Baker (mentioning a salary offer of $250 per month), December 1946, Barnett Papers, Chicago Historical Society (hereafter Barnett Papers), boxes 136, 137.

4. Frank Marshall Davis letters to Dunnigan, April 29 and May 20, 1947, Barnett Papers, box 136.

5. Alvin White, ANP's Washington, D.C., correspondent from 1939 to 1942, described Barnett's unsuccessful efforts to get him accredited to the Congressional Press Galleries in a letter (November 19, 1976) to Lawrence D. Hogan. Hogan, *A Black National News Service*, 99. Barnett had arranged for White to represent the *Atlanta Daily World* in order to satisfy the galleries' requirement that members represent a daily paper, but the application was denied anyway.

6. Barnett letters to Dunnigan, September 8, 1959, and August 8, 1960, respectively. Dunnigan Papers, box 182.

7. *Pittsburgh Courier* letters from P. L. Prattis and George F. Brown to Dunnigan, December 13, June 5, and December 23, 1957, Dunnigan Papers, box 182.

8. Dunnigan would likely agree, having told an interviewer in 1977 that of her several careers, journalism was the most important, as she believed she had done the most in that field to help people and to bring about better race relations. Black Women Oral History Project Interviews (hereafter Oral History Project), April 8, 1977, OH-31, T-32/ Dunnigan, Schlesinger Library, Radcliffe Institute, Harvard University, Cambridge, Mass., http://pds.lib.harvard.edu/pds/view/45168261?n=44&printThumbnails=no.

9. "'From Schoolhouse to White House,' Alice Dunnigan's Story" (undated).

10. Oral History Project, http://pds.lib.harvard.edu/pds/view/45168261?n=44& printThumbnails=no.

CHAPTER 1. NO GREATER THRILL

1. The White House press corps grew during the Truman administration to the point that it became too large for press conferences in the Oval Office, where some reporters were jammed against the back wall and couldn't hear and where ink from reporters' fountain pens sometimes spoiled the carpet. Conferences were moved to the Indian Treaty Room at the State Department, then housed next to the White House in what later was called the Eisenhower Executive Office Building. That room was used until President Kennedy's administration, when again the press corps grew too large and presidential news conferences moved to the auditorium of the new State Department building. Oral history interview, Edward T. Folliard, August 20, 1970, 69, Truman Library, http://www.trumanlibrary.org/oralhist/folliard.htm.

CHAPTER 4. SCHOOL DAYS

1. Change came slowly in Kentucky, as elsewhere in the South, after the U.S. Supreme Court declared racial segregation in schools unconstitutional in *Brown v. Board of Education* in 1954. Statewide school desegregation in Kentucky reportedly did not occur until September 1975. For an excellent overview of African American education in Kentucky during this period, see Alicestyne Turley-Adams, *Rosenwald Schools in Kentucky: 1917–1932*, prepared for the Kentucky Heritage Council, State Historic Preservation Office, and the Kentucky African American Heritage Council, January 1997, http://heritage.ky.gov/NR/rdonlyres/ACF24D83-59B1-4C83-AC25-80173291C4B8/0/RosenwaldSchoolsinKY.pdf.

2. Federally assisted school lunch programs were unheard of at this time. Congress passed Public Law No. 320 in 1935, authorizing a certain amount of money for the development of new outlets for farm products. Much of this food supplied by the Department of Agriculture was used to expand school lunch programs. Such programs did not become widespread, however, until President Truman signed into law the

National School Lunch Act on June 6, 1946. Tuskegee *Negro Year Book*, 1952, 208. —AD (Editor's note: The *Negro Year Book*, compiled by Tuskegee's Department of Records and Research and published by the Tuskegee Institute for forty years beginning in 1912, was used extensively as a reference by agencies, educational institutions, and individuals.)

CHAPTER 10. MOVING ON

1. The Rosenwald school in New Hope, completed in 1924, was one of thirty-three African American schools built in Kentucky between 1917 and 1920 with support from Chicago philanthropist Julius Rosenwald, the Tuskegee Institute, and the General Education Board. Turley-Adams, *Rosenwald Schools in Kentucky*, http://heritage.ky.gov /NR/rdonlyres/ACF24D83-59B1-4C83-AC25-80173291C4B8/0/RosenwaldSchoolsinKY .pdf. Stephanie Deutsch, *You Need a Schoolhouse* (Evanston: Northwestern University Press, 2011) is an excellent history of the collaboration between Julius Rosenwald and Booker T. Washington that led to these and other projects, including the building of Negro YMCA branches.

CHAPTER 11. WADING THROUGH THE DEPRESSION

1. While Dunnigan knew of no law applicable to this particular situation, there were a number of Jim Crow laws on the books in Kentucky prohibiting miscegenation, integration in schools, public carriers or accommodations, and so on.

2. Called the Logan County Tobacco and Heritage Festival, it continues to this day as the county's largest annual event.

3. Much has been written about the WPA, which was the largest and most famous of President Roosevelt's New Deal programs. Dunnigan's experience illustrates how both sexism and Jim Crow distorted its goals in terms of both women and blacks. Only 13.5 percent of WPA employees were women in the peak year of 1938, and contrary to original policy, in practice women were consigned to lower-paying activities such as those described by Dunnigan. "The Works Progress Administration," Public Broadcasting Service website, http://www.pbs.org/wgbh/americanexperience/features/general-article /dustbowl-wpa/.

4. The county attorney, John A. Whittaker, was later elected to the U.S. Congress while I was working on Capitol Hill as a newspaper reporter. He was always courteous, polite, and respectful of my new status in life when our paths crossed in the Capitol building. —AD

CHAPTER 12. SEEKING IDENTITY, EXPERIENCE, AND RECOGNITION

1. Chicken thieves were considered the lowest of crooks, as a family often depended on its barn fowl for meat and eggs for daily sustenance, and as a commodity that could be sold to buy other necessities. Harsh penalties for chicken theft applied well beyond Kentucky. See more at Lawrence P. Gooley, "Adirondack History: Dannemora

Prison's Chicken Thieves," *Adirondack Almanack*, April 22, 2013, http://www
.adirondackalmanack.com/2013/04/adirondack-history-dannemora-prisons-chicken-
thieves.html#sthash.j5HDbF4U.dpuf.

2. Cole founded the *Leader* in 1917, and by the 1930s, the weekly reportedly employed
twenty people and had a circulation of twenty thousand.

3. Woodson founded the Association in 1915 in response to the lack of information on
the accomplishments of African Americans. He is also credited with establishing Negro
History Week in 1926, which fifty years later grew into a month-long observance every
February. Headquartered in Washington, D.C., the organization is now the Association
for the Study of African American Life and History. It continues its mission to "promote,
research, preserve, interpret, and disseminate information about Black life, history, and
culture to the global community."

4. According to the *Old Time Radio Catalog*, "Many of the applicants were poor black
men from the south, hoping to tap dance, sing or harmonica their way to fame and
fortune. Most were turned away, as only 500–700 were auditioned and only 20 appeared
on the show. Even after making the cut-throat audition and appearing live on the show,
many were gonged off before finishing their act, a cruel practice that made the audience
roar with laughter." A few contestants went on to great careers, including Frank Sinatra,
Beverly Sills, and Robert Merrill. See *Old Time Radio Catalog* website, http://www
.otrcat.com/major-bowes-p-1575.html.

5. Described in a brochure for the event as "the first real NEGRO WORLD'S FAIR in all
history," the exposition was held at the Chicago Coliseum, July 4–September 2, 1940. The
"Official Program and Guide Book" states that the Exposition would "promote racial
understanding and good will[,] enlighten the world on the contributions of the Negro to
civilization[,] and make the Negro conscious of his dramatic progress since emancipation"
while also "substantiat[ing] the black man's claim that he has made large and valuable
contributions to both American and world history." The Internet Archive website, http://
archive.org/stream/americannegroexpooamer/americannegroexpooamer_djvu.txt.
(Dunnigan's future boss, Claude Barnett, is listed as a member of the exposition authority.)

6. Located halfway between Memphis and Vicksburg in Bolivar County, Mississippi,
Mound Bayou was established in 1887 by former slaves as a place where blacks might
work for themselves instead of for whites. The origin of its fame as "the Jewel of the Delta"
as well as the town's important role in the birth of the modern civil rights movement are
described by Simeon Booker in *Shocking the Conscience: A Reporter's Account of the Civil
Rights Movement* (Jackson: University Press of Mississippi, 2013), 3–17.

CHAPTER 13. CONVERGING ON WASHINGTON

1. The gracious, four-story Phyllis Wheatley YWCA still stands at the corner of Ninth
Street and Rhode Island Avenue NW, where it was dedicated on December 19, 1920,
as the first "colored" YWCA in the United States. Named for an acclaimed black poet,
a woman brought to America from Senegal as a slave in 1761, the YWCA still provides
housing to women regardless of race, creed, or color. It is not currently affiliated with the
national YWCA.

2. Formed in 1937, the militancy of the union's leadership and its association with "leftist" ideals led to accusations that it was Communist controlled, in turn leading to legislation to restrict its political activities. One of those measures was the Hatch Act of 1939. In 1946, the State, County, and Municipal Workers of America merged with the much smaller UFWA to form the United Public Workers of America.

3. The ANP's membership included most of the national and regional papers, many smaller black weeklies, and by the 1950s over seventy-five African newspapers, for which weekly releases were prepared in French as well as English. Hogan, *A Black National News Service*, 9, 66.

CHAPTER 14. BREAKING DOWN RACE—AND GENDER—BARRIERS

1. When the Senate convened in January 1947, it had two reports to consider on Mississippi senator Bilbo. One concerned an investigation of his campaign activities, and the other addressed charges of illegal conversion of campaign contributions to personal use. Senate action on both reports was tabled while Bilbo returned home for treatment of oral cancer, from which he never recovered, dying on August 21 of that year. United States Senate website, http://www.senate.gov/artandhistory/history/minute /Members_Death_Ends_a_Senate_Predicament.htm.

2. The SCHW grew out of a study of the economic conditions of the South that caused President Franklin D. Roosevelt to issue a statement to the effect that poverty in the South was America's public enemy number one. Southern liberals got together to do something to help improve this situation.

3. Ross, a highly trained newspaperman who for many years had been Washington correspondent of the *St. Louis Post-Dispatch*, was considered a first-rate press secretary. He also had gone to school with Mr. Truman in Independence, and they were very dear friends. Oral history interview, Edward T. Folliard, August 20, 1970, 4, Truman Library, http://www.trumanlibrary.org/oralhist/folliard.htm.

4. Although Dunnigan reports no difficulty, two other black reporters had applied for admission with mixed results. Harry S. McAlpin, the first African American reporter credentialed to the White House, where he covered Presidents Roosevelt and Truman for fifty-one black newspapers, was refused membership in the association. The NNPA continued the fight, and in 1951, its correspondent, Louis Lautier, was admitted to the WHCA. In 1962, the organization finally allowed its female members to attend its annual dinner, frequently attended by the president and vice president, after United Press International's Helen Thomas raised this issue of blatant discrimination with Kennedy press secretary Pierre Salinger. The White House News Photographers Association's refusal to admit black photographers accredited to the White House also ended under the Kennedy administration, when the organization finally admitted Maurice Sorrell of the *Afro-American* newspapers after *Jet/Ebony* Washington bureau chief Simeon Booker raised the issue at a presidential news conference. President John F. Kennedy news conference, April 12, 1961, http://www.jfklibrary.org/Asset-Viewer/Archives /JFKPOF-054-011.aspx.

CHAPTER 15. A TRIP WITH THE PRESIDENT

1. Franklin D. Roosevelt's election in 1932 saw the beginning of a shift in the black vote, which continued into 1936, when black support for the Democratic ticket was tallied at 71 percent. The change in party affiliation was indisputable when Harry Truman garnered 77 percent of the black vote in 1948. David A. Bositis, "Blacks and the 2008 Democratic National Convention," (Joint Center for Political and Economic Studies, 2008), 8, http://jointcenter.org/sites/default/files/Dem%20guide.pdf.

2. Judge Hueston, also a native Kentuckian, was, among many other notable achievements, for many years grand commissioner of education of the Elks.

3. Dunnigan doesn't identify the aide by name, but he may have been David K. Niles, who worked as administrative assistant to Presidents Roosevelt and Truman from 1942 to 1951 with responsibility for Jewish affairs, the Democratic Party, and civil rights. Harry S. Truman Library and Museum, David K. Niles Papers, https://www.trumanlibrary.org/hstpaper/niles.htm.

4. Young later ran unsuccessfully against Rep. Adam Clayton Powell Jr. in the Democratic congressional primaries in 1968 and 1970. —AD

5. Considered a trailblazer for women journalists, Fleeson was the first nationally syndicated female political columnist. —AD

6. The MV *Kalakala* was a luxurious ferry that operated from 1935 until its retirement in 1967, for most of those years carrying passengers across Puget Sound from Bremerton, the largest city on Washington's Kitsap Peninsula, to Seattle, about a fifty-five-minute ride. *Kalakala* website, http://www.kalakala.org/history/history_WA-ST-Ferry.html.

7. Seventeen blacks were among the 1,234 delegates to the Democratic Convention in 1948, or 1.3 percent of the total, as compared with 14.6 percent in 1972 (seven years after the Voting Rights Act of 1965) and 24.3 percent in 2008, when Barack Obama received the presidential nomination. Bositis, "Blacks and the 2008 Democratic Convention," 13.

8. Founded as Lincoln Institute in 1866 by members of the Sixty-Second and Sixty-Fifth United States Colored Infantry for the benefit of freed African Americans, the school was designated a university by the state of Missouri in 1921.

9. Founded as a two-page church bulletin in 1897, the paper reported on both local and national events, eventually becoming one of the top African American papers in the nation. Indiana University–Purdue University Indianapolis, www.ulib.iupui.edu/digitalscholarship/collections/IRecorder.

10. After the trip, Dunnigan wrote a very touching letter to her son, Robert, then a fifteen-year-old high-school student still living with her parents in Russellville. She explained that she had not sent him spending money over the summer because of her debt for the trip but that she would make it up to him during the school year. She also revealed that she felt other black newspeople in D.C. were "mad and jealous" of her because she had accomplished something none of them ever had, and in so short a time, as a journalist. To keep them from saying she was "foolish" or worse for paying her own way, she told people Barnett had paid for the trip, which, she wrote, had paid off in experience and was worth "all that I put in to it and more." Dunnigan Papers, box 136.

CHAPTER 16. THE CIVIL RIGHTS FIGHTS OF THE FORTIES

1. Thurmond left the Democratic Party permanently in 1964 in opposition to the Civil Rights Act and was reelected to the Senate as a Republican.

2. In spite of Mr. Wallace's supposed stronghold in California, President Truman received almost two million votes in that state. This was a margin of nearly eighteen thousand over his leading opponent (Dewey) and more than 1.5 million over Wallace. Nearly thirty-one thousand of Truman's Los Angeles votes came from Negroes. Less than six thousand Negro votes went to Dewey and four thousand to Wallace. Truman's twenty-one thousand margin of black votes could have been attributed to his strong civil rights commitment in Los Angeles, which was widely publicized through the nation's black press. Report of a Survey on Negro Votes of 1948 compiled by the NAACP, released January 1949. *The World Almanac* 1972, 722. Tuskegee *Negro Year Book*, 1952, 298. —AD

3. Henry Wallace was badly defeated in his bid for the presidency in 1948. He had served as agriculture secretary under President Roosevelt (1933–40) before being elected vice president on the Roosevelt slate in 1940, serving one term before being replaced in the 1944 election by Senator Harry S. Truman. At the time of Roosevelt's death (1945), when Truman became president, Wallace was serving as secretary of commerce, a position he held until fired in 1946 by Truman—the man he ran against for the presidency two years later. At the time of Wallace's death in 1965, the name of this seventy-seven-year-old New Dealer had practically been wiped from political history, but his fame as a plant geneticist lingered on. After returning to the soil, the former Iowa agriculturist distinguished himself as a developer of a new hybrid corn and was working on a theory to improve the yield of chicken eggs. —AD

4. Pollsters and many others were so sure of a Republican victory that the *Chicago Daily Tribune* hit the street with the front-page banner headline "Dewey Defeats Truman" even before the final vote count. Iconic photos show the victorious and broadly smiling President Truman holding the newspaper high.

5. Some years later (prior to the 1952 campaign), Congressman Dawson recommended newspaperwoman Venice Spraggs, chief of the *Chicago Defender*'s Washington Bureau, to a newly created position with the DNC similar to the one I had proposed but with the additional duties of organizing black Democratic women around the country, a job that she handled extremely well. She remained with the DNC until her death soon after the 1956 campaign. —AD

6. William Houston's son, Charles, also an attorney, was very active in civil rights and was the subject of a petition bearing the signatures of thousands of D.C. residents urging that Truman appoint him city commissioner. While the effort failed, it was the seed of a movement that eventually saw a black man, John B. Duncan, appointed to Washington's three-man governing body during the Kennedy administration. —AD

7. Founded in 1934, the council connected black churches nationally on common social issues. For more, see Mary R. Sawyer, "Black Ecumenical Movements: Proponents of Social Change," *Review of Religious Research* 30 (1988): 151–61.

8. President Roosevelt created a Fair Employment Practices Committee by executive

order in 1941 to prohibit discrimination based on race, creed, or national origin in defense industries and the government. While the FEPC had success enforcing the president's order in the North, it took a hands-off position in the South and had mixed results in border states. President Truman's support for a permanent FEPC, as well as antilynching legislation and the abolition of the poll tax, were blocked in the Congress in 1948. In 1950, a filibuster by southern senators again blocked passage of a bill to create a permanent FEPC. —AD

CHAPTER 17. PROFILES OF INJUSTICE

1. This description is from the second of a series of articles on the visit to the Ingram family in Georgia by a delegation from the National Committee to Free the Ingram Family: "Mrs. Ingram Receives Guests," *Baltimore Afro-American*, April 23, 1949, 11. Accessed from ProQuest Historical Newspapers.

2. Marcantonio served six terms in Congress between 1935 and 1951, distinguishing himself as a champion of civil rights legislation, including antilynching and anti–poll tax bills, and a federal watchdog to ensure fair employment practices. He also supported independence for Puerto Rico. —AD

3. The Civil Rights Congress (CRC) was founded in Detroit in 1946 with the merger of three left-wing organizations that focused on legal defense strategies and political action on behalf of victims, particularly blacks and political dissidents, of questionable prosecutions. It folded during the height of anticommunism and the Cold War. —AD

4. The concept of an antilynching law was not new. Tuskegee Institute, through its Department of Records and Research, had carried on an educational antilynching program since 1913. The NAACP made investigations of lynching and sponsored federal antilynching legislation as early as 1921. Tuskegee *Negro Year Book*, 1952, 275. —AD

5. President Harry S. Truman, Special Message to the Congress, February 2, 1948, http://www.presidency.ucsb.edu/ws/?pid=13006.

6. Each of these legislative proposals presented by President Truman in 1948 eventually became law but not for several years. The first civil rights act in eighty-two years, e.g., was enacted in 1957, another in 1960, and the most comprehensive in 1964. A temporary Commission on Civil Rights was established in 1957. The Voting Rights Act proposed by Truman seventeen years earlier was adopted in 1965. A permanent Fair Employment Practices Commission was created as the Equal Employment Opportunity Commission under the Civil Rights Act of 1964. Alaska and Hawaii were both finally awarded statehood in 1959. Some measure of home rule for D.C.—by no means complete—was passed by both houses of Congress in 1973. —AD

CHAPTER 18. THE PRESIDENT PROPOSES; THE CONGRESS DEBATES

1. The Industrial Bank of Washington was the district's only black-owned bank when it was founded in 1913 by laborer and entrepreneur John Whitelaw Lewis as the Industrial Savings Bank. Like many other banks during the Depression, it was forced to close in 1932, but it reopened in 1934. —AD

2. President Harry S. Truman, Annual Message to the Congress on the State of the Union, January 5, 1949, http://www.presidency.ucsb.edu/ws/?pid=13293.

3. Davis served in Congress from January 3, 1947, to January 3, 1963, and in 1956 was a signatory to the "Southern Manifesto" opposing integration. —AD

4. Born in Itawamba County, Miss., in 1882, Congressman John Rankin (D-Miss.) was openly racist, anti-Semitic, and a supporter of the Ku Klux Klan. He served sixteen terms in Congress between 1921 and 1953, during which one fellow member, New York Democrat Emanuel Celler, described listening to his harangues on the House floor as "agony." Once I found myself standing next to Rankin as we ate from an elaborate buffet set up at the Veterans Administration for some special occasion. I couldn't resist telling him, "Congressman, now you cannot say again that you have never eaten with a Negro." He looked at me strangely, made no comment, and kept eating, making no attempt to move. He died in Tupelo, Miss., November 26, 1960. Theodore G. Bilbo (born in Pearl River County, Miss., in 1887) served twice as governor of his home state and in 1934 was elected to the first of successive terms in the U.S. Senate, where he served until the Eightieth Congress in 1947, when having been diagnosed with cancer and facing a Senate investigation of his conduct, he died without taking the oath of office. Like Rankin, he was a symbol and defender of white supremacy and peppered his speeches with racist diatribes. —AD

5. The Civil Rights Act of 1964 established a permanent Equal Employment Opportunity Commission with limited powers. It was not until eight years later that some extra "teeth" (enforcement powers) were put into the measure. On March 24, President Nixon signed into law the Equal Employment Opportunity Act of 1972, giving the EEOC power to go into court to obtain enforcement through its own general counsel. Prior to this act, it could only obtain redress by private suits. —AD

CHAPTER 20. FREEDOM FIGHTS OF THE FIFTIES

1. In the late 1970s, all were released or pardoned and returned to Puerto Rico.

2. President Truman supported a plebiscite in Puerto Rico to determine its future relationship to the United States. The result was an overwhelming vote in favor of commonwealth status under a new constitution. —AD

3. When his passport was finally returned, Dr. DuBois left this country for Ghana, where he became a citizen and where he died on August 27, 1963, at the age of ninety-five. —AD

4. President Dwight D. Eisenhower, News Conference, March 19, 1953, http://www.presidency.ucsb.edu/ws/index.php?pid=9798-title=Eisenhower.

5. In downtown Washington, the flagship of this large, family-owned department store chain wasn't entirely committed to racial equality two decades earlier. Dunnigan had reported on black and white demonstrators picketing outside the Hecht Co. store in 1951 against racial segregation in its cafeteria, which had become an international embarrassment. Under the headline "Dark-Skinned Foreigners Find D.C. Doesn't Care Who They Are," Dunnigan's article for ANP papers described how a lunch counter waitress, supported by the manager, had repeatedly refused to serve dark-skinned

women despite their protests that they were not Negro but foreigners. After demanding and receiving proof of their national origin, the manager apologized and offered to serve the first woman himself, but she declined, irate, and left the store. He served the second woman, from India, himself, after the waitress still refused, saying she'd been instructed not to serve colored people and would quit before doing so. The embassy of India had declined to comment for the article. *Philadelphia Tribune*, July 31, 1951.

6. Evermont Robinson was the first black man appointed Senate doorkeeper (as far as could be determined). This appointment was made during the Eighty-First Congress (1949) upon recommendation of Senator Taft. William Belcher became the first known black doorkeeper for the House of Representatives around 1954. —AD

7. Charles Vernon Bush, the first Negro page on the Hill, was appointed in October 1954 to serve the U.S. Supreme Court. Upon graduation from the Capitol High School for Pages, he was appointed to the U.S. Air Force Academy, graduating in 1963. —AD

8. The economic squeeze against black would-be voters was a tool promulgated by White Citizens' Councils throughout the South, where it typically included everything from firing to refusing credit, calling in existing loans, refusing to gin the cotton, and even evicting or refusing to rent to anyone who defied the whites-only voting tradition. Soon after the practice began in the Mississippi Delta in the mid-1950s, the NAACP established a "war chest" to help blacks denied loans or credit by white institutions.

9. Just eight minutes into the news conference, Dunnigan was the first female, as well as the first black, reporter recognized by President Kennedy. Her question was also the only one regarding civil rights. Audio of the conference can be heard on the JFK Presidential Library website: http://www.jfklibrary.org/Asset-Viewer/Archives /JFKWHA-004.aspx.

10. A quarter of a century later, much ado would be made when other women joined the ranks of sportswriters, but I received no special attention in the general press when I was the first to break through this gender barrier. —AD

11. Built in 1911 between Georgia Avenue and Fifth Street NW, with Florida Avenue and W Street to its south and north, respectively, Griffith Stadium was home to the American League's Washington Senators and hosted three World Series. It was also home to the Negro League's Homestead Grays in the 1940s. The stadium was torn down in 1965 and is now the site of Howard University Hospital. —AD

CHAPTER 21. EISENHOWER'S PIQUE

1. Founded in 1806 as the Washington Infirmary and renamed D.C. General Hospital in 1953, Gallinger was the district's first public hospital. —AD

2. Founded in 1862, Freedmen's was the first D.C. hospital to treat former slaves, and for years it was the major hospital for the Washington Negro community. After the Civil War, it became the teaching hospital for the Howard University Medical School. —AD

3. The suit to abolish discrimination in D.C. public facilities was filed in the courts in 1950, before twhe Eisenhower administration. It was three years later, in June 1953, that the final decision was handed down by the Supreme Court. *District of Columbia v. John R. Thompson Co., Inc.*, 346 U.S. 100 (1953). —AD

4. Until Ethel Payne joined the White House press corps in 1954, Alice Dunnigan was the only reporter who asked Eisenhower about racial or civil rights issues.

5. Eisenhower didn't call on Dunnigan again until almost a year later, January 19, 1955. That was the first Eisenhower press conference that was filmed for later distribution to television stations, which the president referred to as an "experiment." According to press secretary James Hagerty's personal diary entry for that day, the president told him "that he deliberately recognized Alice Dunnigan toward the end of the conference so that a Negro reporter would have a chance to ask a question." Hagerty Papers, Dwight D. Eisenhower Presidential Library, box 1a.

6. President Eisenhower news conference July 7, 1954. The American Presidency Project website, http://www.presidency.ucsb.edu/ws/index.php.

7. The date was July 8, 1959, and the reporter was William H. Lawrence of the *New York Times*.

8. Transcripts of the Eisenhower news conferences reveal that after his February 8, 1956, conference, Eisenhower did not call on Dunnigan again until August 20, 1958, when she asked him to comment on news stories that had (correctly) reported that Assistant Secretary of Labor J. Ernest Wilkins, the only black person at the subcabinet level, had been asked for his resignation so that the position could be given to George Lodge (son of U.N. Rep. Henry Cabot Lodge). Eisenhower claimed it wasn't true but that Wilkins had been talking about resigning. He also ridiculed, "I never heard of any contemplated replacement for someone whose resignation I have not yet accepted."

9. June 16, 1957.

10. June 6, 1957.

11. Barnett wrote Alice about this again in July 1957, confiding, "We are entirely in sympathy with your portrayal of what seems to be President Eisenhower's weakness in dealing with the South." However, he repeated his warning that Dunnigan be careful about her reputation for impartiality as a reporter since there was no telling what Eisenhower's "people" "may have told the man in warning about your Fleeson like pen." Barnett Letter to Dunnigan, July 16, 1957, Dunnigan Papers, box 182.

12. Through all of this, Rabb and I remained friends until he left the White House, at which time he sent Claude Barnett a letter stating, "Mrs. Dunnigan has been in constant touch with me and I have always found her to be both capable and friendly." —AD

13. *Jet*, February 9, 1961, 6–7.

EPILOGUE

1. Alice Allison Dunnigan, *A Black Woman's Experience—from Schoolhouse to White House* (Philadelphia: Dorrance & Co., 1974), 569.

2. Dunnigan, *Black Woman's Experience*, 662.

Index